THE MNEME

THE MNEME

BY

RICHARD SEMON

LONDON: GEORGE ALLEN & UNWIN LTD.
RUSKIN HOUSE, 40 MUSEUM STREET, W.C. 1
NEW YORK: THE MACMILLAN COMPANY

First published in 1921

PREFACE

In translating the *Mneme* during the years 1912–14 I had the benefit of the constant advice of its distinguished author, whose great wish it was to present his theory, in English, to the scientific world.

The translation was completed in July 1914, but the publication of the work could not be arranged for until six years later, after the death of the author.

Professor Semon died at Munich in 1919, in his sixty-first year.

A sequel to the *Mneme* (*Die mnemischen Empfindungen*) was published in 1909 by Wilhelm Engelmann, Leipzig. A posthumous work, *Bewusstseinsvorgang und Gehirnprozess*, has just been published by Bergmann, Wiesbaden.

I desire to acknowledge my indebtedness to the Rev. Lawrence Schroeder, M.A., of Halifax, and Mr. L. H. Edminson, M.A., of London, for their valuable help in revision.

LOUIS SIMON

Altrincham, Cheshire,
January, 1921.

THE ENGLISH EDITION OF
THE MNEME
IS DEDICATED TO
SIR FRANCIS DARWIN

CONTENTS

PART IV

INTRODUCTION

THE attempt to discover analogies between the various organic phenomena of reproduction is by no means new. It would have been strange if philosophers and naturalists had not been struck by the similarity existing between the reproduction in offspring of the shape and other characteristics of parent organisms, and that other kind of reproduction which we call memory. Should the present or any subsequent author succeed in proving that this similarity is more than superficial, there will be no lack of critics who will remind us that some ancient or modern thinker has already conceived the idea. Have we not already heard heredity described as a kind of racial memory (memory inherent in the species)?

The first serious enquiry into the nature of this coincidence was made by the celebrated physiologist Ewald Hering in a paper read on May 30, 1870, before the Vienna Academy, entitled, "Memory, a Universal Function of Organic Matter." In this short paper of only twenty pages Hering, with admirable insight and clearness, summed up the chief points of resemblance between the reproductive powers of heredity, of practice and habit, and of conscious memory.

Satisfied, however, with combining these in a harmonious scheme—thus pointing out the way for future enquiry—Hering refrained from analytically demonstrating that the resemblances between the different reproductive processes were more than accidental, and left behind him the task of proving that all these reproductive processes—whether of heredity, habit, or memory—owe their resemblance to their common origin in one and the same faculty of organic matter.

A few years later the English physician, F. Laycock, evidently unaware of Hering's paper, elaborated a similar thesis in an interesting essay entitled, " A Chapter on Some Organic Laws of Personal and Ancestral Memory " (*Journal of Mental Science*, vol. xxi, 1879).

A more explicit treatment of the problem was attempted in 1878, in *Life and Habit*, by Samuel Butler, the well-known author of *Erewhon*. Butler endeavoured to trace analogies between the various reproductive processes in greater detail than had been attempted by Hering, whose paper came to Butler's knowledge only after the appearance in 1880 of *Unconscious Memory*, his own first publication on the subject. Butler's essay contains brilliant suggestions, but these are mixed with so much questionable matter, that the whole, compared with Hering's paper on the same subject, is rather a retrogression than an advance.

Many years later, similar ideas were set forth by Henry D. Orr in a book entitled, *A Theory of Development and Heredity* (*New York*, 1893), and with as complete independence of Hering as was the case with Laycock and Butler.

Of these four independent attempts to connect the phenomena of memory, heredity, and habit, not one seems to have had any real influence on contemporary scientific thought, for they all omitted to explain definitely why such dissimilar processes should possess in common an obviously repetitive nature.

Mere repetition is of course not confined to these three classes of phenomena, nor yet even to the organic kingdom. Repetition of similar modes and peculiarities occurs frequently in the inorganic world without our ever being tempted to compare such repetition with the phenomena of memory. Indeed, we expect repetition of this kind, that is to say, of modes and qualities, whenever there is a repetition of the original conditions. But the peculiarity of memory is that its kind of repetition is independent of a *complete* repetition of the original conditions.

The periodic eruptions of a geyser, or the recurrence

of spring tides each time a given lunar phase and a given position of the sun coincide, do not suggest any comparison with the phenomena of memory. We simply recognise that when all the specific conditions are present, then, and only then, certain phenomena are invariably repeated. But if we wish to distinguish from these the various phenomena of organic reproduction, such as memory, habit, periodicity, and heredity, as a group by themselves, we must show that these latter possess a common quality which differentiates them from all other kinds of repetition. This characteristic they possess in the capacity for repetition, even when the original conditions are varied to an extreme degree. An infinitesimal portion, indeed, of the original conditions often suffices to cause the reproduction.

To show this demands a thorough analysis of these phenomena, not only in all their details and connections, but also in their verbal and logical formulation. As such an analysis is necessarily a complicated piece of work, requiring considerable patience and attention on the part of the reader, it may be well to acquaint him with the aim and scope of the following chapters, and to present a general outline of the problems discussed. He must also be familiarised with some of the words I have coined in the hope of avoiding the misleading connotations inherent in everyday speech.

First of all I wish to point out that, instead of speaking of a factor of *memory*, a factor of *habit*, or a factor of *heredity*, and attempting to identify one with another, I have preferred to consider these as manifestations of a common principle, which I shall call the *mnemic* principle. This mnemic property may be regarded from a purely physiological point of view, inasmuch as it is traced back to the effect of stimuli applied to the irritable organic substance. But the immediate effect of stimulation on the irritable substance is only one half of the problem with which we are concerned, although it happens to be that which has mainly occupied the attention of investigators. The other and distinctive half of the mnemic problem underlying the problems of memory, habit, and heredity, is the effect which remains in the stimulated substance *after* the excitement produced by the stimulation has apparently ceased. The capacity for such after-effect of stimulation constitutes what I have called the *Mneme*. Its result, namely, the enduring though primarily latent modification in the irritable substance produced by a stimulus, I have called an *Engram*, and the effect of certain stimulations upon certain substances is referred to as their *Engraphic effect.*

Now, it is attested by numerous observations and experiments that the engraphic effects of stimulation are not restricted to the irritable substance of the individual, but that the offspring of that individual may manifest corresponding *engraphic modifications*. Nor is there anything surprising in this, once we recognise not only that the offspring is produced from the germ-cells of the generation which has been submitted to the particular engraphic stimulation, but that these germ-cells are in continuous organic connection with the rest of the irritable substance of the organism. This once demonstrated, it should not be difficult to prove that the *engraphic* effects of stimulation are subject to the same laws, whether these effects are manifested in the individual which originally experienced stimulation, or in what we call the particular inherited character of that individual's offspring.

So much for the general nature of engrams, engraphic action, and effects, and of the principle which has given the name of *Mneme* to this book.

The second part of the book endeavours to trace all mnemic phenomena to a common origin. In doing this we deal with the influences which awaken the mnemic trace or engram out of its latent state into one of manifested activity, a process to which is given the name of *Ecphory*. Our study reveals the laws regulating the various associations between the latent and the revived, or *ecphorised*, mnemic traces or engrams. Going still further into the subject, we deal with the manner in

which the stock of engrams has been originally acquired, and also with the way in which this stock
has been partially transmitted by heredity. Meanwhile, the reader is given some notion of the con-
cordant action of closely allied mnemic and original
excitations, a consonance which I have found it convenient
to call *Homophony*. Broadly, the aim at this point in
the enquiry is to reduce the phenomena of individually
acquired reminiscences and the phenomena of individually
acquired habit to the same common mnemic elements
as are discernible in the large group of reproductive
phenomena usually referred to heredity. These common
mnemic elements are dealt with in special reference to
their capacity for making and reviving impressions
(Engraphy and Ecphory). Everyday expressions which
have hitherto led to many mistaken verbal analogies are
thus excluded.

The third part of the book seeks to furnish concrete
proof that the development of the individual ontogeny
is explicable by mnemic processes, especially by what I
have called *homophony*, the consonance of original and
mnemic excitations. Under such ontogenetic development
are included both the normal processes of growth and the
processes of regeneration and regulation.

This part of the book further undertakes to prove
that the above view of the relations between the Mneme
and the processes of genetics is not opposed to, but is
in accordance with, the results of modern experimental
research (Mendelism).

In this way I have tried to deduce from a common
property of all irritable organic substance—namely, that
of retaining revivable traces or engrams—a number of
mnemic laws, equally valid for the reproductions commonly grouped under memory, habit, or training, and
also for those which come under the head of ontogenetic
development, inherited periodicity, and regeneration
—laws common, in fact, to every kind of organic
reproduction.

I should like, however, to make it clear that while

putting forward the *mnemic principle* as the explanation of a vast group of vital phenomena, I am far from imagining that it explains the entire course of organic evolution or the present state of the organic world. What I have dealt with is merely the conserving principle necessary for the maintenance of the alterations produced by constantly changing environment. The adaptation of the individual organism to the surrounding organic and inorganic world is, of course, not explicable solely by this purely conserving principle; but, taking the latter in conjunction with the principle of natural selection, we shall, I think, find that the interplay of these two great factors affords us an adequate insight into the methods of organic evolution. The theory here developed will be found to be based solely upon causality, and to require no help from either vitalism or teleology.

PART I

CHAPTER I

ON STIMULUS AND EXCITATION

MY purpose in this book is to examine a specific kind of stimulation, or more properly, of excitation. An exact definition of the terms "stimulus" and "excitation" is therefore an indispensable preliminary to any study of the subject; still, notwithstanding the brilliant results already achieved by physiological research into stimuli and their effects on animals, plants, and protists, a precise meaning has not yet been assigned to the all-important terms in question. In the first two German editions of this work the greater part of the first chapter was devoted to this task; but having since treated it in a separate essay, I will content myself in this chapter with embodying its conclusions.

I will begin by stating the generally accepted definitions of the terms employed. "Stimuli" are certain actions on living organisms *accompanied by specific effects*. This implies that we determine the nature of a stimulus by the specific result thereby produced in an organism. It is this result or effect which characterises the stimulus as such.

What now is the specific nature of such action, as distinguished from the nature of action not followed by such result? We may begin by advancing a negative criterion:—"No action is a stimulus which does not produce some corresponding *physiological* change." Thus there can be no stimulus in the case of an inorganic body, nor in that of an organism after extinction of life. We are accustomed to define the changes referred to as *a reaction of the living organism.* Such reactions can be regarded as falling into two main groups according to the way in which we perceive them. One group embraces the sensory reactions resulting from impressions such as those of light, sound, pressure, etc., given to us in immediate sensation. These impressions can only be perceived by the individual himself and the corresponding reactions are therefore described as subjective. On the basis of extensive physiological observations and experiments, we premise from these respective sensations certain excitation - processes in definite parts of an irritable substance.

The second main group consists of objectively perceptible reactions, when an organism responds to a definite action by a corresponding change perceptible by the observer, i.e. a change which can be physico-chemically demonstrated. This change may be a process of growth, or the contraction of a muscle, or processes of metabolism such as secretions or chemical redistributions. It is characteristic of a great many of these objectively perceptible reactions that they do not become manifest in that part of the irritable substance subjected to the action of the stimulus, but in a remote part of the organism. The most striking examples of this are afforded by those tissues in which the function of irritability has reached the highest degree of specialisation, as in the nerve tissues of animals. But examples may also be found amongst plants As regards nerve tissue, no immediate change can be noted either in the exposed brain, or in the spinal cord, or in the nerves originating in the same, when stimulated either electrically, mechanically, chemically, or otherwise; but according to the part of the nervous system acted on, may be observed the contraction now of this, now of that muscle group, acceleration of breathing, change of heart action, secretion of saliva and of tears. The result of a given stimulus is to be observed not in the irritable substance—the nerve tissue to which the stimulus was applied, in which no change is demonstrable either morphological or chemical—but in possibly remote organs possessing the capacity of reaction to the given agent. We assume with reason, however, that the primarily irritated substance *is* affected, and it is now generally agreed to describe this primary change as excitation, upon which the visible reaction in the reactive organ follows only as a secondary effect.

Long after this assumption had been generally accepted as a clear explanation of the process involved, Du Bois Reymond demonstrated in the electro-motive behaviour of the nerves a state of excitement of the nervous substance itself. So by means of the reversed polarity of the nerve during stimulation (negative variation), we can prove that the nerve substance is affected by the stimulus, and we can in the same way directly demonstrate the result of the stimulus on the irritable gland substance by the negative variation of the gland current, and on the vegetable cellular tissue by the negative variation of the parenchyma current.

To sum up, if we group together all these specific results of stimulation, the group will comprise certain heterogeneous effects. First, the immediate sensations ; secondly, effects observed on organs far remote from the part directly subjected to the action ; and finally, effects observed on the irritable substance of this part itself.

We assume, however, one common feature in this heterogeneous group, viz. the process of the excitation in the irritable substance. The question as to the characteristic effects of the action of stimuli may now be answered in this way :—The effects of stimuli are known in all cases by the appearance of an excitation in the irritable substance.

The existence of an excitation, as we have already insisted, is purely a matter of inferential reasoning, and the same reasoning points to excitation being some form of energy ; for whether we base our reasoning on immediate reactions in consciousness, or whether we argue indirectly from our observation of motor or plastic reactions, metabolisms, or the negative variation of the electric current, we are obliged in all cases to assume an " energetic " process in the irritable organic substance. It is impossible

at present to state definitely what these energetic processes
are. Some writers believe that they are essentially
chemical energy. Others, in summary fashion, prefer to
speak of " physiological energy," or even of " nervous
energy," but they admit the possibility of reducing this
into the well-known forms—mechanical, thermal, electrical,
radiating, and chemical—which may be termed elementary
energies. We prefer, however, to speak only of the energetic process of the excitation, which may manifest itself
in many ways, differing according to the stimulus-receptor
which transforms the excitation.

Experience and experiment show that the entire,
highly complex state of excitement of the irritable
substance of an organism, which may be described as
its irritative-energetic condition, or, more briefly, as
its irritable condition, stands in close relationship to
the surrounding elementary-energetic condition which
is ceaselessly changing. We can, however, analyse this
relationship more precisely, for in many cases the specific
dependence of single components of the irritable condition
on single components of the elementary-energetic condition
can be traced.

This special relationship consists in the fact that the
initiation, duration, and termination of a component
of the elementary-energetic condition determines the
initiation, duration, and termination of a component of
the irritable condition.

The former component we term " stimulus," and the
latter " excitation." In ordinary speech we describe
such a relationship as one of cause and effect ; but in
all cases where we trace causal connection, that which
we call " effect " depends on a plurality of conditions.
There can be therefore no question of the production
of a single effect by a single independent factor. This
also obviously applies to the relation between the stimulus
and what has been defined as its " effect "—the single
excitation. In describing this relationship, therefore,
in terms of cause and effect, the presence of all other
essential conditions is implied.

" Stimulus " may thus be defined as that elementary-energetic condition whose initiation, duration, and termination in the presence of the requisite general conditions are followed by, or, as we commonly say, " cause " the initiation, duration, and termination of a single component of the irritable condition or single excitation. This component, the single original excitation, will thus not only be initiated, but also maintained by the stimulus. Further, a definite relation may be discerned between the magnitude of the stimulus and the intensity of the excitation resulting therefrom.

The above definition of the relation between stimulus and excitation sets the time-relation in the foreground. It describes the dependence, as regards time, of the excitation on the elementary-energetic condition. For the stimulus is immediately followed by the corresponding excitation, which lasts while the stimulus continues, and which ceases when the stimulus is withdrawn. For though the excitation may not then immediately disappear, yet it diminishes so rapidly that after a short interval no traces of the same are to be found.

The time-relation between stimulus and excitation is proved by observed and verifiable facts, and in my judgment must be a chief factor in any close analytical description of stimulation. I have already mentioned that immediately on the cessation of the stimulus, not complete disappearance, but rapid diminution of the excitation takes place. The excitation exists in full vigour only during the continuance of the stimulus, appearing immediately after it, and rapidly subsiding on the cessation of the stimulus. This, which we characterize as " synchronous," is the main phase of stimulation, and the excitation in this phase may be termed " synchronous excitation."

On the cessation of the stimulus, the excitation rapidly diminishes ; but always some seconds and sometimes minutes elapse before the last demonstrable traces of the excitation vanish, and the parts affected return to the condition in which they were prior to the commencement of the stimulus. This phase of the diminishing excitation, i.e. from the moment of the cessation of the stimulus and the rapid fall of the excitation until its total extinction, may be called the " acoluthic " phase of the excitation. This phase also may be regarded as a product of stimulation, or rather as a mediate product ; the immediate product being the synchronous excitation, upon which the acoluthic excitation follows. Regarding the latter as a mediate product of the stimulus, we can speak of an acoluthic or after-effect of the stimulus.

The study of acoluthic excitation has hitherto been pursued very sporadically. Amongst sensory excitations only visual acoluthic sensations have received detailed attention. Some study has been given to auditory acoluthic sensations ; but as regards the other fields of sense, hardly any research work has been undertaken so far.

In the department of peripheral, especially motor excitations, those phenomena of acoluthic excitation manifested on electrical stimulation of the muscles and of the nerves have been very closely studied (opening contraction, opening tetanus, etc.).

It must here be mentioned that the phenomenon of stimulus-summation to be treated in the next chapter implies a summation of acoluthic and synchronous excitations, new synchronous excitations being added to the already existing acoluthic excitations.

In the realm of plant-physiology, also, several cases of " after-effects " have been observed. Unfortunately, however, the acoluthic effect of stimulation has been hardly, if at all, discriminated from the engraphic effect, and the acoluthic and the mnemic excitations have in most cases not been sufficiently distinguished. So far as I am aware, only Sir Francis Darwin and Miss D. F. M. Pertz have been alive to the fundamental distinction between these two conceptions, and emphasised the inaccuracy of applying the term " after-effect " indiscriminately to both.

The acoluthic excitation is characterised by being the

immediate continuation of the synchronous excitation, which it terminates with a rapid diminution in intensity.

In many, perhaps in all cases, it possesses an oscillating character, but the lowest point of the oscillations seems to register not total absence, but merely a great weakening of the respective acoluthic excitations, but in a few seconds, or at most a few minutes after cessation of the stimulus, the acoluthic excitation entirely vanishes, and no further traces of it as such, i.e. as a demonstrable excitation, can be discerned. The condition of the irritable substance as regards the special excitation which has now died away is apparently the same as before the application of the stimulus. This state of renewed indifference may be called the secondary state of indifference, in contrast to the primary state of indifference which existed prior to the application of the stimulus. The ordinary understanding is that primary and secondary states of indifference are practically, if not absolutely, identical. They are so in respect of the immediately manifested reactions, but it will now be our task to show that they are not so in respect of their capacity for reaction. Plant-physiologists have given more attention to this matter than animal-physiologists, but both have somewhat neglected the systematic handling of the problem. The view here taken is that the problem is of fundamental importance in the investigation of the physiology of stimulus and for the theory of descent.

CHAPTER II

ENGRAPHIC ACTION OF STIMULI ON THE INDIVIDUAL

WHEN an organism has been temporarily stimulated and has passed, after the cessation of the stimulus, into the condition of " secondary indifference," it can be shown that such organism—be it plant, protist, or animal —has been permanently affected. This I call the *engraphic* action of a stimulus, because a permanent record has been written or engraved on the irritable substance. I use the word *engram* to denote this permanent change wrought by a stimulus ; the sum of such engrams in an organism may be called its " engram-store," among which we must distinguish inherited from acquired engrams. The phenomena resulting from the existence of one or more engrams in an organism I describe as mnemic phenomena. The totality of the mnemic potentialities of an organism is its " Mneme."

In adopting original expressions for the conceptions defined in this book, I am not unmindful of the words " Memory " and " Memory image," already in use. But for my purpose I should have to use these in a much wider sense than is customary, and the way would thus be opened for innumerable misconceptions and consequent controversy. It would be a mistake to give a wider interpretation to a term which is ordinarily used in a narrower sense. or to use an expression like " Memory image," which invariably suggests phenomena in consciousness.

In quoting experimental examples of engraphic stimulation in higher and lower organisms, one thing must be borne in mind. The ability to retain the engraphic stimulations—the so-called engraphic susceptibility—varies in irritable organic substances, just as the irritability in respect of synchronous excitation differs greatly in various organisms, and in the varieties of tissue and cell within the same organism. In animals, during the evolutionary process, one organic system—the nervous system—has become specialised for the reception and transmission of stimuli. No monopoly of this function by the nervous system, however, can be deduced from this specialisation, not even in its highest state of evolution, as in Man. To quote a significant case, it has been demonstrated by indisputable observation and experiment that muscle is still irritable even after entire elimination of all nervous influence.

Just as the synchronous irritability of the nervous system has gradually increased in the evolution of the species, so its engraphic susceptibility has increased. Yet neither of them has become a monopoly of the nervous system, but has remained in the higher organisms as a property of irritable substance as such, thus seeming to be indissolubly bound up with the mere quality of irritability. Observations on the nervous system lead us to the conclusion that the engraphic susceptibility grows with the increase of irritability. Weak and momentary stimuli may fail in any decisive engraphic effect on the non-nervously differentiated organic substance, and yet exercise a strong influence so far as nerve substance is concerned.

This idea is advanced in order to prepare the reader for the demonstration of the fact that the engraphic action of stimuli on nerve substance is simpler and more direct than on non-nervously differentiated substance, especially in cases of the experimental production of such engraphic action. On non-nervous substance, as contrasted with nerve substance, the stimuli have as a rule to act much longer, or repeat themselves much more frequently, in order to produce engraphic effects. But in the nervous substance of the higher animals a single momentary stimulus suffices to produce an easily demonstrable, durable engram.   In principle little significance attaches to this difference, but it is strikingly evident in experimental illustrations, which gain in effectiveness and simplicity in proportion to the amount of nervous differentiation in the material employed.

For this reason we may take as our first example of engraphic stimulation one on the nerve substance of a higher animal.   The supposition that we are best able to study the physiological properties and capacities of organic substance by experiments with unicellular living creatures is an error, though common enough in the scientific literature of the present day.   Where the division of labour amongst cells and tissues is far advanced, and specific organic functions have been evolved, our study of these functions is made more simple and the results of our work are less ambiguous than in those cases where functions are merged in each other, and it seems almost impossible to differentiate them.

Although in our study of engraphic stimulation both nerve and other substance must be taken into account, it will be easier and better to proceed in our research from the more to the less differentiated.

Let us take first the case of a young dog whose simple trust in humanity has not yet been shaken.   He is pelted with stones by boys at play.   Two groups of stimuli act upon the creature :—(Group "a") the optical stimulus of the boys picking up stones and throwing them, and (Group "b") the tactual stimulus of the stones striking the skin, resulting in pain.   Both stimuli groups act engraphically, for after the cessation of the synchronous and the acoluthic effects of stimulation, the organism now appears permanently changed in relation to certain stimuli.   Previously, the optical stimulus of a stooping boy was accompanied by no definite reaction, but now this stimulus acts regularly—generally until the death of the animal—as a pain-causing stimulus.   The animal puts its tail between its legs and runs away, often with loud howls. We may express this by saying that the reactions belonging to stimulus group " b " are henceforth elicited not only by these stimuli, but also by stimulus group " a."

The illustration affords a deeper understanding of the nature of the engraphic stimulation. We perceive that the change of the organic substance is of such a nature that the synchronous state of excitement belonging to stimulus " b " may be aroused not only by the entry of stimulus " b " as in the primary state of excitement, but also by other influences, such as the stimulus group " a " in the above-mentioned case. The influences which produce this result may be termed " ecphoric " influences, and if they possess a stimulus character, ecphoric stimuli. But, as we shall find later, not all ecphoric influences can simply be called " stimuli."

It is only when the synchronous and acoluthic action of a stimulus has ceased, and the substance has entered the secondary state of indifference, that we are able to recognise whether the effect left behind is an engraphic change, and this we are able to do by the following method :—We have to find out whether the state of excitement belonging to that stimulus may now be called up by influences differing quantitatively and qualitatively from the engraphically acting stimulus. A stimulus which on its first appearance acts engraphically may be called an original stimulus. The synchronous excitation with its acoluthic sequence may be termed an original excitation.

It is self-evident that the stimulus produces at each action its corresponding synchronous state of excitement, and that this is in itself no proof of a preceding engraphic change. A stimulus must therefore differ either quantitatively or qualitatively from the original stimulus before one can say of it, from the standpoint of objective analysis, that it acts ecphorically. To prove this fully, it is necessary to demonstrate by experiment that this ecphoric influence is either quantitatively or qualitatively insufficient by itself to elicit the given reaction without the preceding action of the original stimulus. In the case before us it is easy to obtain proof by comparing the behaviour of the animal before the painful experience with its behaviour after it. The essential points of the case quoted, to which many other cases of animals, birds, reptiles, and cephalopods might be added, can be stated in the following propositions :—

(1) Stimulus " a," as original stimulus, generates only excitation " a."

(2) Stimulus " b," as original stimulus, generates only excitation " β."

(3) Excitation $(a + \beta)$, as original excitation, is generated only by stimulus ("a" + "b").

(4) But excitation $(a + \beta)$, as mnemic excitation, that is, after former action of stimulus ("a" + "b") and the creation of the engrams $(A + B)$, may be generated by stimulus " a " alone, acting as ecphoric stimulus.

In the case of lower animals, plants, and protists, it is as a rule impossible to obtain an engraphic effect by the action of a single momentary stimulus. A prolonged or frequently repeated stimulation is required. But we are still of opinion that further research will furnish convincing experimental evidence of engraphic effects of all kinds in the case of the lower organisms.

Proof of clear and permanent engraphic effects may be gathered from observations made during the last decade by Bohn, Jennings, van der Ghinst, and others on non-vertebrates, such as the lower Molluscs, Echinoderms, Coelenterates, and the more highly organised Crustaceans. Hodge and Aikins as long ago as 1895 noted such effects, traces of which remained for several hours.

Since the first edition of *The Mneme* Sir Francis Darwin, pursuing the line of investigation suggested in that book, has collected various examples of united (associated) engrams in the realm of the physiology of plants. Even earlier, the same distinguished worker in collaboration with Miss D. Pertz succeeded in associating the photical or geotropical engrams in plants with metabolic engrams.

Engraphic effect can readily be demonstrated by the application of one single kind of stimulus. For after repeated or prolonged action of the stimulus, and after return of the organism to the secondary state of indifference, a much feebler stimulus of the kind which produced the original state of excitement suffices to produce the same effect. Such effects may be produced in animals with moderately high nervous systems by a few momentary stimuli. Thus Davenport and Cannon, in the course of experiments made for quite a different purpose on Daphniæ, discovered that their reaction to the stimulus of light—a positive heliotropic reaction—altered perceptibly on the application of a limited number of momentary stimuli. After this application only a quarter of the original light-stimulus was required to produce the original or an even stronger reaction. This result was a constant one. Observations frequently made by botanists and students of the Protista on the alteration of the so-called " light disposition," under the influence of photic stimuli, fall into the same class. The reactions by which these alterations, surviving the supervention of the secondary state of indifference, become manifest may be motor reactions as well as those of growth. In connection with the latter, Oltmanns, experimenting on fungi, exposed them for ten hours to the electric light. For a further fifteen hours the plants were kept in the dark, and then again subjected to intense light. " Under the influence of the renewed exposure the sporangia at first made some strongly negative curvatures, which were soon neutralised. Then within a relatively short interval positive movements set in, which were maintained with far greater energy than previously, and which also brought about sharper endings. It is clear that the latter phenomenon was caused by the preceding exposure to intense light, that is, that the movements became more energetic in consequence of increased " light disposition."

The essential points of this and the previous observation may be expressed in propositions corresponding to those in which we summed up the results of our first example (p. 28).

(1) Stimulus "a," as original stimulus, generates original excitation "a."

(2) Stimulus $\frac{"a"}{2}$, as original stimulus, generates original excitation $\frac{"a"}{2}$ only.

(3) But stimulus $\frac{"a"}{2}$, as ecphoric stimulus, may liberate excitation "a" as mnemic excitation (i.e. after the previous action of stimulus "a" and the creation of an engram "A").

Further proof of the engraphic effect of the stimuli in respect of the excitations, both in the individual subjected to them and in his progeny, will be given later. For the present it will be more to our purpose if, instead of quoting further cases, we begin the specific analysis of engraphic stimulation and its manifestations, an analysis, however, which is merely provisional at this stage, and will be more fully elaborated in the second part of the book.

We may begin by considering the organism in its primary state of indifference.

PRIMARY STATE OF INDIFFERENCE.—Under this definition we have simply to conceive the state of the organism at the beginning of the observations and experiments. Into this state it is absolutely essential for us to enquire minutely. At the outset we are met by difficulties of a two-fold order ; for the objects which we choose for analysis possess—unless they are germs just separated from the parent organism—a sum of individually acquired engrams, and also engrams resembling those whose genesis we wish to observe, or which we wish to produce artificially. Suppose we choose a one-year-old specimen of the sensitive plant *Mimosa pudica,* and try to influence it

engraphically by photic stimuli, it will not be sufficient
to register at the beginning of the experiments its reactions
to light during the previous twenty-four hours. The
reactions given at the end of September by a one-year-
old plant grown in Christiania may be almost identical
with the reactions given by a plant imported direct from
the Equator, but we must not forget the possibility of
the manifestation to pronounced differences a few months
later, which would be inexplicable did we not take into
account the engrams which the plants acquired in their
different places of origin. One way out of this difficulty
would be to cultivate the demonstration objects, whenever
practicable, directly from seeds and ova, and keep them
under conditions which safeguard a study of the engraphic
action of such stimuli. A mimosa, which for one year had
been subjected alternately to twelve hours' artificial
light and twelve hours' artificial darkness in a room kept
at an equal temperature, is a much more controllable
object than one which has been exposed only to natural
conditions of light and darkness. The best results, however, are obtained from those objects upon which, in
their individual lives, relatively few stimuli have acted,
e.g. the seed plant just emerging and exposed for the
first time to the light of day, or the young chick at the
moment of breaking its shell. Whatever object is chosen,
the attempt should be made to secure individuals which
hitherto have not been subjected to that particular
stimulus, of which it is intended to study the engraphic
action.

So far, our method of determining engraphic change
by simple observation with a minimum of inferential
reasoning, has consisted in demonstrating the change of
the capacity to react between the primary and the
secondary states of indifference. The fewer individually
acquired engrams that exist in the primary state, the less
complicated the task.

The individual, which in its unicellular stage has just
separated from the parental organism, is virgin soil as
far as its individual Mneme is concerned ; but as we shall

see later, it already possesses inherited engrams, indeed a considerable stock of them. Accordingly, since on our planet it is impossible to obtain fresh, spontaneously generated organic material, there is no single organism available for examination which, mnemically considered, can be regarded as *tabula rasa*. The germ cell, which a moment before was part of the parent and shared its Mneme, does not by the act of separation from its parent and by its entrance into a new individual phase obliterate entirely its own Mneme. This might, of course, be assumed a priori, but it can be demonstrated by an abundance of evidence.

Later on it will be our task to see to what degree the germ cells share in the individual and acquired engrams of the entire organism, and to what extent they retain their share after separation.

ENGRAPHICALLY ACTING STIMULUS —Energetic influences from those energy-groups, of which we know that they produce synchronous excitations in organisms, may act engraphically simply by the medium of those excitations. Such are mechanical, geotropic, acoustic, photic, thermal, electric, and chemical influences. Magnetic influences appear to be altogether unable to act as stimuli on organisms. If this assumption be correct, then neither can such influences act engraphically. Again, it is possible that energies which have hitherto escaped our observation may produce synchronous excitations in organisms, and thereby also act engraphically. Within recent years, the " X " rays—a hitherto unknown kind of radiant energy—have been discovered. Shortly afterwards, their capability to act on organic bodies as stimuli was demonstrated. Of Radium radiation the same may be said. The above enumeration does not exhaust the list of energies which act as original stimuli, and in a secondary degree as engraphic stimuli. It suffices, however, for the present phase of our research.

The question now arises.—When does a stimulus that is capable of originating an engraphic effect act engraphically, and when does it not ? To answer this question we must examine some general laws of stimulation. To produce a synchronous effect each energetic action must be of a definite strength and duration, and these vary in value according to the nature and state of the organism to be influenced. In this sense, we may speak of the "threshold" of the stimulus. Careful observation shows that this "threshold" or liminal value depends not only on the strength and duration of the energetic action, but also on a third factor, namely, its continuity or its discontinuity. Whilst the first two factors in their significance for synchronous stimulation do not require further comment, the third factor demands more minute treatment. It is well known that electrical (as also mechanical) actions on contractile substances, lying usually under the threshold, become effective after repeated action. Evidently, by the continued application of stimuli, the irritability of the organic substance is increased by "addition latente" (Richet), which lowers the threshold of the effective intensity of such stimulus for the given substance, so that a hitherto subliminal intensity becomes a liminal one. Biedermann, demonstrating the stimulus-summation of non-striated muscles, writes :—" Even under the most favourable conditions a visible effect (contraction) can hardly be obtained by strong, but detached induction shocks ; whilst the same objects, namely, the muscles of Molluscæ—all of which are non-striated—and the muscles of the intestines and of the ureter, manifest tetanus with even a relatively weak current, when the stimulus acts in quick succession under Neef's oscillating hammer. Even in the application of constant currents, according to Engelmann, one can often induce an effective excitation by frequently making and breaking a current which otherwise would not act. The capacity of stimulus-summation, although graduated according to development, seems to belong to all irritable plasm—to ciliated cells, to nerve cells, and to vegetable plasm such as that of Dionæa, etc.—so that the recorded manifestations in the above-mentioned experiments on muscles represent only a specific case of a general law."

Recent investigations by Steinach regarding the flagellates, infusoria, and plant and animal tissues, have fully confirmed the accuracy of Biedermann's view that all irritable plasm is susceptible of stimulus-summation. We may instance the very great capacity for summation of vegetable cells and the still greater capacity of the luminous cells of Lampyris.

In considering the engraphic action of discontinuous stimuli, we shall have to differentiate two distinct classes of effects. It is apparent that no stimulus acting engraphically does so directly, but only through the medium of the excitation produced by it. If a discontinuous stimulus produces a continuous excitation which occurs regularly under short intervals of stimulation—as in the cases described by Biedermann and Steinach—the excitation so produced does not differ in its engraphic action from that produced by continuous stimulation. The former may be stronger quantitatively as a result of stimulus-summation, but is otherwise identical.

The engraphic action is, however, altogether different if the repetition of the stimulus takes place at longer intervals of time, and if the periods of stimulation are sufficiently separated for the excitation produced by the preceding stimulus to have died away before a re-application, and for the irritable substance to have returned to its corresponding state of indifference. In such cases, not only the stimuli, but also the excitation produced by them, are discontinuous, and each repetition of the stimulus then produces a fresh engram qualitatively equal to, but distinct from, its corresponding predecessors. This discontinuity and independence of engrams which owe their existence to the repetition of the same stimulus is of great importance, as will be explained in detail in Chapter VII on the subject of Homophony and the significance of stimulus-repetition.

So far we have spoken only of the engraphic action of a single continuous or discontinuous stimulus. Each organism, however, is affected by conditions of distance and volume and motion in regard to the various kinds of energy to which it is permanently exposed. We defined these conditions as its external energetic situation.

Now, it appears hardly possible, even in the best planned experiment in a laboratory, to alter the energetic situation in relation to a single energy alone, and we can hardly expect to meet with such a case under natural conditions. When the sun breaks through the clouds and shines on a plant, not a simple, but a highly complex change of the energetic situation is produced, and different kinds of radiant energy, such as ultra-red heat rays, various light rays, and chemically acting ultra-violet rays, act as so many stimuli on the organism.

Only in the laboratory are we able in a measure to allow purely photic influences to act on the organism— for instance, by applying red rays of a definite wave length which exercise hardly any chemical effect, and the thermal influence of which has been reduced almost to zero by passing them through interpolated films of ice. A mimosa standing in a darkened room may be subjected suddenly to the influence of sunlight. By this single cause is produced the simultaneous action of at least three stimuli, the synchronic effect of which we can demonstrate by the appearance of three different reactions. To the photic stimulus the plant responds by unfolding its leaves, to the chemical stimulus by metabolic reactions known as the absorption of carbonic acid and the emission of oxygen, and to the thermal stimulus by acceleration of growth. By eliminating either the thermal, photic or chemical rays, we can demonstrate how the previous simple change of the external energetic situation was the occasion of different simultaneous stimuli. The energetic situation of the organisms on our planet is continually subject to change, not in one, but in many, respects. Such changes may have a manifest connection with each other. For example, a thunderstorm produces simultaneously photic, thermal, acoustic, mechanical and numerous other stimuli affecting those organisms with whose energetic situation it interferes. Often various stimuli simultaneously influence the same organism, and we are unable to trace their relations of origin. Such a coincidence we describe as fortuitous.

We conclude that each organism is continually subjected to stimulation, and in most cases to the simultaneous action of various stimuli.

We may now ask whether two or more stimuli, acting simultaneously on an organism and producing synchronous effects, can also influence it engraphically in juxtaposition.

The answer is readily given in the case of those organisms where the engraphic effects of stimuli are easily observed. If the organism be a man, a monkey, a dog, a horse, or a bird, it is comparatively easy to demonstrate the engraphic action of two simultaneous stimuli. If I whip a young dog which has never been punished before, both the optical stimulus—the sight of the whip—and the tactual stimulus—producing sensations of pain—act engraphically and, what is of particular importance, the engrams produced by these simultaneous stimuli enter into a certain indissoluble relationship to each other. This relationship can be defined by stating that henceforward the application of only one stimulus will suffice to act ecphorically on the engram simultaneously produced by the other stimulus. The mere sight of the whip in the hand of its master will ecphorise in the dog the mnemic excitation of the definite sensation of pain, and produce the corresponding reaction, namely, curling of the tail, howls, and flight. We describe such engrams, where the application of the engraphic stimulus of one serves as the ecphoric stimulus of the other, as *associated* engrams. We may state it as a rule without exception that all simultaneously-produced engrams are associated even when the effective stimuli are of different kinds and have no relationship in respect of the cause of their appearance. Two stimuli of very different kinds and without recognisable relationship once acted upon me simultaneously—the view of Capri from Naples, and a specific smell of boiling olive oil. Ever since, a similar smell of oil unfailingly acts ecphorically on the photogenic engram of Capri.

Apart from this association of engrams created by the simultaneous action of their engraphic stimuli, which, in keeping with the terms already introduced, we may describe as association of simultaneously created engrams, a second and equally important association may be observed, which is also dependent on the time-relation of the action of the engraphic stimuli. Not only the simultaneous engrams, but also those generated immediately after, are associated in such a manner that the application of the original stimulus of one may serve as an ecphoric stimulus to the others. In this case, too, an association is established, even when the respective engrams owe their genesis to widely differing kinds of stimulus, and where a causal nexus between these engraphic stimuli cannot be traced. We may describe this latter condition as the association of *successively created engrams*. We shall examine more closely in the second part of this work the derivation of the successive from the simultaneous association.

SECONDARY STATE OF INDIFFERENCE. (Latent state of the engram.)—After the cessation of the synchronous state of excitement, followed by a transient acoluthic state of excitement, the organism passes into a state which may be.termed the secondary state of indifference. This is distinguished from the primary state solely by the possession of the new engrams due to the action of the various engraphic stimuli. These, however, being latent are not perceptible in the secondary state. Ecphoric influences are necessary for their manifestation.

The intervention of a latent phase between the synchronous and the mnemic states of excitement is highly characteristic of mnemic phenomena, and presents the mnemic excitation in the light of a reproduction.

The results of our researches so far may be summarised as follows :—A stimulus induces in an organism a specific state of excitement which manifests itself by definite reactions. On the cessation of the stimulus, the state of excitement is at once modified, and a little later altogether subsides. The irritable substance, so far as the stimulus is concerned, returns to the state in which it was before the action of the stimulus, and the return marks the secondary state of indifference. But the two states of indifference, the one before and the other after the interference of the stimulus, are not identical. They differ in that the irritable substance in its secondary state may, by the action of certain ecphoric influences, manifest the intermediary state of excitement, a result which would not be possible in its primary state. The question arises whether there are not cases where the irritable substance, after the cessation of stimulation, does not pass into the secondary state of indifference, but maintains permanently the state of excitement originally created by the stimulus. I believe we are to-day already in a position to answer this question with a decided negative, notwithstanding that our re-searches are not yet completed. Of course, there are subsequent *results* of the excitations which do not dis-appear with the cessation of the excitation, for instance, the results which appear as phenomena of growth.

More difficult to judge are those cases which Pfeffer (*Plant Physiology*, vol. ii, p. 167) describes as continuous (static, inherent) induction. In these cases, a temporary stimulus creates a continuous induction. May this not be explained on the assumption that here also the stimulation results in growth, which itself conditions new growth by acting as stimulus to that end? In none of these cases can we speak of persistence of the irritable substance in its primary state of excitement. The case of *Marchantia polymorpha* seems to present considerable difficulty. The gemmæ of this liverwort can be so influenced by a few days' exposure to light from one side, that it becomes definitely determined which is going to be the upper and which the lower side of the plant before the anatomical differentiation has become pronounced in the seedling.

It may be, however, that future research will show that the action of stimuli creates permanent states in the morphological structure of the growing seedling, and that these states, acting as stimuli of position, continue to influence new acquisitions. But until such a structure has been demonstrated, this interpretation of the difficulty must be regarded as merely an assumption. Further, since other explanations are also conceivable, the case of *Marchantia* need not be taken as proof that under certain circumstances a state of excitement becomes permanent in the organic substance, instead of ultimately resolving itself into the secondary state of indifference. The general order of things is as follows, and may be stated as an established rule :—After the cessation of a stimulus the organism returns sooner or later into the state of indifference. A permanent effect on the irritable substance is produced by the stimulus only in so far as it leaves an engram behind. The irritable substance is therefore altered in this respect that, from now, the synchronous state of excitement peculiar to the stimulus may be resuscitated not only by the latter, but also by other influences, which may be termed ecphoric.

Ecphoric Influences.—From the preceding exposition it follows that the engram of a stimulus—that is, the engram of the state of excitement produced by a stimulus—is simply the altered disposition of the irritable substance in its relation to the repetition of the state of excitement. The organic substance reveals the working of a new law, in that it is now predisposed to the state of excitement by influences other than that of the original stimulus.

The state of excitement arising from the ecphorizing of an engram may be described as the *mnemic state of excitement*. And so far as a mnemic excitation manifests itself as a sensation, the latter may be termed a *mnemic sensation*.

Surveying the mnemic phenomena in the three organic realms, we find that the following groups of influences may act ecphorically on an engram :—

First :—The repetition of the original stimulus either in a qualitatively and quantitatively identical—or almost identical—form, or in a form which, while similar, varies somewhat quantitatively and qualitatively.

Second :—The ecphory of other engrams generated at the same time as the engram, or immediately before. Engrams may be associated simultaneously or in succession.

Third :—Certain influences which appear to us at first only as definite periods of time or development also act ecphorically.

These may all be reduced, as we shall see later on, to the one principle which underlies all three groups. This principle is the *partial* recurrence of a definite energetic condition.

The simplest of all quoted cases is apparently that in which a stimulus, identical qualitatively and quantitatively with the original stimulus, acts ecphorically. But in this particular case it is hardly possible to prove the ecphoric action of the stimulus objectively. For one has no right to differentiate between the effect of a stimulus at its first and at its later action if, on its recurrence, it shows exactly the same phenomena as on its first appearance. Nevertheless good reasons may be given for speaking of an ecphoric effect even in the case of a mere repetition of the original stimulus. These reasons are based in the first place on subjective observation or introspection. This essential aid is regarded dubiously by many scientific men, whose work may not have allowed them to become intimate with the methods of physiological and especially sense-physiological research. But as we shall often have occasion to refer to introspection, some remarks on its value as a method for scientific research may well be made.

All that we name the " external world " is cognisable by us objectively, that is, by occurrences and processes within our own organism. A number of retinal and brain processes result in the consciousness of what we call a " tree," which we regard as external to us. Other processes involving the olfactory epithelium we describe as " fragrances," referring them also to something external. Consciousness involves the perception of stimulus effects. We gradually learn to argue from these effects to the stimuli causing them. Experience helps us to differentiate " inner " and " outer." The developing child thus builds up for itself an image of the outer world which, like the unsophisticated adult, it refers to something not itself. It is altogether unaware of the subjective foundation of its external world. At no time must we lose sight of the fact that subjective states of consciousness are for us the prime foundation of the external world. From them we fashion the world of images which represents for us external reality, and which, by the use of analogy, we come to regard as objective. So much at least must be acknowledged, even if for the purposes of this book —as for science—the reality of this external world is unquestioned. The necessity of employing the subjective (introspective) method in the analysis of many fundamental problems of biology and physiology lies in its being the only one whereby knowledge based on sense-perception can be obtained. By the objective method the analysis of sense-perception is impossible. Even when to the methods of observation and experiment we add the method of verbal communication, the ideas we form by such objective means of the sensations of our fellow creatures are not particularly well defined, and probably only quite exceptionally, if at any time, absolutely correct. The application of the subjective method to the problems of biological science is, therefore, perfectly legitimate. It has been applied in proper places by physiologists such as Johannes Müller, Helmholtz, Hering, and many others, men of the highest repute in their profession. We owe the most valuable results of sense-physiology to this method, without which the imposing and securely founded edifice of this science would never have been built. But we need to be on our guard against a non-critical intermixture of the objective with the subjective method.

The latter method is purely personal, but the use of the objective method gives material for comparison, whereby we can check the observations of our own stimulations by reference to the experience of others.

But as soon as we begin to apply conclusions from the observation of reactions occurring in our own muscles, glands, etc., to the sensations of other individuals we at once enter the field of hypothesis.

This hypothesis is perfectly justifiable as long as we are concerned with those creatures which closely resemble us morphologically and physiologically, and whose physiological reactions speak to us in a language hardly to be misunderstood, especially when human speech is available as an auxiliary. Only I myself know the qualitative and quantitative values of the sensation of pain caused in me by the prick of a needle, and can estimate them to a fairly correct degree; but it would be hypercritical to reject the conclusion that this stimulus causes a sensation nearly identical with that in my fellow men who react in a similar manner by a twitch and a sudden cry, and who can minutely describe to me in words the sensation they feel. It is very probable that a monkey or a dog, reacting against a needle-prick by a twitch and a specific vocal sound, feels something similar to my own sensation. We are, however, on less certain ground when we consider the reactions that a frog or a fish may make to such a stimulus as a needle-prick, although it is probable that the sensations are not unlike our own.

Our conclusions become still less valid when we approach the invertebrate Worms, the Coelenterates, and similar creatures, even though these react against the pin-prick by a sudden withdrawal of the part touched. But an assertion that a Mimosa feels something like our sensation of pain at a touch, against which it reacts by the sudden folding up of its leaves, falls entirely outside the limits of scientific discussion because of the lack of those convincing inferences from analogy which might make it appear probable.

The subjective method of the investigation of Self gives results which are denied in great measure to the objective method. We may apply the former in unlimited measure in our perceptive knowledge of nature. It is legitimate, moreover, to make analogical use of such knowledge in our estimate of the sensory reactions of other creatures. Human intercourse is largely dependent on such a use. But we must bear in mind the uncertainty of the conclusions based on analogical reasoning, for the validity of them diminishes as we extend them from our fellow men to the remaining warm-blooded species, from these to the cold-blooded ones, from the Vertebrates to the Non-vertebrates, and from these to the Protozoa and Plants. In the course of our present investigation we are fortunately able to dispense with such a transference of the subjective method. We apply this method only to the Self, so that each reader may form for himself a clear idea of the ecphory of an engram by a stimulus resembling qualitatively and quantitatively the original stimulus. Everybody may observe in himself, on the repetition of a stimulus which has already once acted upon him—for instance, the optical stimulus of an arabesque or the characteristic design of a carpet or wall-paper—that the state of sensation which arose at the first action of this stimulus is not simply repeated, but that a new element appears in consciousness, namely, the sensation of having been subjected once before to this specific stimulation, that is, of having already experienced this characteristic state of excitement. We describe this state of consciousness which responds to stimuli of all kinds, and which we do not intend to analyse here any further, as "recognition." The point we wish to emphasise is that the irritable substance in the secondary state of indifference, as compared with it in its primary state of indifference, has undergone a change, or, as we say, has been influenced engraphically. If this repetition of the original stimulus produces the same synchronous effect as at its first appearance, and if my consciousness tells me clearly that my organism has retained traces of having already passed through this state of excitement, then here surely is first-hand evidence that the second stimulus does not only exercise a synchronous effect, but also an ecphoric one in making me aware of the existence of an engram by means of a specific reaction, namely, that of consciousness.

With the assistance of the objective method it is possible to show in a fairly convincing but more uncertain way that the existence of an engram may be traced by the simple repetition of the original stimulus. This less direct proof is based on the fact that the objectively traceable reactions frequently appear in quicker or stronger fashion on repetition of the stimulus than when the stimulus was first applied. We may remind the reader of the previously-quoted observations of Davenport and Cannon, which show that Daphniæ in their heliotropic movements towards the source of light require at the third application of a strong light-stimulus about half the necessary time (twenty-eight instead of forty-eight seconds) to swim the distance of 16 cm. The investigations of Oltmann into fungi lead to similar conclusions. The experiments cited lead to cases where a stimulus coinciding qualitatively with the original stimulus, but differing from it quantitatively, can be regarded as an ecphorising stimulus. After repeated stimulation of an organism, a stimulus of far less intensity and duration than was required in the first instance will suffice to produce the same reactions (lowering of stimulation threshold). Evidence of this being an ecphory of engrams, however, is given only by those cases where the repetition does not take place at too short intervals, so that the organism has time to pass entirely into its second state of indifference and to allow of the subsidence of the synchronous and acoluthic states. It is not necessary, therefore, for us to consider the phenomenon of stimulus-summation, for, as already suggested on page 34, such summation is not a case of the ecphory of mnemic excitations by the rapid repetition of stimuli, but rather a case of synchronous excitations freshly generated by these stimuli, added to acoluthic excitations which have not yet subsided. We may see engraphic and ecphoric action in the experiments by Davenport and Cannon on the Daphniæ, where, after repeated stimulation at gradually longer intervals, a stimulus possessing but a quarter of the strength of the original stimulus produced after a few repetitions the same reactions as the original stimulus, and after many repetitions even quicker reactions than were given by the original stimulus on its first application.

Similar conclusions may be obtained from observations made on the higher animals and on man. In the breaking-in of a horse, e.g. while training it to canter, the trainer may reduce the force of the pressure-stimuli, which induce definite positions and movements of the horse, so much that comparatively weak stimuli which at the beginning were not even noticed will at the end be quite effective. By the repeated action of stimuli it is possible, therefore, to lower their stimulation threshold. Most frequently, these are instances of ecphoric action on engrams ; and, exceptionally, of the general increase of sensitiveness in the respective sensory areas. A good wine-taster is not necessarily also a good tea-taster ; and although perhaps better qualified to be a taste expert than an ordinary mortal, he first must acquire hundreds of new engrams from the chemical stimulus of tea in order to be able to react to the finely-graded differences of stimuli which would be bewildering to the non-expert. Similar examples might be adduced in reference to the engraphic training of the visual and oral senses, but in these cases it is more difficult to exclude from these reactions the co-operation of subsidiary brain-processes than from those of the senses of touch, taste, and smell, which are less complicated with accessory processes. Slight qualitative deviations from the original stimulus do not, however, invalidate the ecphoric action of a stimulus on the engram belonging to the original stimulus. Thus, it is sufficient to see the picture of a landscape in order to be able to ecphorise the engram belonging to the landscape itself ; to hear a tune hummed in order to ecphorise the engram belonging to the original full orchestral performance. If the smell of Selene gas ecphorises in us the olfactory engram of rotten radish, it is clear that one ecphoric stimulus has vicariously replaced another which from a chemical point of view is altogether different. How far these deviations may extend without diminishing the ecphoric action or entirely preventing it is a question to which a general answer cannot be given. Each case must be considered in its specific action.

We will now consider those influences, the ecphoric action of which can in a certain sense only be described as intermediate, inasmuch as they do not act on the engram (A) itself which is "focused," but in some engram (B) associated with the former. We find that the ecphory of B, that is, the mnemic excitation β, acts ecphorically on engram A.

Already, in the section on the engraphic action of original stimuli, attention has been drawn to the peculiarity of engrams generated in an organism either simultaneously or in quick succession. These are described as associated. This association or connection is latent in the engram, and only becomes manifest when owing to a strongly marked association the ecphory of one engram unfailingly affects the ecphory of the other ; the association having been established by the frequent repetitions of the simultaneous or successive engraphic stimulation.

To demonstrate the presence of such intermediate ecphory we ought, of course, to be able to produce such associated engrams experimentally. But we have already pointed out the difficulties of experiment on organisms where no differentiation in the irritable substance as such has yet taken place. If it is then difficult to create by individual stimulation a single clearly defined engram, how much more difficult will it be to produce two different engrams simultaneously or successively associated? The reader is referred to the remarks on page 28. We shall, however, meet with many cases of simultaneously or successively associated engrams of lower organisms in the later chapters of this book, especially in that part which deals with the action of mnemic processes in ontogenesis. For our present purpose we prefer to select examples from the realm of the higher animals where, on account of the high specialisation of their irritable substance in the shape of a nervous system, the general production of engrams, and consequently also the simultaneous and successive production of different engrams, is the readier.

It has already been described how in a young dog the single simultaneous experience of stimuli—such as (1) the optic stimulus of a man picking up stones and (2) the tactual stimulus caused by stones which strike the dog —suffices to generate for life two engrams, so closely associated as to allow of the ecphory of the one engram by the single repetition of the original stimulus belonging to the other.

Any other dog without a like experience reacts as the first one did before the generation of the associated engrams, that is, either it is indifferent at the sight of a stooping man, or if it has been previously engraphically influenced in the way of playing at recovering stones—the dog reacts to the optic stimulus by the tension of muscles ready for the jump, and by an accurate focussing of the man's hand with the eyes in order to be able to judge the fall of the stone immediately it is flung.

For examples of associated ecphory in vertebrates not so highly organised as the dog we may consider the birds, although they also are comparatively highly organised creatures.

Lloyd Morgan has observed that the offspring of chickens, pheasants, guinea fowls, water fowls, etc., on their emergence from the shell, and in the absence of parental guidance, peck indiscriminately at things of a certain size, at grain, small stones, breadcrumbs, wax matches, bits of paper, beads, cigarette-ash, cigar-ends, their own toes, and those of their companions, maggots, bits of thread, specks on the floor, their neighbours' eyes—anything and everything about the size of a pea or less. But soon the optic engram of an object becomes associated with an engram of taste, and the bird ceases to peck at things non-edible or unpleasant to the taste. When Lloyd Morgan threw before the chickens certain distasteful caterpillars conspicuous by alternate rings of black and golden-yellow, the larvæ of the moth *Euchelia jacobiæ*, the young birds picked them up at once, but dropped them immediately after-wards. The one experience sufficed, in most cases, to produce an optic and a chemical engram in an association which became manifest on repetition of the experiment ; for the optic stimulus induced the ecphory of the optic engram, and indirectly that of the chemical engram, to prevent the picking up of the striped caterpillars, while other caterpillars, coloured brown and green, were taken and readily devoured. After the second or third repetition, both engrams were, in all cases, so well fixed and associated that the black and gold striped caterpillars were either no longer noticed, or the sight of them stimulated flight and warning notes of disapprobation.

To produce clearly manifest and well-established engrams in fishes, frequent repetitions of stimuli are necessary. But Edinger's researches in that realm show most clearly that such repetition of stimuli succeeds in producing an association of engrams, and that with such simul-taneously or successively produced engrams, the ecphory of one effects the ecphory of the other. The engram produced in the fish by repetition of the optic stimulus of a man casting food upon the water becomes associated with the optic and chemical engrams established by the sight and taste of that food. The ecphory of the appearance of the man suffices to act ecphorically on the associated engrams, and liberates the reactions appertaining to the latter, such as swimming to the side of the pond, etc., even when the actual distribution of the food is suspended. It could also be proved here that these engrams survived a period of latency of four months without disappearing or losing their associated or ecphoric capacity. I have myself observed in the peculiar sucking fish (Echeneis) in the Torres Straits, that such an engram-association can be produced by a single experience, and remain fixed for at least some hours or even for days. It was sufficient to catch with a hook one fish out of the large shoal of fishes unsuspiciously swallowing the food thrown to them for disgust of this feeding to be created in the rest of the shoal for days. The experiment was repeated many times, and always with the same result. Edinger mentions similar observations on *Abramis brama* and *Idus melanotus*, and further reports a number of well-authenticated observations which prove that several associated engrams remaining effective for days and weeks can be generated in fishes by a single stimulation. Among the most highly developed non-vertebrates, chiefly certain insects such as wasps, bees, and ants, it is relatively easy, as compared with experiments on the lower vertebrates, to produce by a single stimulation engrams whose existence may be determined with all necessary accuracy. Some cuttlefishes respond to a like experiment in a similar way. But the stimulus effect on these forms is always restricted to specific stimuli, differing according to groups ; and the lower we descend in the animal kingdom the more frequent must be the repetition of the stimuli in order to generate clearly demonstrable engrams.

We have entitled this portion of the chapter " ecphoric influences," and not ecphoric stimuli. The title of stimuli, however, would cover all the ecphoric actions enumerated so far. But now we pass on to consider influences which cannot exactly be described as stimuli, although their character is an undoubtedly ecphoric one.

We may take our first example from a very common experience. Suppose I am in the habit of having my first meal at eight o'clock in the morning, my second at noon, and my third at eight o'clock in the evening, the complex stimuli connected with each partaking of food produce the following reaction amongst several others. The sight and taste of the dishes are accompanied by a peculiar reaction of our sensory areas which we describe as hunger or appetite, and which under ordinary circumstances is absent in healthy well-nourished individuals during the intervals between meals. If I now suddenly interpose between these meals two slight repasts—one at eleven and the other at five o'clock—I shall experience at first some disinclination. But I force myself to them, let us say, on the doctor's recommendation, and adhere to the order for half a year. If at the end of that time I try to dispense with the eleven and five o'clock meals, a strong feeling of hunger makes itself distinctly felt at those times. Apparently, the lapse of a definite period acts ecphorically on this reaction of my sensory areas.

"Time" also apparently influences other reactions of our body. We need not dwell on respiration and pulsation, because the intervals between the single reactions are so short that it appears unlikely that a return of the irritable substance into its state of indifference can actually take place, and that these phenomena can be regarded as mnemic at all. The real nature of the rhythm may be explained equally well in other ways, although the manner of its expression in various species of animals is probably influenced by inherited engrams. I shall not however, discuss this question further in our analysis.

On the other hand, the time interval connected with the periodical maturation of the ovum and the changes in the mucous membrane of the uterus, which we call menstruation, bears distinctly the character of an ecphory. In all periodical phenomena in the animal and vegetable kingdom, whether acquired or inherited, time is commonly supposed to determine and regulate the appearance and disappearance of reactions. This may be explained by the help of a well-known example which, however, happens to be a case of inherited engrams ; but as for this present analysis the nature only of the ecphoric influence matters, and not the origin of the engrams, the choice may be permitted. Most plants of the temperate and frigid zones possess an annual period, that is, a definitely determined alternation between the pause in growth and the progress of vegetation. The turning-points are, as is well known, very distinctly marked in our deciduous trees by the fall of leaves in autumn and the sprouting of new buds and leaves in spring. This order is unmistakably connected with the climatic periods we call seasons, and naturally depends primarily on the geographical latitude, and among other things on the height above sea-level, vicinity of mountains or sea, predominating air currents, and peculiarity of position. We need not labour the point that in the frigid and temperate zones the change of temperature is the determining factor in the dependence of the vegetation periods on the seasons. In the tropics, however, the relations between the seasons and the vegetation periods depend on variation in humidity. Examining the plants of our own zone, we find that in the case of a few the change from cold to warm determines in each instance the transition from rest to new growth. Some of our shrubs will certainly sprout in winter, if in January or February we have mild weather with plenty of sunshine. Then snowdrop, crocus, scilla, auricula, and daphne will begin to flower, the honeysuckle will unfold its leaves, and the lilac-trees show the first shimmer of green. All these are plants which can be made to grow and blossom prematurely in a forcing house. An attentive observer, though he may be but a layman in natural science, will soon notice that the various plants behave differently under forcing. Whilst a great number of the most varied plants can be regularly forced without difficulty—mostly those which sprout early in spring—others offer more resistance to the process, while on some plants forcing has but a feeble effect. Observations carried on for years on plants grown in the open air gave similar results. The Munich winter of 1899–1900 was very long and very cold. Heavy snowfalls and severe frosts occurred in March and in the beginning of April. One night in early April the thermometer fell to 15° C. Not until after the middle of April did the warmer weather set in. Consequently, vegetation in the Isar valley near Munich was still very backward in April. Snowflakes (*Leucojum vernum*) and crocuses did not bloom in our shaded garden until mid-April had passed. In donning their vernal robes most bushes were late ; *Lonicera tartarica* was clothed about mid-April, and Spanish lilac only towards the end of the same month. The leaf buds on most branches of a certain copper beech opened out on the first day of May.

The winter and spring of 1901–1902 offered a strong contrast to the corresponding seasons of 1899–1900. The winter was mild throughout, the spring without severe frost or snowfalls. The temperature was fairly even and moderate, and now and then we had spells of sunshine. In this year the first snowflakes bloomed in our garden on the 17th of March, the first crocuses on the 20th of March, that is, nearly four weeks earlier than in the year 1900. The first green leaf of the Lonicera bushes appeared on the 20th of March, and the lilacs started to unfold their leaves on the 10th of April. The before-mentioned beech began to leaf this year on the 23rd of April, that is only one week earlier than in the year 1900, a fact worthy of note in a year when the majority of the other plants growing under the same conditions were three or four weeks ahead of the corresponding phase of vegetation in 1900.

Observations continued for several years in order to illustrate a fact which had long been known to botanists and gardeners gave convincing results. The following table shows that the unfolding of the leaves of our beech-tree between the years 1900 and 1905 varies as to time within the narrow limits of the 22nd of April and the 4th of May; thus evidencing a far higher degree of independence of the annually changing climate influences than most other plants:—

Year.	*Leucojum vernum* commenced to blossom.	The Crocus commenced to blossom.	The Leaves of *Lonicera tatarica* commenced to unfold.	The Leaves of *Syringa vulgaris* commenced to unfold	The Leaves of Isolated Specimens of *Fagus silvatica* commenced to unfold.
1900	15 April	17 April	17 April	17 April	1 May
1901	—	—	—	—	—
1902	17 March	20 March	20 March	10 April	23 April
1903	25 February	20 March	8 March	26 March	4 May
1904	13 March	19 March	25 March	8 April	22 April
1905	9 March	11 March	—	17 April	23 April

It is clear that the periodicity of a number of plants does not stand in immediate and pre-eminent relation to the lack or excess of vernal warmth, but that a second factor—the element of time—has a predominating influence. Even in those plants which can be forced the time factor makes itself known. In very few plants, indeed, is it possible without considerable difficulty to overcome the influence of the time factor. Plant-physiological researches and experiments by nurserymen show that even those plants which are relatively easily forced resist in the first part of their resting period the stimulus of temperature, even, of all external influences, and only reach a state in which forcing becomes possible after the lapse of a definite period which differs according to species and geographical distribution.

In order to observe the direct simple action of the time factor, one must eliminate as far as is possible the stimulus of temperature. This was done by potting in the spring of 1903 a one-year old beech and cultivating it in an even temperature side by side with two beech seedlings, likewise potted. From the 1st of September onwards the plants were kept in the room in order that they might be protected from the night-chills. Nevertheless, the leaves commenced falling on the 22nd of September, and were all off by the 15th of November. All through the winter these three branches stood in a room of the same temperature both day and night, and were watered with water of moderate temperature. No unfolding of leaves showed itself of any of the trees until the 1st of May, when the beech, now two years old, started. Of the two seedlings, now one year old, one began to unfold its leaves on the 25th of May, but the other started only in mid-June. The retarded leafing might be explained by the harm the plants suffered through having been entirely withheld from the winter cooling. It is known that this interference can be endured without harm by only a few plants of the temperate zone. In this connection it is interesting to note how the hereditary character of these dispositions can be deduced from the retention of the periodicity of those two seedlings, which during their individual lives never were subjected to the least periodical influence.

But what do we mean by the expression " time factor " ? Or, as we are not desirous of discussing the theory of knowledge as such, how can we form a conception of a time period which in its influence will resemble or represent the action of a stimulus ?

All life processes as experienced appear to us to be regulated by time. We find that the state of excitement of any specific organism requires definite time to propagate itself through equal extents of irritable substance. The beginning and course of all other reactions is, under given circumstances, equally determinable in time. Is there not here some clue to the nature of the time influence ? To a plant or an animal a time period means the elaboration of a definite number of life processes in its system. A man, who knows the average rate of his pulse and respiration, could without reference to a chronometer fairly correctly estimate the passing of minutes and even of hours, if he were willing to go to the trouble of the prolonged counting.

A prisoner in a subterranean prison, artificially lighted and heated, denied communication with the outer world, and receiving his food at quite irregular intervals—by calculating the rate of growth of his nails and hair, by reference to pulse beats, thus making his own body serve as a watch—could register the run of the weeks and months and years with approximate accuracy.

The chronometer of the organism, which one might call its " body watch," is thus regulated by the rate of speed of its life processes. But how does the organism read the close of a time period from this chronometer without conscious counting ? Or, to speak less in simile, how is it that a quite definite reaction sets in after the close of a specific series of life processes ? Simply because at the end of a definite series of metabolic or other life processes, a state of the organism results which partially or altogether corresponds to the state which ruled at the time of the production of a definite engram, and by the repetition of which state this engram becomes now ecphorised. A Central European beech, which stands in full vegetation from May until September, reaches in the latter month an organic state which acts ecphorically on that engram whose successive reactions consist of food circulation from leaves into branches and root-stems, and of the fall of leaves. This ecphory takes place in the beech in autumn irrespective of those specific influences of temperature which rightly are expected to act at that time of the year, and which by abnormal mildness fail to come into play. We must remember, however, that otherwise normal temperature would also act ecphorically on the engram.

We conclude that the time period as such does not act ecphorically, but that the ecphory is due to the appearance of a definite state associated with the respective engram, and that this appearance is determined in time, in so far as it takes place on the conclusion of a definite number of life processes which may be estimated from the moment chosen as the starting-point.

That these processes are the result of the ecphory of an engram is proved by the fact that by the frequent repetition of a new and appropriate stimulus leaf-fall can be associated with some earlier or later engram of metabolism. I term such engrams and their ecphory "chronogeneous." From some cause that is still unknown to us, this can only be effected with great difficulty in the case of the beech, but in the case of most other plants it is sufficient to expose them to a different temperature and light for a number of years for the engram of, say, leaf-fall, or the engram of forcing to associate itself with some other chronogeneous engram. Numerous instances are furnished by the science of plant-acclimatisation.

The ecphoric influence which the appearance of a definite phase of development in the life history of an organism exercises on a definite engram has to be classed with this chronogeneous ecphory. Here, also, it is a case of the association of a certain engram with a specific phase of organic development. Further, this ecphory is based on the association of various engrams ; but that conception we shall analyse more minutely in the second part. We may simply note that the time factor here is pushed more into the background than in the previous cases of chronogeneous ecphory. We shall describe such a state as " phasogeneous ecphory," which means that on reaching a certain phase of development a state of the irritable substance has been generated which acts ecphorically on a certain engram.

Such expressions as " chronogeneous " or " phaso-geneous " ecphory will be simply used for the sake of ready reference, and not with any idea of making them specific categories distinct from other ecphories. It is characteristic of them, as well as of all other ecphories, that the partial return of an energetic condition acts ecphorically on the engram-complex of the total situation. But these questions will receive more detailed treatment in the second part of this book.

CHAPTER III

ENGRAPHIC ACTION OF STIMULI ON PROGENY

In our analysis of mnemic phenomena we have preferred to consider engrams acquired during the individual life of the organism under examination, and only occasionally have we considered engrams inherited by the organism from its ancestors. To ignore these entirely was impossible, for they exist in each organism from the ovum stage onwards, and interfere in manifold ways with the course of all our experiments.

Proceeding now to their closer analysis, we have first to consider a point of fundamental importance, namely, whether engrams persist through the individuality phase in which they have been generated into the immediately succeeding phases.

To answer this question we will consider various crucial tests taken from four distinct groups of observations which, to our mind, demonstrate clearly the inheritance of engraphic actions.

In the first group the inherited engram, or rather, the inherited engram-complex, manifests itself by reactions, which concern primarily, though not exclusively, the sphere of instinct. The experiments cited here are those which P. Kammerer elaborated.

The so-called fire newt, *Salamandra maculosa*, which is viviparous, ordinarily gives birth to larvæ measuring on the average 25 mm. and carrying gills. The broods may number anything from fourteen to seventy-two. These larvæ are deposited in the water, and there pass a long transitional stage, until after several months they lose their gills, leave the water, and completely change into land newts. By change of conditions Kammerer succeeded in forcing the females to retain their offspring for a longer time in the uterus. Then, by repetition of the coercion, these retarded parturitions became habitual. In order to induce the females, so far bearing normally, to retain their offspring in the uterus beyond the usual time, Kammerer kept them from the water-trough in which ordinarily they would have deposited their larvæ. The keeping of the animals in a cool temperature, which rarely was higher than 12° C, proved of assistance.

By artificial conditions *Salamandra maculosa* can thus be compelled to retain her offspring in the uterus until they are fully developed, as is normally the case with the black Alpine newt, *Salamandra atra*. This remarkable change is effected in four stages :—(1) Numerous larvæ, 25–30 mm. in length, are deposited on land instead of in water. (2) Later, a smaller number, but still further advanced in development, are similarly deposited. (3) A still smaller number of larvæ, seven at the most, with reduced gills, either ready for their immediate metamorphosis into the adult newt, or just past it, are deposited. (4) The number of individuals in a brood grows gradually less from one gravid period to another, until, as in the case of the *Salamandra atra*, the number of offspring remains constant at two, that is, one fœtus in each uterus.

Kammerer now reared a number of young ones, born after their mothers had reached the highest stage of habitual late parturition, and mated them amongst each other. He then subjected the fertilized females of this second generation to normal conditions during their pregnancy by supplying them with a water-trough and sufficient moist air, and by maintaining them at a moderately high temperature. Although there was no longer any external coercion to a late parturition, the creatures departed from the normal breeding mode of their species, and without exception from the beginning made late and sparse births. It is true that they did

not bear fully metamorphosed newts, but their newt
larvæ stood in all cases nearer to their metamorphosis
than the normal larvæ. Further, the number of each
brood had decreased from the average thirty or forty
to five, four, or two larvæ.

If, on the basis of previously enunciated views, we
analyse this effect of change in external conditions inherited from one generation to another, we find the
following elements :—

I. *A primary state of indifference.* By this we refer
simply to the state of the organism at the commencement
of our observations and experiments. In the case before
us it means the state of the maternal generation before
coercion.

II. *Stimulus to be tested for its engraphic action.* This
is of a complex nature, and may be defined comprehensively as the coercion of the females to retain the
young in the uterus beyond the normal time of pregnancy.
This end was effected partly by keeping the animal in a
relatively dry, cool state, but mainly by the withdrawal
of the water-trough. When at each subsequent pregnancy
this coercion was repeated, the effect of its action increased
from case to case until the retarded parturition finally
reached the fourth stage. We conclude from this that
the complex coercion-stimulus effected an unmistakable
engraphic action on the individuals of the first generation.
So far our observations warrant us in speaking only of
engraphic action in the case of individuals directly subjected
to the stimulus, and with these, of course, it is a case
of an individually acquired and not an inherited engram.

To establish proof of the *inheritance* of the engram
we must turn from this generation on which the stimulus
has directly acted as original stimulus to the next generation, and keep the animals under conditions where they
are withdrawn from those influences which have acted
engraphically on the mother.

III. *A secondary state of indifference.* This is the state
in which the second generation, born of the habitually
late-bearing mothers, remain from their first pregnancy

until that moment which corresponds to the normal bringing forth of the young of *Salamandra maculosa*. During this time they do not differ in anything from newts born of normally-bearing mothers.

IV. *Ecphoric influence*. Proof that the repeatedly practised forcing of the mothers to retain their young ones in the uterus beyond the ordinary time has not only acted engraphically on them, but also on their offspring, is furnished by the following data:—When the gravid offspring reach the phase of the normal parturition, the delivery is retarded, and late parturition regularly takes place instead, although the mothers of the second generation during their pregnancy were kept under normal conditions of moisture and temperature, and with a water-trough at their disposal.

The external means used to cause the first generation to retain their young in the uterus were not applied to the second generation. The engram, ecphorised on reaching the corresponding stage of pregnancy or, as we may say, the mnemic excitation ecphorised phasogeneously, manifested itself in this case by the retardation of the normal act of parturition.

On the other hand, in the case of the Alpine newt, *Salamandra atra*, the inherited engram manifests itself during its phasogeneous ecphory by a *positive* reaction, and not by retardation. *Salamandra atra* normally deposits fully developed land newts on dry soil. By keeping the animal in a relatively high temperature and by supplying it with abundance of water—means very different from those used with the spotted newt—Kammerer succeeded in introducing premature parturition in the Alpine newt, gradually increasing the brood and finally making the change habitual. The induced change was transmitted to the offspring which, kept under conditions normal to their species, without exception produced a more numerous but less developed progeny at a time earlier than the normal act of parturition. In this case, the phasogeneously-ecphorised engram manifested itself not by the retardation of a process normally due, but by its acceleration, that is, by a relatively premature parturition.

In a similar way the ecphory of the inherited engram expresses itself positively in the case of the change of the development and instinct in the Axolotl described by Miss v. Chauvin, and to which reference will be made later, as well as in the manifold changes of instinct in Butterfly-caterpillars and Beetles, Lymantria, Gracilaria, Phratora, experimentally brought about by Pictet and by Schröder. In a later passage we shall treat in detail the successful experiments in heredity made by Kammerer on the Obstetric Toad, *Alytes obstetricans.*

For the moment, however, leaving those cases of inheritance which manifest themselves in their ecphory principally by reactions of instinct, as also by certain morphological and physiological characters in the newly born, let us concern ourselves with equally convincing researches in which the inherited engram manifests itself by plastic reactions in the bodily development of the offspring. Let us begin with the experiments made by E. Fischer on the Tiger Moth, *Arctia caja,* experiments which leave nothing to be desired as regards the unequivocal nature and force of their evidence. Earlier than Fischer, Standfuss had made similar experiments on butterflies, with similar results.

Later, Schröder, Pictet and Tower, among others, obtained analogous results from butterflies and beetles. Stimuli of different kinds were applied in these experiments. In those of Fischer, stimuli of temperature were applied, the pupæ being kept at the low temperature of 8° C. The reaction produced by this stimulus manifested itself as a plastic one, by alterations in the pigmentation of the wings of the emerging imago.

I. *The primary state of indifference* was traced with sufficient accuracy by Fischer in this experiment by keeping permanently at a normal temperature half of the number of pupæ collected for these trials.

These pupæ, with the exception of five from which no imagos emerged, gave moths that showed *no* appreciable alteration in colouring and marking. Neither the brown spots of the frontal wings nor the black ones of the back wings showed any deviation from the normal. The development of such normally coloured moths may in this case rightly be described as the primary state of indifference.

II. *The stimulus, whose engraphic action* we are now examining, consisted in Fischer's experiments of an intermittent decrease of temperature until it reached 8° C. This stimulus was applied to the brood in its pupal stage, with the result that the emerging moths "showed aberrant colouring of the wings. Seven of the total number of forty-eight pupæ died. The aberration lay in an enlargement of the brown spots on the front wings and the black spots on the back wings. In some of the male specimens the dark colouring affected the whole of the wing."—"The moths also showed a corresponding change on the lower part of their bodies." An unmistakable melanotic aberration had taken place.

III. *Secondary state of indifference.* This we defined as that state where the excitation of the engraphic substance produced by the stimulus had subsided, having effected a latent engraphic change. Exactly when this state supervened in the generation of *Arctia caja*, exposed to the stimulus of cold, need not here specially concern us. The point is that this secondary state of indifference persisted until, on the application of the stimulus, the reaction was given. During the time of development from the egg to the pupal stage, no reaction deviating from the normal can be observed, either in growth or in any other biological phenomenon.

Of the descendants, we need but to consider the offspring of two moths which had been affected melanotically by the stimulus of cold. The male had been much altered ; the female less so. Fischer gives a drawing of them both. From the pairing of these two abnormal specimens resulted 173 pupæ, *which were kept at a temperature of from* 18° C *to* 25° C.

VI. *Ecphory of the engram.* In the absence of that

stimulus of cold which had acted engraphically on the parent generation, the case proved to be one of phasogeneous ecphory. For when the pupation was finished seventeen out of the 173 specimens showed melanotic aberration entirely along the line of aberration in the parents. Comparison with the parents shows that " the offspring represent generally a combination of parental characteristics. The marking of the male preponderates in some, that of the female in others. It is worth emphasising, however, that the aberration had taken place most strongly in the male moth. Further, in these descendants the under side of the wings is altered similarly to the upper side."

The stimulus of cold on the parents not only generated engrams which manifested themselves in descendants by morphogenetic reactions, but generated also others, which found expression in other reactions. For the seventeen affected specimens were amongst the latest of the emerging moths, whilst those which came out at the beginning were entirely normal. In the first edition of this book it was suggested that the stimulus of cold might generate another inheritable engram, namely, retardation of the rate of development. This idea has since been confirmed, for Pictet discovered that accelerated pupation regularly accompanies melanotic aberration, whilst retarded pupation accompanies albinotic aberration.

Here then are two perfectly clear cases of engraphic effects, which are open at any time to be tested anew. They are representative of a great series of related cases. Let us now turn to a third group of cases demonstrating inherited engraphic changes in plants.

It has long been known that some trees, when transplanted from the temperate zone into moist tropical regions, gradually relinquish their periodical fall of leaves, and change from deciduous into ever-green plants. Bordage, during his twelve years' stay at Réunion, investigated the question whether this alteration climatically induced might not be transmissible by seed. The idea of grafting was not entertained. He found a suitable object for his experiments in the peach-tree. Plants grown in Réunion from European peach kernels continued for ten years to drop their leaves annually at the ordinary time, even when cultivated in the hot coast districts. At first they remained entirely leafless for about a month and a half, but gradually the period was shortened. After ten years some specimens were so much changed that they continued in leaf the whole year through. But it was not until after twenty years that they reached a state in which they might be described as practically evergreen plants. Bordage speaks of this as " subpersistance du feuillage." If now the seeds of these evergreen trees are sown, the resultant plants are evergreen like their parents. This occurs even when the seeds are sown, not in the hot coast lowlands, but a thousand metres above sea-level, where those peach-trees, the descendants of parents not changed by the climate, permanently retain a periodical fall of leaves. A more detailed enumeration of cases is given in the *Problem of the Inheritance of Acquired Characters*.

We now arrive at the conclusion that the numerous stimuli which continually act upon an organism have not only synchronous and acoluthic, but very frequently also engraphic effects. Further, it has been shown that these engraphic effects extend beyond the individuality phase into later phases of the continuous line of development, that is, they are inherited. From this it follows that each organism, linked up as it is with the history of millions of years and consequently representing the millionth or billionth phase in a continuous line of development, must contain a great many such engrams ancestrally acquired which have been transmitted to it through the generations. In our investigation of organisms, do we find in their irritable substance properties that possess the character of inherited engrams ? Whether they are inherited or not will, of course, be determined by the observation of several generations. But it will be exceedingly difficult to decide whether we are dealing with an engram, that is, a latent residue of a previous stimulation.

The inherited engram is the product of a stimulation upon a previous generation. We therefore have to deal with an historical occurrence, and as a rule in such a case the experimental method is denied us. Even if in thousands of organisms we show that we are able to generate engrams which become inherited, this by no means proves that the inherited dispositions we find in organisms are actual engrams.

We have arrived at a critical point in our analysis, for we are about to enquire into the nature of the dispositions hereditarily transmitted from generation to generation. Hitherto, we have had the solid ground of immediate experimental experience beneath our feet. For a time our further journey will be in the realms of conjecture. Before we enter fully into the matter, perhaps we may be permitted a short but somewhat necessary digression.

To begin with, every conclusion which tells us something really new, which adds something to our knowledge, is after all an inference from analogy. The mathematical and purely logical conclusions termed " necessary " are only transformations of what is already contained in the premises. They do not tell us anything new in fact. Experience alone gives us that which is new. And the method is by analogical inference. Hence originate our conceptions of time and space, the mathematical theorems and the fundamental propositions of science. That a stone thrown up in the air will fall to the earth we know only *per analogiam*. For knowledge of the existence of the force of gravity is not innate in the human mind, but is an inference drawn from a great mass of analogous experiences. The same may be said of the law of the conservation of energy, and of every conception of natural science.

Now we can divide the things which present themselves to the mind in causal series into two groups—those which repeat themselves or are capable of being repeated, and those which appear but once and cannot be repeated. Strictly speaking, only those occurrences which can be repeated are matter for experiment. The laws of falling

5

bodies find continual confirmation in new experience. The presuppositions and conditions of the test experiments may be varied indefinitely, but the same result always follows. Conclusions which can thus be confirmed continually by immediate experience acquire for us the character not merely of probability, but of inevitability.

Occurrences which cannot be repeated escape the direct control of fresh immediate experience. It cannot be proved by new direct experience that the Triassic cretaceous rocks have been formed by the precipitation of solid ingredients from a liquid medium. An experimental imitation of the process is merely an imitation, not a test experiment. But the fact that in this deposit we find creatures like the Echinoderms known to be living at the present time exclusively in the sea, whereas terrestrial creatures are absent, considerably increases the force of the probability that the chalk strata were originally laid in the sea. But the sceptic, clamouring for direct experimental evidence, is not easily satisfied even by the most cogent indirect reasoning. In this case, he may perhaps argue that the fact that present-day Echinoderms are exclusively marine animals does not prove anything in respect of the Echinoderms of the Trias. But that non-recurring physical and biological phenomena may nevertheless warrant conclusions convincing to any normal human being may be demonstrated by any number of examples. Is there any thinking man who seriously questions the idea that the fossilised animals and plants have once actually lived ? Or that the fossilised vertebrates possessed nerves ? Is he justified in rejecting the idea because the fact cannot be proved by direct experimental evidence ? It has recently become the fashion among a certain group of biologists to deprecate the value of the historical method because of the indirect conclusions involved. It would be interesting to know how far these men of science would allow their scepticism to affect their reading of social history. Is the account of Erasmus and the Reformation to be rejected because it is not possible to set out an experimental repetition ?

Why should natural science be denied the valid use of the historical method ? It is a comfort to know that the majority of men, learned and unlearned, will continue to devote thought and attention to mere historical, non-recurring phenomena.

The problem, whether vital and physical phenomena can be made to recur at all in identical fashion need not here be investigated. It is admitted that many occurrences in the inorganic world lend themselves to such uniform repetition that, as far as the results are concerned, the deviations are hardly appreciable, and need not be reckoned. But in the organic world the deviations in each occurrence of an event are much greater. No single organism can serve in repeated experiments in exactly the same way. And in the case of different organisms, for instance, of two individuals of the same species, the innate differences may be considerable. Nevertheless, we may speak of recurring phenomena also in the organic world, as long as we limit the expression to those characteristic features, in comparison with which the infinitesimally small deviations at each recurrence do not count. It is, however, well to remember that in the strict sense the identical recurrence of organic events is impossible. We fully acknowledge the superiority of the direct experimental conclusion over the indirect historical conclusion, but we shall not give up the latter, since it affords us the sole key to the understanding of non-recurring historical phenomena, and because its results may, in favourable cases, possess such convincing force of evidence as to approach the results obtained by direct experimental methods so nearly that the difference of value becomes infinitesimally small.

By the historical method, which of course involves logical process, we conclude that fossils are the remains of animals and plants that formerly lived, and that they are not "freaks of nature." This is a demonstrable conclusion. The perfectly accurate assertion that the laws of mechanics are, by the experimental method, still more definitely demonstrable does not affect our conclusion. The point is that conclusions by either method are valid. Applying these considerations to the problem of the inheritance of engrams, it is clear that as regards the genesis of these engrams we have in the majority of instances to deal with non-recurring events. This is indeed always the case when the engrams have been acquired by ancestral generations which differed considerably in form and function from the animal and vegetable generations now living. All these age-long acquisitions are beyond the direct experimental method of proof. They can only be established by an inferential proof.

If now we set forth our argument—that the great majority of the dispositions inherited by organisms are to be regarded as engrams, asking for its acceptance on the grounds of strong probability—we shall have first to enquire into those particular features by which an engram is recognised.

The surest signs of an engram are derived from the observation of the phases of its genesis. We note (1) the state of the organism before the existence of the engram, that is, the primary state of indifference; (2) the action of the engraphic stimulus; (3) the secondary state of indifference, that is, the phase of latency; and (4) the ecphory or the phase of manifestation.

In the historical engrams which concern us now, the action of the engraphic stimulus belongs to the past. The organism as presented to us for investigation is already in its secondary state of indifference. Our examination, therefore, can only deal with the phases of latency and manifestation. The argument that in this case we are really concerned with an actual engram must proceed on two considerations. First: On the fact that it concerns properties of the organic substance which at times are latent, and at other times are manifest; and secondly: on the manner in which the transition from the phase of latency to the phase of manifestation is made, that is, on the evidence that this transition bears the character of an ecphory.

Now, all the inherited properties which concern us here are in a state of latency, out of which at each recurrence of the liberating influence they pass into the corresponding state of excitement.

The reaction by which an engram becomes manifest to us naturally does not differ as such from any of the reactions effected by an original stimulus. The difference lies rather in that which evokes the reaction. But can we learn from the liberating influence itself whether its action is ecphoric, or whether it is indeed an original stimulus? Here we venture on grounds of probability. As we have already seen, the existence of an engram is recognised by the fact that the unaltered original stimulus is no longer requisite for the production of the corresponding reaction. Instead, there may be only the action either of the quantitatively or qualitatively changed original stimulus, or of a stimulus acting ecphorically on an associated engram, or the mere lapse of a definite time period, that is, chronogeneous ecphory, or, finally, the initiation of a definite development phase in the continuous line of the successive generations, that is, phasogeneous ecphory.

Now, in all organisms, protozoa, plants, and animals, we meet with an extraordinarily large number of excitation-dispositions, the corresponding stimuli of which have in all probability to be classed in one or other of the above mentioned categories.

The first named categories of ecphoric influence, where the merely quantitative or qualitative change of the original stimulus comes into play, are no less important and uncommon than the others mentioned. But as they more or less resemble the original stimuli, it is clear that for our present exposition they are of far less value than are the cases of associated chronogeneous and phasogeneous ecphory. Still, what they offer is by no means unimportant. In many species of birds the reaction of pecking at first sight at grains and other minute objects is inherited. That this is a case of an inherited engram on which the mere optic stimulus of the object acts ecphorically seems to me most probable. It sometimes happens, however, that the optic stimulus alone is not sufficient to produce the reaction, and with many a young chicken and pheasant, bred in the incubator, it takes some time for the optic stimulus of the scattered grains to produce the reaction of pecking. This reaction can, however, be initiated by the example of older and more sophisticated chickens, or by touching the grains before the eyes of the young creature with the finger-nail or a pencil, in imitation of the pecking of the hen. This is especially the case with young ostriches bred in the incubator, which, according to Claypole, do not pick up the food unless one first touches the ground where it is scattered. Of the explanations of this phenomenon, the most probable, in my view, is that it is the ecphory of an inherited engram. The engram is that of which pecking is the corresponding reaction ; the ecphoric stimulus is the recurrence of a primary stimulus somewhat altered qualitatively. So instead of the demonstration of pecking by the mother hen, we have the touching of the food with fingernail or pencil—a case of vicarious ecphory.

Still more convincing as to the engraphic character of many inherited dispositions, and the ecphoric character of the influences liberating them, are the observations made on young birds which on the first contact of their beaks with water, were induced to go through the whole ceremonial pretence of a bird-bath. Lloyd Morgan reports in the fourth chapter of the book previously cited several cases, one of which, observed by Charbonnier, is here given. " A magpie about five weeks old, which he had reared from quite an early stage of its life, when placed in a cage and supplied with a pan of water, made one or two pecks at the surface, and then, outside the pan, without entering the water at all, proceeded to go through all the gestures of a bird bathing—ducking its head, fluttering its wings and tail, squatting down, and spreading itself out on the ground. It afterwards and by degrees acquired the habit of real bathing, and seemed always

anxious for a bath in rainy weather." The strangeness
of the bird's conduct becomes intelligible when regarded
in the light of engram-inheritance. The stimulus of the
contact with water, slight though it was relative to body
area, acted ecphorically.

The cases so far given are instances of more or less
direct ecphory. We may meet, however, with numerous
inherited dispositions whose manifestation depends on
indirect ecphoric influences. The next case is one of
many which are intelligible only on the assumption of
several associated engrams. P. Huber gives an account
of a caterpillar which in a series of about a dozen processes
constructs for its pupation a very complicated cocoon. A
caterpillar that had reached the sixth stage in the spinning
of its cocoon, when placed in one not so far advanced,
immediately took up the work at the earlier stage and repeated the third, fourth and fifth processes in the making
of the cocoon. But when Huber placed a caterpillar
from a cocoon in its third stage of development into
one which had reached the ninth stage, the animal was
unable to take advantage of the work already done and
proceed from the ninth stage, but neglecting the intermediate stages, had to start from the third at which it
had been interrupted, so that the fourth to the eighth
stages of the cocoon were spun twice. The case finds a
natural explanation in the idea that the complicated
act of spinning is the manifestation of a chain successively associated inherited engrams. The ecphory of each
engram acts in its turn ecphorically on the next successively
associated engram.

In the engrams hitherto discussed, the reactions manifested themselves in muscular contractions such as pecking,
the stretching of wings of the young bird, and the complicated spinning activity of the caterpillar. It has already
been emphasised, but I should like to lay stress on it
again, that it is absolutely immaterial to the fundamental
questions occupying us now whether the reactions under
observation by which the states of excitement of the
irritable organic substance become manifest to us consist

in muscular contractions, or in changes of the cell turgidity, or in processes of secretion and metabolism, or in cell divisions and other processes of growth, or, finally, in sensations whose existence can only be inferred by us.

We now turn to inherited dispositions whose corresponding reactions are produced by time influences, that is, by the lapse of a definite time period. These reactions have already been classed under the heading of chronogeneous ecphory (p. 55). The manifestation of inherited dispositions by chronogeneous ecphory may be discerned in a very great number of animals and plants. Mention need only be made of the periodic ovum maturation in woman and of the mating periods of most animals. The reactions by which these engrams become manifest consist primarily in processes of growth. The " migration impulse," innate in so many species of birds, is the motor reaction of an inherited engram, a reaction produced by chronogeneous ecphory.

The vegetation periods of the plants are phenomena in which chronogeneous ecphory plays a very important part. This is most obvious in plants which resist forcing, that is, in those plants where the reaction of growth admits of little interference. When a beech kept at an even temperature in a heated room withers and drops its leaves in November, despite the absence of that direct stimulus of cold which at other times is necessary to this reaction, it is clearly a case of a chronogeneous engram manifesting itself in a chronogeneous ecphory. For otherwise, in the absence of the stimulus of cold which usually produces the leaf-fall, we should expect the beech to retain its foliage. That this is a case of an inherited engram is readily proved by using for these experiment seedlings which have always been kept at an even temperature, and which, having been grown from seed, have never yet been engraphically influenced in this particular way during their individual lives.

The matter, however, is somewhat complicated in so far as natural selection has determined the specific annual periods of those plants, interference with whose growth by way of forcing is almost an impossibility. For it must be of great importance to plants sensitive to frost not to be tempted by the warmth of an early spring to unfold their buds prematurely, and thereby risk the blight of later frosts. The case of the annual period, therefore, is by no means so clear as the one of the diurnal period next to be discussed, in the hereditary determination of which natural selection apparently has little to do. The diurnal periodic leaf movements of plants are ecphorised chronogeneously for some time after the cessation of the light-stimulus that normally liberates them. That this recurrence of the diurnal period, which may be observed in plants kept in constant darkness or in constant exposure to light, is a case of inherited, and not, as Pfeffer thought, of exclusively individually acquired dispositions, may be proved by the following experiments :—

Seedlings of the Acacia, *Albizzia lophanta*, kept hitherto in the dark, were subjected by me to intermittent artificial light and darkness, a cycle of six hours being chosen in one series of cases, and a cycle of twenty-four hours in another series. When, after several weeks' exposure to this kind of thing, intermittent illumination was discontinued and the plants were left altogether either in light or in darkness, they continued for some time their movements of leaves, but not in the cycle of six and twenty-four hours respectively which I had tried to induce, but at intervals of twelve hours ; from which it may be gathered that the tendency to a cycle of twelve hours is an inherited one. Seedlings, which from the beginning were left either in complete darkness or in continual light, did not show periodic movements at all. Those in the dark kept their leaves closed, while those constantly exposed to the light took up and maintained with unfolded leaves an angular position, which varied in different individuals from 135° to 180°. From these observations, we conclude that periodic illumination and obscuration contribute to the ecphory of engrams whose corresponding reaction manifests itself in regular leaf-movement every twelve hours. The periodic change in illumination is necessary for the *ecphory* of the engram. But that the exposure to light itself has not generated the engram, that is, the tendency to move in cycles of twelve hours, may be gathered from the fact that after the cessation of the intermittent illumination, the opening and closing of the leaves do not take place in cycles of six and twenty-four hours, the experimental periods, but in one of twelve hours, a period to which the individual under observation has never been exposed, but which its ancestors for many generations have experienced, and which may, therefore, be regarded as inherited.

Further evidence of mnemic periodicity, the engraphic factors of which are readily recognisable, may be derived from the work of Bohn, Schleip and others. A diurnal period of an undoubtedly mnemic character may be observed in Crustaceæ. In the case of a shrimp, *Hippolyte varians*, the periodicity has been thoroughly investigated. Certain observations of Gamble and Keeble on *Palæmon squilla* suggest that among the Crustaceæ there has been an *hereditary* fixing of this periodicity. Of many other animals it might be said that they show a mnemic diurnal periodicity, that is one which persists after the discontinuance of the periodical exposure to light. But it has not yet been determined in these cases whether the periodicity has acquired an *hereditary* character. Special mention may here be made of Bohn's observations on Actiniæ, Worms, and Molluscæ, and of Schleip's recently published investigations on the " Sceptre " locust, *Dixippus morosus*. Schleip gives a good index to the literature of the subject.

The diurnal periodicity, however, is but a part of the mnemic periodicity. Bohn showed, for instance, that the alternation of tidal ebb and flow produced a six hours' cycle in the shore-dwelling Actini, Turbellaria, and Snails.

Many pertinent observations on this subject might be quoted, but a comprehensive treatment of the problem of the engraphic, and of the *hereditarily* engraphic determination of periodic stimulation, will be given later.

In the course of the preceding chapter we have traced phasogeneous ecphory amongst the various ecphoric influences (p. 56), and described how, when a definite phase of development is reached, a state of the irritable substance is produced which acts ecphorically on a definite engram. Inherited dispositions, becoming manifest by phasogeneous ecphory, may be met with in very great numbers in plant and animal organisms. To mention but one case :—The segmentation of the ovum of *Synapta digitata*, an echinoderm, occurs, according to Selenka, in nine phases ; the co-existing cells dividing equally in nine successive stages. When the cells number 512, a process regularly takes place, which is usually described as "gastrulation." A rapid cell-multiplication by division begins at one pole of the ovum, and this part invaginates into the cleavage cavity. Simultaneously all the cells develop cilia on their exterior, and the organism begins to rotate within the membrane of the ovum. May we not, therefore, say in the case of Synapta that the reaching of the " 512 cell stage," or, as we may phrase it, the energetic condition of the " 512 cell stage," acts ecphorically on an inherited disposition which becomes manifest to us in a number of plastic and motor reactions such as gastrulation, cilia formation, and ciliary motion ?

We must bear in mind, however, that the description "phasogeneous ecphory" covers a state which in each individual case is open to a more exact analysis. By the specific development-phase of an organism we understand its entire morphological and physiological state at any given moment. In members of the same species the development of the organism occurs with a certain regularity, but by no means in an absolutely identical manner. The corresponding phases, or stages, or total states are similar but not identical, even in twins. We shall, therefore, find it impossible to define in a universally acceptable manner a total phase other than that of the concrete case with which we are at any one moment concerned. However, no serious difficulty arises from that as regards our conception of phasogeneous ecphory. For it is conveniently characteristic of each ecphory that a *partial* return of a definite energetic condition suffices to awaken the engram from its latent state. A new internal energetic condition marks each entry into a new phase of development. Slight deviations in the developmental phase will, in the greater number of cases, be practically of no consequence so far as the ecphoric action is concerned, seeing that for the ecphory the partial return of the energetic condition is sufficient.

This general statement, of course, is not to be regarded as the final word. The great symphony of single components, which each organic development represents, contains, in addition to that general dependence of each successive total phase on its predecessor, numerous specific dependencies within the separate developing organic systems.

A simile may be useful. In the reproduction of a piece of music, say a pianoforte sonata, the whole progresses from phase to phase, each new bar growing, so to speak, out of its predecessor, and its mode of exit determining the mode of entry of its successor. But, in addition, there co-exist as many specific dependencies within the single parts as there are such parts. Each of these parts is closely knitted with the whole, but it also progresses with a certain independence within its own succession ; and in the case of a not very skilled pianist it may happen that the bar he is playing with his right hand may finish slightly in advance of the bar played with his left hand, as, for instance, when he has to play one rhythm in triple time with his right hand, and another in common time with his left. Nevertheless, both parts, although progressing independently, will coincide again either at the conclusion of the movement or at the entry of the new phase—in this latter case, a new bar. So also in the wonderful symphony of an organic development there exist, besides the general relationship of succeeding simultaneous complexes, numerous specific relations, which again are subordinated to the whole. Within the separate cycles, slight oscillations in the ensemble may occur, corresponding to what is called "Heterochrony" in embryology. Here, also, the common association of the single components within the simultaneous complexes usually forces the vagaries of specific cycles back into the general rhythm. In the second part of this work (p. 96) we shall have an opportunity of a closer consideration of the more or less intimate relations existing between the single components of successive simultaneous complexes.

From the point of view just enunciated, it is incumbent upon us to search within the total phases for specific changes, which are either connected with specific ecphories or indicative of ecphoric manifestations. Thus, in the above quoted case of the gastrulation of a definite Echinoderm ovum, reaction took place on the attainment of the " 512 cell stage." Is it now possible to trace within the total state of the phase those specific appearances on which the ecphory depends ? The observations and conclusions of a large number of scientific workers, among whom special mention may be made of Th. H. Morgan, Driesch, and Boveri, suggest the answer. In inducing segmentation in fragments of the Echinoderm eggs, as also in isolated blastomeres, gastrulation resulted, not simply after the characteristic numerical segmentation phase of the normal egg had been reached, but after the cells had been reduced to a certain size by continued subdivision. The true ecphorising factor here was, therefore, not simply the completion of a certain number of cell-divisions and the attainment of a definite number of cells, but primarily the attainment of a certain size of cell in division. The creation of a definite relation, variable within certain limits, between the chromatin mass and the protoplasmic mass within the cell was necessary to the ecphory.

Yet another example more exactly defining the most important element in specific phasogeneous ecphory may be given. When a vertebrate embryo has reached a certain stage of development, the formation of the lens takes place. Herbst and Speman, independently of each other, have demonstrated that the formation of the lens does not follow on the mere realisation of one or the other total phase, but specifically is dependent on the stimulus exercised by the retinal layer of the optic vesicle when it comes into close contact with the epidermis.

Speman was able to furnish experimental evidence that in the case of the common frog (*Rana fusca*) no lens formation takes place unless the optic vesicle touches the epidermis. The moment, however, the optic vesicle comes into contact with the epidermis, lens growth begins at the point of contact. Otherwise the epidermis retains its dark pigmentation, and the growth of transparent corneal epithelium is impossible.

With these facts before us it would seem necessary, at least in this case, to narrow the conception of phasogeneous ecphory, and to make it dependent on a single element, namely, contact-stimulus exercised by the retinal layer of the optic vesicle on the epidermis. It has, however, been discovered since the work of Herbst and Speman that there are cases where the lens formation does take place on the mere entry into a total phase, even though the main component, the contact-stimulus of the optic vesicle on the epidermis, be lacking in this state of the energetic condition. Mencl, in his work on the embryo of the salmon, found that lens formation can take place in the entire absence of the optic vesicle. Speman himself admitted that while in the case of the common frog (*Rana fusca*), the toad (*Bombinator igneus*), and probably also *Triton tæniatus*, contact-stimulus seems to be indispensable, in the case of the edible frog (*Rana esculenta*) lens formation takes place regularly without this contact, that is, as soon as the respective total phase has been reached.

The American *Rana palustris* seems to resemble in this respect *Rana esculenta*, according to experiments by King. It is interesting in this connection to note that a small fragment of the optic vesicle in *Bombinator* suffices to start lens formation.

Speaking generally, we may say in regard to this problem that there is a developmental component, namely, contact-stimulus of the optic vesicle on the epidermis, which exercises a strong ecphoric action on the engram complex, and that the ecphory manifests itself in the reaction of lens formation. As first shown by Lewis in his work on *Rana silvatica*, this contact-stimulus of the optic vesicle on the skin can also ecphorise lens formation on parts of the epidermis other than those which the normal development demands.

He removed the optic vesicle at a very early stage from the brain, and inserted it beneath the epidermis of some other part of the body, such as the abdomen, etc. In numerous cases he succeeded in obtaining the formation of a lens in parts of the body where normally this never occurs. Speman, after repeated experiments on the toad *Bombinator*, considers it probable that, if not the skin of the abdomen or of the trunk, at any rate that of the head behind the eye, is able to form a lens on contact with the optic vesicle. Recent investigations by G. Ekman have even shown that during a definite period the entire ectoderm of the green frog (*Hyla arborea*), with the possible exception of the ear and nose primordia, is capable of lens formation. In comparison with the ecphoric action of the stimulus, the other components of the energetic conditions of that phase play but a minor part in their ecphoric action on this engram complex; they are, however, not altogether without effect, as may be demonstrated in the cases of *Rana esculenta* and *Rana palustris*, where they suffice for ecphory on elimination of such contact-stimulus. In our conception of the process as one of phasogeneous ecphory the apparent irregularities and exceptions, which otherwise would loom large, disappear. Indeed, the very facts just given—material available since the first edition of *The Mneme*—show us in the clearest manner that an understanding of these processes can be gained *only in the light of the theory of ecphory.*

From what has been said we reach this important conclusion. In the irritable substance of protists, of animals, and of plants are properties, "excitation-dispositions," which as a rule are characterised by latency. Like the individually acquired engrams, they are evoked from this state of latency by stimuli, on the cessation of which they sooner or later lapse into latency. Each recurrence of the ecphoric influence effects the return of the respective state of excitement, and this becomes manifest to us by its own proper reactions.

What finally determines our conclusion that these are inherited engrams is the nature of the influences calling them into activity. They bear, as we have briefly demonstrated, the definite character of an ecphory in part direct, in part associative, or chronogeneous, or phasogeneous. Finally, we note that these inherited excitation-dispositions behave in every respect like engrams. Only their origin, not their nature, is problematical.

We have still to deal with the problem of differentiating the characteristics of those inherited excitation-dispositions, which in our view are to be regarded as engrams, from those of other inherited dispositions which have not so to be regarded. It is natural enough to look for distinguishing marks in those characteristic properties of the inherited engrams which are typical also of the engram as such. The engram, we may repeat, is characterised, first, by a latent condition ; secondly, by the fact that each recurrence of the liberating influence effects the return of the corresponding state of excitement ; thirdly, by the ecphoric character of the liberating influences ; and finally, by its power, through addition of new engraphic influences, to affect the function of the inherited dispositions.

According to their possession or non-possession of these characteristics, the inherited excitation-dispositions may or may not be regarded as inherited engrams.

The first characteristic, a condition of latency, is useless for the purposes of differentiation, simply because in this discussion we have regarded all properties of the organic substance as dispositions or predispositions. The whole problem is concerned with dispositions which are generally latent.

The second characteristic is that with each recurrence of the liberating influence there is a return of the corresponding state of excitement. Are there now any inherited dispositions in which this is not the case? Personally, I am unaware of any dispositions of the organic irritable substance which, without the occurrence of other changes of state—for example, the entry into a totally different stage of development—have exhausted themselves by having been repeatedly roused into their corresponding states of excitement. But too frequent repetition and too long duration of the excitation may produce a state of fatigue, leading to the enfeeblement of the excitation and of the reactions caused by it. If, however, sufficient time is given for the organism to recover, no exhaustion takes place, or, at any rate, not while it remains in a state of primitive energy ; but on the contrary, an increase in the predisposition to react usually sets in. Many dispositions are only elicited once in the individual life of the organism, as witness the lapse of the different development phases in onto-genesis, and of instincts which normally become manifest only once in the individual life. In these cases it is not that the disposition has been exhausted, but only that the end has been reached of the situation which acts ecphorically on the disposition ; for by artificially throwing back an organism to a state through which it has already passed, the disposition can be roused again. Mention need only be made of the numerous cases of regeneration in embryos and fully developed animals in order to show that the disposition, normally evoked once only in the individual life, is not thereby exhausted. This is the case, too, with those excitation-dispositions, the reactions of which belong to the motor or secretive area. We have already on page 71 related how caterpillars, which normally make only one cocoon in their lifetime, can be induced to spin parts, or the whole, over and over again.

The latent condition of inherited dispositions can readily be inferred. Further, such dispositions are characterised by a persistent vitality ; for far from being enfeebled or slowly exhausted by repeatedly being roused into activity, they, on the contrary, with proper regard to time for recovery are strengthened by it.

Perhaps, in dealing with the third characteristic of an engram, we may succeed in tracing inherited dispositions which differ in their response to ecphoric influences from those whose activity cannot be traced to such ecphory. An exact determination of the difficulty is impossible, for a liberating influence can only be called ecphoric with certainty, provided we know the engraphic stimulus, and are thus in a position to distinguish by comparison between the ecphoric and the engraphic influences. Our real difficulty lies in the fact that, in the great majority of inherited dispositions, the engraphic stimuli are unknown to us, and that in cases of immediate manifestations we are able only under especially favourable conditions to recognise their ecphoric character. Reference may be made to the elaborate pantomime of a bath without water that a young magpie was induced to go through by the contact of its beak with water. On the other hand, we are not justified in eliminating cases where the ecphoric character of the actuating factor is less apparent, or in denying the engram-nature of the respective reactions.

Amongst inherited dispositions the irritability as such is not, of course, to be included, for that is the indispensable condition for the acquisition of engrams. But the specific evolution of this irritability is brought about by its one fundamental property of susceptibility to engraphic influences. The irritability, as it presents itself to us to-day in the single organism after a history of many millions of years, is charged with innumerable engrams, whose presence renders the irritability an exceedingly complex thing.

Earlier in our investigation, when we defined the primary state of indifference, we said that we wished thereby simply to imply the state of the organism at the beginning of our various observations and experiments. Even if our subject is an organism just separated from its mother, it will only be a blank sheet in respect to its individual mneme. If we submit such an organism for the first time to a stimulus and describe the result as a simple synchronous stimulation, the stimulus can only be regarded relatively as original. In the majority of such instances it will be partly a case of the ecphory of inherited engrams, or it may be that such ecphories will mingle with the action on the primary, so to say, pre-engraphic irritability. We are, therefore, unable to eliminate with absolute certainty the ecphoric co-operation in any stimulation. If we were in a position to examine organic matter newly produced by spontaneous generation, then, and only then, should we be able to observe purely synchronous stimulation without any trace of ecphory. This difficulty will also prevent us, in dealing with inherited dispositions, from distinguishing by the ecphoric or non-ecphoric character of the actuating influences the engraphic from the non-engraphic.

Finally, we turn to the consideration of the fourth characteristic of an engram, and enquire as to the kind of inherited disposition which can be influenced by newly generated engrams. The mere possibility of influencing such a disposition engraphically is sufficient justification for regarding it as an inherited engram. But the impossibility of so doing is no sure argument in favour of the opposite conclusion, simply because our failure to influence the disposition engraphically is partly caused by the imperfection of our experiments ; some new experimental method may prove the possibility of influence. The degree of difficulty in influencing inherited dispositions engraphically varies greatly. For example, those inherited dispositions of the higher animals, for the ecphory of which a definite specialisation of parts of the central nervous system is required, are more easily influenced engraphically than less specialised dispositions. But, indeed, I do not know of any class of inherited dispositions which is entirely exempt from engraphic influence, nor of any group of organisms which possess rigid, non-modifiable, inherited dispositions. Among the Bacteria, many inherited dispositions can readily be affected by newly acquired engrams ; with comparative ease it is even possible to secure the hereditary continuation of the engraphic influence. So also with many other inherited dispositions, such as the heliotropism of uni-cellular organisms like the Flagellates, and the tropisms, periodic movements, rate of growth, and many other characteristics of Plants.

In a limited but fairly imposing number of cases we are able to influence inherited dispositions so effectively that the newly added engram not only remains in force during the individual life of the organism, but is transmitted to the offspring. Attention is directed to those cited on pages 57–64. The cases are limited partly by reason of the imperfection and too brief duration of our experiments, and also because of the short period during which the germ-cells of many, perhaps of all, organisms are to any considerable extent sensitive to any engraphic influence. From our prescribed human point of view the hereditary engraphic variability might almost be described as capricious.

Thus it appears impossible to me to divide inherited dispositions into two categories, namely, those that are to be regarded as engrams, and those that are not. If, therefore, we look upon each specifically evolved form of irritability as engraphically complicated, we have to prove the value of the conception, and ask whether it is possible to apply it logically in concrete cases. Does it help us to a "complete description in the simplest manner," to quote Kirchoff's criterion ? If we can furnish proof that facts do not contradict our idea of the engram-nature of inherited dispositions, and also that such a conception throws new light on this aspect of organic phenomena, we have added a new and important link to the chain of probability we are endeavouring to forge.

This part of our task will be attempted in the third

part of this book, where the action of mnemic processes in Ontogenesis will be investigated, and where it will be shown how the enigmatic phenomena of the normal ontogenetic processes and of those modified by interferences, as well as the phenomena of regeneration, are brought within closer reach of our understanding by·our conception of them as a function of the Mneme. Before we elaborate this phase of our subject, we shall in the second part of this work deepen and extend our foundations by subjecting the mnemic fundamental phenomena to a systematic investigation.

POSTCRIPT TO THE THIRD GERMAN EDITION

Since the appearance of the first edition in 1904, the material from which evidence in support of the engraphic origin of dispositions acquired in the long process of evolution can be drawn has been extraordinarily increased. New experiments by Blaringhem, Klebs, Bordage, Kammerer, Pictet, Przibram, and Summer, to name but the principal workers in this field, are in entire harmony with the earlier investigations of Chauvin, Standfuss, Fischer, Schröder, and others. It has been most clearly demonstrated that, with appropriate experimental arrangements, dispositions of all kinds can be created *de novo* ; that changes in the manner of manifestation of the already existing dispositions can be obtained without difficulty ; and that the new acquisitions of the organism, of whatever origin they may be, present themselves without exception as products of stimulation or induction. They are to be regarded as engrams, and we can prove their hereditary nature, if in appropriate circumstances they are generated during the sensitive period of the germ-cells. They also behave like dispositions acquired during evolution, for, as the crossing experiments of Tower and Kammerer show, they can under suitable conditions be transmitted according to Mendel's principles of segregation. On the strength of these numerous indisputable agreements, the conclusion seems fully justified that dispositions acquired during evolution also have arisen engraphically.

I have just completed the compilation of relevant data in a special work entitled, *The Problem of the Inheritance of Acquired Characters* (*Das Problem Der Vererbung Erworbener Eigenschaften*, Wilhelm Engelmann, Leipzig, 1912).

As shown in that book, experimental research has proved that all new acquisitions of the organism must be regarded as products of stimulation or induction. We are, therefore, driven to elaborate some such Engram Theory as the one with which we are now concerned. In the following sections of this book it will be our task to show how our general understanding of organic processes will profit by the working out of this theory.

PART II

CHAPTER IV

*THE MUTUAL RELATIONS OF ENGRAMS:
SIMULTANEOUS AND SUCCESSIVE
ASSOCIATION*

In the introductory part we discussed the genesis of engrams and the various phases of their existence. From an analysis of organic states we formulated the following definition :—" An engram is the result of engraphic action, and implies an altered disposition of the irritable substance towards a recurrence of the state of excitement produced by the original stimulus. The organic substance so affected by engraphic action shows itself specifically predisposed to the state of excitement induced by the original stimulus. On being subjected again to this stimulus, or to other influences, the basis of which is invariably the partial recurrence of a definite energetic condition, the original state of excitement is reproduced."

With this definition in mind, we have next to trace more precisely the relations of the various engrams generated and conserved in the same organism. In the nature of things, the organism can very rarely be affected and influenced by a single stimulus alone, as for instance, by a single light-ray of a definite wave length. The stimulus, even when belonging to a distinct category such as the photic stimuli, is invariably of a complex nature. We need only think of the various elements combined in the visual impressions or sounds which act upon our organism. When we see a landscape, or when we listen to a piece of music, our organism is in both cases simultaneously excited by a large number of stimuli, which, however, do not blend into something homogeneous, but group themselves in juxtaposition. Thus, we are conscious of the juxtaposition of the photic stimuli which impinge on our retina, and such juxtaposition we call a picture. In similar fashion we term simultaneous polyphonic acoustic stimuli a chord or a discord. We do not attempt an explanation of this fact, but accept it as such. In keeping with this co-ordinated reception by the organism of simultaneously acting stimuli, which we may describe as a co-ordinated synchronous effect of stimulation, the engraphic effect of this stimulation is also a co-ordinated one. This means that subsequently, on the ecphory of the respective engrams, a state of excitement arises which corresponds to the co-ordinated effect of those stimuli which previously acted synchronically in juxtaposition.

This statement, which at first sight appears to be only a roundabout way of saying that co-acting stimuli are received by the organism and are mnemically reproduced in juxtaposition, involves far-reaching consequences, and helps us to a surprising perception of the deeper connection of various data which so far we have obtained by the analytical method alone. We have already noted how, on the action of a complex stimulus of a definite kind, a juxtaposition, not a mere diffuse blending, is secured. A co-ordinated synchronous effect of the stimulation also follows on the simultaneous action of various stimuli, not only of the same, but also of different categories.

When an express train thunders past us rapidly, we feel clearly the juxtaposition of visual and auditory impressions, and we are able to reproduce this juxtaposition mnemically after the cessation of the stimuli, if the latter have been sufficiently strong to act engraphically. It in no way affects the problem occupying us here that, at the reception of stimuli belonging to different categories, different receptor-organs are called into action. Co-ordinated vision, for example, is conditioned by the excitation of numerous specific receptor-elements, such as the cones and rods of the retina. Tactual and auditory impressions involve like conditions. What interests us here is the fact that the organism as a whole is able to perceive simultaneously different stimuli in juxtaposition, and always does so perceive them ; and that the effect of these involves elements contiguous and disparate which refuse to blend into something homogeneous. Thus, at any given moment a firmly connected, co-ordinated total of excitations exists in each individual, and this is manifest for Self in the consciousness of the juxtaposition of sensations ; and in the case of other organisms by numerous objectively perceptible reactions. We will call this totality the simultaneous excitation-complex.

From the coherent whole of this simultaneous complex we may, for the sake of theory, abstract the action of a single stimulus or stimulus-category, and thereby facilitate our understanding of this multitudinous complex of simultaneous excitations. But we must remember that in so doing we strain the actual facts of observation and arbitrarily undo the nexus of the whole. This must be borne in mind when we consider not only the synchronous but also the engraphic effect of the stimuli. The individual stimulus does not liberate one isolated synchronous excitation and make an isolated engram Such detachment is well-nigh impossible in Nature. What we find is this : that a simultaneous excitation-complex as such is, after the lapse of the synchronous excitations, engraphically fixed *in its totality*. That which remains is a simultaneous *engram-complex*.

Let us examine more closely the engraphic action which the simultaneous excitation-complex exercises on the organism. We may characterise this simultaneous complex as the product of the excitations resulting from the entire energetic condition. By " energetic condition " we mean not only the external energies affecting the organism, but also its internal energetic state. The latter is at least as important as the forces acting on it from without— a fact which becomes evident on subjecting the organism of a higher animal to the influence of the same external stimuli during sleep and in the waking state. In the waking state the internal energetic state of an organism varies greatly at different times, so that the same external energetic condition produces at various moments altogether different simultaneous excitation-complexes; the subsequent engraphic effect varies accordingly, different engrams corresponding to different excitation-complexes.

As the mnemic reproduction is usually weaker than the original excitations were at the time when they created the engrams, we must not be surprised that on the ecphory of the engram-complex many of the components of the complex do not become manifest at all, that is, they cannot be recognised by reactions. Thus it seems that of successive experiences a few engrams only are conceived. But as already stated, most of these engrams are not simple units, but products of highly composite excitation-complexes.

Because only a small fraction of a simultaneous excitation-complex manifests itself clearly on mnemic reproduction, we get the impression, not of the recurrence of a former complete energetic condition, but only of a specific section. We were once standing by the Bay of Naples and saw Capri lying before us; near by an organ-grinder played on a large barrel-organ; a peculiar smell of oil reached us from a neighbouring " trattoria "; the sun was beating pitilessly on our backs; and our boots, in which we had been tramping about for hours, pinched us. Many years after, a similar smell of oil ecphorised most vividly the optic engram of Capri, and even now this smell has invariably the same effect. The other elements of the simultaneous situation are not ecphorised by the smell of oil. The melody of the barrel-organ, the heat of the sun, the discomfort of the boots are ecphorised neither by the smell of oil nor by the renewed experience of Capri; and on their recurrence as original stimuli they fail to effect the ecphory of those two engram-complexes, but this is no evidence that they have not acted engraphically at all It may be that a friend reminds us of the sufferings we then endured from the heat and our tight boots, or he plays the organ melody on the piano to us, and we then find that these elements of the energetic condition have also acted engraphically, but that for their ecphory some special kind of assistance is necessary.

The case illustrates the fact that the stimulus of which we become most vividly conscious has not always the most powerful engraphic effect. The pressure of the boots was in its way more insistent than the smell from the oil; yet it was the smell-element of the excitation-complex which apparently attained the stronger engraphic position. We need not enter more closely into a discussion of these specific questions, but it is well to emphasise that, as a general rule, the nature of the stimulus and the momentary state of the organism are together the principal factors in determining the intensity of the engraphic influence, and that according to circumstances the influence of the one or other factor predominates.

In the many simultaneous engram-complexes which we retain, we often find that, together with important impressions, there are many commonplace indifferent ones mnemically fixed. One of my earliest recollections is of a garden at Kreuznach, in which as a child of three years of age I had been stung by a wasp. Even to-day I could draw the shape of the flower-beds and the distribution of the rose-trees and my relative position in the garden at the moment I was stung.

Darwin tells us in his autobiography that the solution of an important problem, which furnished him with the key to many hitherto enigmatic cases, came quite suddenly to him during a drive. He adds the remark: " I can remember the very spot in the road, whilst in my carriage, when to my joy the solution occurred to me, and this was long after I had come to Down." It would be easy to quote many more observations which show that in moments of intense emotion, besides the main impressions, relatively unimportant parts of the simultaneous excitation-complex also act engraphically in a surprisingly strong manner. Later, they naturally show themselves indissolubly associated with the main impressions and accordingly act ecphorically on these.

I think our investigations have shown that the facts of simultaneous association follow from the one fundamental postulate that the organic substance responds to a number of simultaneous stimuli with an orderly, coherent juxtaposition of excitations, and that this simultaneous excitation-complex acts engraphically as a complex.

The single simultaneous excitation-complexes are related to each other in a temporal succession marked by specific characteristics due to their varied mode of origin. The succession is continuous ; that is, one complex merges into the next. A break, in the sense of successive complexes separated by a section devoid of excitations, never occurs, not even in sleep or in those periods of rest when there is a discontinuity of consciousness.

Further, the relation of complexes is unilinear. Each simultaneous complex is connected with but two others, its immediate predecessor and its immediate successor. As no complex exactly resembles another, although a periodic recurrence of single components of the complexes is characteristic of many life processes, the sequence of these complexes is non-reversible ; consequently it makes a fundamental difference whether we regard them in the order of their genesis, i.e. from the earlier to the later, or vice versa, from the later to the earlier

Just as the simultaneous engram appears on ecphory as the faithful, if somewhat weakened, image of the simultaneous excitation-complex to which it owes its origin, showing, therefore, the same co-ordinated juxtaposition of the various stimulations, so in a sequence of engram-complexes the same unbroken, unilinear, progressive arrangement, in which the original excitation-complexes were grouped, reappears on each ecphory of the sequence, proving thereby that the succession is engraphically registered.

We have noted that each separate simultaneous engram complex presents a co-ordinated juxtaposition of the various stimulations, and that it is followed immediately by a like co-ordinated complex.

Hereby a situation is created in which each fresh engram has to be allocated to a definite place. From the very beginning, therefore, the engram stands in closer relation to some, and in more distant relation to other, simultaneous engrams.

It follows from this, that within any simultaneous complex there are components already more closely associated with some fellow components than with others, and that this difference of relationship also obtains in the case of successive associations.

In certain circumstances, close associations between engrams may be created which the relative position in the simultaneous complex would not lead us to expect. But this follows only from the specific strength of engraphic *action* exercised on the respective engrams at their genesis, to the exclusion of their fellow components.

Strength of stimuli, frequency of the simultaneous stimulation, the focussing of attention effect the close association of entirely heterogeneous engrams. So a smell of oil becomes more closely connected with the visual image of Capri than with other components of the same simultaneous complex.

Within any simultaneous engram-complex, as well as within successively associated complexes, a more intimate association exists between engrams of like stimulus-quality than between engrams of different stimulus-quality. Further, given the same stimulus quality, engrams of nearly related origin are more closely associated than those of more distant relationship.

The closer or more distant relationship of the engrams refers, of course, to their mutual ecphoric action. A few examples may, however, make the meaning clearer. The execution of an impressive dance to an easily remembered tune generates a double succession of acoustic and optic engrams which, series by series, are easily ecphorised. Generally, one series acts ecphorically on the other. On hearing the tune, I have the visual image of the dancer, or on seeing the dancer, I have the auditory image of the melody. But in the lack of an often repeated experience of dance and tune together, the optic engram does not attain that close association with the acoustic engram whereby the simultaneous movement of the dancer corresponds exactly to each bar of the melody.

Again, in engram-complexes originated from one and the same stimulus-quality, we may discern the existence of more intimate connections between some than between other components of the successions. Any one of fair musical ability, to whom a polyphonous piece of music has often been played or sung, is able after a little time to reproduce as a memory-image, or to sing, or to play the sequence of each single part.

The performance does not demand a highly specialised musical training, as a child can easily reproduce the sequences in the case of a two-part song. But the ability to reproduce in that way can only be explained on the assumption that the tone sequences within each particular part are more closely associated with each other than are the sequences of one part with those of another. Should this not be the case, the reproducer in his attempt to capture a single part would helplessly vacillate between the collateral progressions, especially if he had set himself to render a part other than the dominant.

In the following diagram we trace a case, very much simplified for our purpose, in which the relations of the acoustic components have been worked out. The connections between the four successive engram-complexes can readily be seen.

We have now reached the following position :—

The external and internal stimuli acting simultaneously and successively on the organism generate in it excitation-complexes which represent an orderly juxtaposition in their simultaneous action, and an unbroken, unilinear, and non-reversible sequence in their succession.

The appearance of these excitation-complexes implies a permanent affection of the organism. This we characterised as engraphic, meaning thereby the creation of

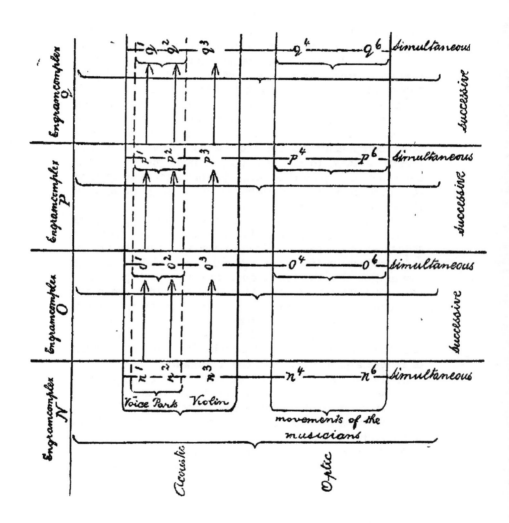

an increased disposition of the organism to reproduce those excitation-complexes. It is obvious, therefore, that things recur as on their first appearance, namely as an orderly juxtaposition, and an unbroken, unilinear, and non-reversible sequence.

It would be the exception to this that would naturally call for a special explanation.

We described the co-ordination of the simultaneous excitation-complexes, and the subsequent engram-complexes as unbroken, unilinear, and non-reversible. The expression " unbroken " implies the continuity in which no division can be observed, division being solely a function of our intellect.

This becomes clear at once when we try to understand what we mean in this connection by the idea of division. In speaking of simultaneous excitation, that is, of excitations existing at the same time, the answer to the question regarding the duration of such simultaneity can only be " infinitesimally short," in view of the enormous number of influences acting on the organism at any one moment.

As each excitation of the organic substance possesses a measurable duration, and consequently is never infinitesimally small, we have, at the juxtaposition of simultaneous infinitesimally brief states, to apply to the objects a purely logical principle of division *ab extra.*

The division is imperative and indispensable, for it is in the very nature of our understanding that knowledge of the world of phenomena proceeds by the aid of division and rearrangement.

By regarding the excitations of an organism in point of time as simultaneous and successive states, we obtain an arrangement objectively justified, although based on an arbitrary and purely logical division. In our examination of two successive simultaneous complexes, I and II, we may find that regarding some components they differ essentially from each other. The components *a, b, c* of I may have disappeared. On the other hand, the components *x*, *y*, *z* of II may have sprung into existence. A number of components, however, will be regularly carried forward from I to II, even if the external energetic condition is suddenly and completely changed. For example, I make a dive out of the bright hot sunshine into the cool dark depths of the river. First, we note that a change of the external energetic condition of my entire organism has taken place, not in an infinitesimally small, but in a measurable, degree ; secondly, that despite the change, many components of the internal energetic condition of the organism remain unaltered.

It follows from these considerations that the simultaneous engram-complexes also represent theoretical and not actual unities, and that in reality they pass into each other without a break, notwithstanding that some of their components are detached. The successive association is not limited to the continuously progressing components in the line of simultaneous complexes, but holds good also in regard to those components which are detached. This becomes immediately evident if one thinks of a melodic succession of sounds, or of noises such as the beats of a drum, or the trampling of feet, or of those lists of grammatical exceptions which in their bareness seem devoid of sense. A little consideration convinces us that one can hardly speak of an association in the permanently continuous and, therefore, unchanging components of the successive engram-complexes. It is only the varying components of the successive complexes, those that come and go, that allow us to apply the idea of connection and association. To them we apply *the objective method*, arguing from the appearance and disappearance of objectively perceivable reactions to the idea of association. The conception of connection and association surely presupposes the discontinuity of what has to be connected.

Direct observation teaches us that the engrams left by the discontinuous components of successive excitations are themselves successively associated, even when the separating interval is appreciably measurable. The engraphic fixation of a melody is as sure when the sounds follow each other " staccato " with appreciable intervals as when they are joined together " legato." But the intervals must not be too long if the engrams are to become successively associated. Tone sequences with intervals of several minutes find it almost impossible to establish themselves engraphically. It will be the task of later experimental research to define for each case the maximum length of interval at which a successive association still takes place. What has been said regarding acoustic engrams applies with equal force to all other engrams. They must not be separated by too long intervals from each other, if the repetition of the earlier has to act engraphically on the later.

The reason for this limitation in time for the successive association becomes clear to us, when we examine the relation of the successive with the simultaneous association, especially with regard to the possible derivation of the former from the latter. The successive association is indeed only a consequence of the simultaneous one. As previously stated (p. 21), to each original stimulus there corresponds a definite synchronous excitation. On cessation of the stimulus the excitation does not suddenly cease, but ebbs gradually with frequent, if faint, revivals, before finally dying away. We described the excitation in this phase of its disappearance as acoluthic excitation. It must be pointed out, however, that the excitation acts engraphically, not only during its stronger synchronous, but also during its weaker acoluthic phase.

It is true that in a succession of discontinuous stimuli there can be no simultaneity of the synchronous excitations. Let us call these C(syn), D(syn), E(syn), F(syn)— but there does exist a simultaneity of the synchronous excitation D(syn) with the vanishing acoluthic phase of its predecessor—which may be denoted by c^1(ac), c^2(ac), c^3(ac), o.

The following diagram shows the simultaneous relations

of the synchronous phase of an excitation with the acoluthic phases of its predecessors:—

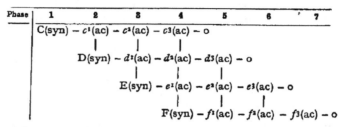

Phase	1	2	3	4	5	6	7
	$C(\text{syn}) - c^1(\text{ac}) - c^2(\text{ac}) - c^3(\text{ac}) - o$						
		$D(\text{syn}) - d^1(\text{ac}) - d^2(\text{ac}) - d^3(\text{ac}) - o$					
			$E(\text{syn}) - e^1(\text{ac}) - e^2(\text{ac}) - e^3(\text{ac}) - o$				
				$F(\text{syn}) - f^1(\text{ac}) - f^2(\text{ac}) - f^3(\text{ac}) - o$			

We see here that simultaneity exists between the
synchronous excitation D(syn) and the acoluthic $c^1(\text{ac})$;
between the synchronous E(syn), the acoluthic $d^1(\text{ac})$
and the already weakened $c^2(\text{ac})$; finally between the
synchronous F(syn) and the acoluthic $e^1(\text{ac})$, the weaker
acoluthic $d^2(\text{ac})$, and the vanishing $c^3(\text{ac})$. This simultaneity of the excitations implies, of course, a simultaneous association of the engrams left behind by the
excitations, and thereby the possibility of reducing the
successive association to a simultaneous one of two
engrams, of which the first has been left by the synchronous
excitation, and the other by the acoluthic excitation of
its predecessor.

A glance at our diagram will also help us to understand the important fact experimentally determined by
Ebbinghaus, that successive association not only exists
between members of a continuous series as from one
member to the next, but that each member is associated,
although less strongly, with its second following member,
and also, but in still weaker connection, with the third
following, and so on. A limit to the formation of such
associations is only set by the continuous diminution and
final complete extinction of the acoluthic excitations.
This also explains why a succession of excitations can
give rise to associated engrams only when, during the
original excitation, the time-intervals between the separate
members have been sufficiently short to allow of the
connection of the acoluthic excitation of the preceding

member with the synchronous excitation of its successor. These ideas, lightly touched on here, are more precisely formulated in the *Mnemic Sensations*.

Despite the derivation of the successive association from the simultaneous one, the final result in each case is very different. This is shown in a striking manner when we compare the ecphory of simultaneously associated engrams with that of successively associated engrams. True, in one respect congruity exists between them. Also at the ecphory of simultaneously associated engrams, one must be ecphorised a little time before the other, in order to ecphorise this other. Simultaneously produced engrams are linked with equal force in both directions, whilst this is not the case with successively produced engrams, which constitutes a difference of fundamental importance. We arrive at this statement from the fact that, if engram *a* is simultaneously associated with engram *b*, then under ordinary circumstances the ecphorising power of *a* on *b* and of *b* on *a* is equal. But if *a* and *b* are successively associated, the ecphory of *a* acts far more strongly ecphorically on *b*, than the other way round.

This varying ecphoric strength in the successive association can be most easily demonstrated in dealing with auditory engrams. Even the skilled musician may be quite unable to recognise the most familiar tone passage if it be played to him in reversed order. The same difficulty applies in regard to the vocal sounds of which the words of our language are composed.

When on my travels in Queensland I passed through the squatter station Degilbo. Afterwards I heard its name frequently mentioned, but I had no idea that the name was simply the word "obliged" in reversed spelling. If chance had not enlightened me, I should have regarded this word as a typical native name. Again, it is not possible to recite a poem in reversed sequence of words, nor a meaningless combination of words like the lists of gender, for example. If in a recitation we misplace the words, this may only be evidence that the engrams have been acquired in a false sequence, or that during the learning of the poem we sought the assistance of simultaneous association. If, for example, a boy learning the Latin rules of gender pictures to himself as an aid to memory, while reciting the list " Men, people, rivers, winds," how the men of a seafaring people enter the mouth of a river under favourable winds, the normal succession by the use of such simultaneous associations becomes disturbed, because the components of the simultaneous association ecphorise each other indiscriminately.

We have seen that successively associated engrams act ecphorically more strongly on each other in the order of their genesis than conversely. But the evidence for this rule becomes, as we have just seen, somewhat obscured in the successions of auditory engrams by the co-operation of simultaneous associations. This difficulty arises oftener in cases of the succession of engrams which have made their entrance through some other sense receptors. Let us take the succession of visual impressions during a walk. The succession of visual excitations, and consequently the generation of successive visual engrams, often occurs so slowly, and so many components continually pass from the earlier into the later stages, that the ecphoric predominance of the succeeding engram over its predecessor in the chain might become almost unrecognisable simply through the interplay of numerous simultaneous connections.

That visual engrams in a succession act ecphorically with unequal strength may be adequately shown in the following way:—The image of a movement is physiologically represented by a succession of visual excitations, which, if of mnemic origin, represents a succession of visual engrams. If the order of the movement be now reversed—and this can easily be done by photographing small phases of the movement, and then with the help of either kinetoscope or cinematograph viewing these photographs in the reversed way—we find that the reversion affects us quite as strangely as would a reversed tone-succession or the word " Degilbo " for " obliged."

That is, its connection with the original movement is not recognised at all.

Among human beings, engrams of the olfactory sense, and also of the gustatory sense, often enter into simultaneous association with engrams of other origin, but very rarely with engrams of their own kind. Among simultaneous olfactory excitations, the co-ordination is not as definite and clear as among simultaneous visual, auditory, or tactual excitations. Frequently, the olfactory excitations so blend that they mutually neutralise each other so far as their individual quality is concerned. Nor do they form successive sequences of distinct units as do tone-passages. Forel has rightly argued that this defect can be chiefly attributed to the irregular manner in which the stimuli enter our organism. The principal cause of the inability of the stimulus-successions to act sufficiently clearly and quickly in the generation of successively associated engrams lies in the nature of the sense-organs, which serve as receptors of such stimuli.

In many insects, the engrams entering into the organism through the receptor of the olfactory sense show themselves much more perfectly associated, simultaneously and successively, than do the olfactory engrams in man. Forel has convincingly argued that this distinction between insects and man rests not so much on the greater or lesser acumen of the senses as on the different mode by which different organisms receive these stimulations. With the ant the antennæ are the sense-organs. By these the ant cognises the objects in its way olfactorily. Through such an organ it receives simultaneously and successively associated excitations, and the immediately subsequent corresponding engrams ; just as we human beings, and especially those of us who are born blind, receive them in the area of the tactual sense by the help of the groping finger points. This olfactory sense of the insects, which involves so remarkable a power of exact localisation in space, has been described most adequately by Forel as a topochemical sense of smell.

Forel, and afterwards Wasmann, have shown that

many phases in the biology of the ant are greatly elucidated by an accurate knowledge of the peculiar nature
of this topochemical sense, and by the idea that the
impressions acquired through it are retained in the memory
of the animals or, as I should say, act engraphically.

But in all directions precise investigation goes to prove
that the successive engrams of smell are, in respect to
their mutual ecphoric action, non-reversible. Of course,
each series of engrams may also be acquired in reversed
sequence. We are able to learn the list, " panis, piscis,
crinis, finis " in that sequence, as also in the sequence
" finis, crinis, piscis, panis." The latter by frequent
repetition is engraved on my organism as an associated
succession of engrams. But we have done nothing beyond
acquiring a second succession of engrams which exists
independently. Like most ants, an ant of the species
Lasius follows the same track forwards and backwards.
On the strength of chemical stimuli frequently repeated
and acting in two definite sequences, two successions of
topochemical engrams are then gradually impressed on
it, but these impressions are almost as independent of
each other as if a different road had been chosen for the
return journey, which also exceptionally occurs.

Ebbinghaus by ingenious experiments succeeded in obtaining extremely interesting and important data on the
mode of connection—that is, on the mutual ecphoric
action—of successive engrams. The method devised by
him consists of the learning by heart of meaningless lines
of syllables until these can be faultlessly recited, the
forming of new combinations out of the previously learnt
lines, and learning by heart of these new combinations,
and finally a comparison of the number of repetitions
and of the time-periods required for the learning by
heart of the differently prepared combinations. By this
method Ebbinghaus discovered, first, that " at repeated
creation of lines of syllables, the separate members not
only associated with their immediate successors, but
that connections were also formed between each member
and several of its more remote successors. " The strength

of the connection is a decreasing function of the time
or of the number of the intermediate members, which
separate the respective syllables in the original line.
The function is a maximum for those members succeeding
each other immediately. The intimate nature of the
function is unknown, only it decreases for growing distances of the members, at first very rapidly, and afterwards very slowly." A second important result of the
experimental investigations by Ebbinghaus was expressed
as follows :—" In fact, in the learning of a line certain
mutual connections of the members move in two directions, backwards as well as forwards. The strength of
the disposition thus created was again a decreasing function
of the distance of the members in the original line. At
equal distances, however, it was considerably less for
the backward than for the forward connections. On
lines being repeated in equal frequency it was found that
each member is connected with the one preceding it
not much more closely than with the *next but one* succeeding it ; and with the next but *one* preceding it, hardly
as closely as with the next but *two* succeeding it."

Ebbinghaus has elsewhere calculated the ecphoric
influence of a member on the next but one succeeding
it at a third of its ecphoric influence on the immediately
succeeding member, as shown in the diagram :—

Preceding Engrams. $\longleftrightarrow$ Successive Engrams.

γ β a b c

If we express the ecphoric strength in the successive
association of a on b by 1, the ecphoric strength of a on
c is one-third, or expressed in the form of an equation :—

$$\left.\begin{array}{l} \text{if}\quad a \text{ on } b=1 \\ \text{and}\quad a \text{ on } c=\tfrac{1}{3} \\ \text{and}\quad a \text{ on } c=a \text{ on } \beta \end{array}\right\} \text{according to Ebbinghaus.}$$

then a on $\beta=\tfrac{1}{3}$ or a on $b=3$ (a on β)

One may therefore accept this calculation as also
representing the relative ecphoric influence of a member

on its successor and on its predecessor, and say that in the case under observation, the ecphory of an engram has an ecphoric effect on the engram succeeding it thrice as strong as on the one preceding it.

Later investigations carried on by Müller, Schumann, and Pilzecker have confirmed in all essential points the results obtained by Ebbinghaus on "nonsense-syllables." Wohlgemuth's experiments gave identical results for syllables learnt aloud. This author, however, inferred from his experiments with optical stimuli that associations of visual engrams have equal ecphoric value in both directions, backwards and forwards. Wohlgemuth's extension of the experiments to visual engrams is undoubtedly of great value. They might with advantage be made to embrace the remaining classes of engrams. In view of Wohlgemuth's experiments, it seems to me certain that there exist differences depending on the nature of the sense-organ which serves as the receptor of the stimulus and transforms it into the excitation which acts engraphically. There are, however, equally good grounds for assuming that these are only differences of degree, and that they are in no way fundamental. We have first of all this fact, which is in no way shaken by Wohlgemuth's experiments, that we are absolutely unable to reverse a long mnemic succession of stimuli—whether visual, auditory, or tactile ; and secondly, we find that if the stimuli which originated the series of engrams in question are repeated in the original order there is an immediate recognition of the succession as familiar ; but when they are repeated in the reverse order, the succession strikes us as new and strange, even though it consists of the characteristic movements of some familiar object or the tones of some well-known melody. Wohlgemuth's experiments on visual engrams, confined to two consecutive members of a series and neglecting longer courses, do not appear to me to affect these fundamental facts. It would be well for us to await the results of the continuation and extension of these promising experiments, suggesting meanwhile that they be carried on under a variation of the experimental conditions, especially as regards time and the intervals of exposure. I might be rightly expected to show where we may look for the *real cause* of the unequal ecphoric strength of the successive connection, for this is not self-evident in the diagram given on page 101. Why does the ecphory of E(syn) through d^1(ac) not act as strongly ecphorically on D(syn) as through e^1(ac) on F(syn) ? I have dealt more fully with this problem in the *Mnemic Sensations* (p. 205–216), and believe I have found a satisfactory solution which, however, cannot here be explained in detail.

The successively connected inherited dispositions also show an unequal ecphoric strength similar to that of the individually acquired engram successions. It has already been argued above that we have many reasons for treating inherited dispositions as engrams also. Sufficient justification of this view will be given in the third part of this book.

In any case, we find the series of all such inherited dispositions, in respect of the mode and strength of their connections, subject to the same rules as the succession of the individually acquired engrams. A reversion in the course of the series of reactions by which those dispositions manifest themselves does not occur, and for them also the strength of the connection is a decreasing function of the intermediate members, and is at its maximum for the members immediately succeeding each other. The ecphoric action of member a on b is stronger than on c, of b on c stronger than on d. It is therefore impossible for a to overleap b and ecphorise c, or for b to ecphorise d to the utter neglect of c.

A burrowing wasp (Sphex) burrows a hole, and then flies out to catch insects, which, paralysed by the sting, are dragged to the entrance. The wasp, however, before taking its prey into the hole, always enters it first to see whether things are all right. Whilst the wasp was in the burrow, Fabre removed the insect to a short distance away. When the wasp came out again, the prey was found and again brought to the entrance of the burrow, when the instinct to examine the burrow before depositing the prey in it reasserted itself, and the insect was once more left at the entrance. As often as Fabre removed the prey, so often did the other action follow, so that the unfortunate wasp had to examine the burrow forty times.

Let us now analyse the case more precisely, denoting the successive reactions of the dragging along of the prey, by a, the laying down before the burrow, by b, the examination of the burrow, by c, and the carrying into the burrow, by d. The inherited dispositions corresponding to these reactions let us denote by a, β, γ and δ. We then have the following clearly ordinated succession of engrams :—

Dragging along — Laying down — Examination — Carrying in.
$\quad\quad a \quad\quad\quad\quad \beta \quad\quad\quad\quad \gamma \quad\quad\quad\quad \delta$

Fabre's experiment shows that when the wasp, after manifestation of the series of dispositions a, β, γ, is placed in a situation which renders a fresh manifestation of a necessary, the manifestation of a commands that of β and that of the latter the manifestation of γ. That is, if we conceive the dispositions as engrams, the earlier ecphorises the next. The association of disposition (or engram) a with δ is so much weaker than with β and γ, that, even with the experience of forty fruitless journeys, the wasp was unable to effect the direct ecphory of δ by a, and dispense with the ecphory of β and γ. We do not wish to convey the idea, however, that this succession is eternally immutable for Sphex and its descendants, and that it could never be altered under the influence of synchronically and engraphically acting stimuli. On the contrary, in the Hymenoptera as well as in the Vertebrates, we meet with many cases where inherited series of engrams are liable to become transformed by new individually acquired engrams.

We note exactly the same laws of association in the

successions of those inherited dispositions whose reactions manifest themselves as phenomena of growth. This fact is of great significance for the understanding of the normal ontogenesis of the organisms as well as of that experimentally disturbed. As this subject will be dealt with more in detail later on, I shall for the present leave it, and in conclusion discuss one special peculiarity of successive association.

A succession need not always continue in one series. In many cases a line of excitations divides at a certain point into two branches, and later, perhaps, into three or more. A simple case is the distribution of the engrams of a mnemically preserved piece of music that begins in one part and develops into two parts.

Phase 1	2	3	4	5
c —	d —	$e <$	$\begin{matrix} g\text{---} \\ \mid \\ d \end{matrix}$	$\begin{matrix} c\text{---} \\ \mid \\ e\text{---} \end{matrix}$

It is evident that in these equal phases the members of the two branches of the bifurcation or dichotomy are simultaneously associated. We may, therefore, describe such a dichotomy of a series of engrams as a simultaneously associated dichotomy.

But there also exist dichotomies, trichotomies, etc., of such successions, where the members of equal phases are not simultaneously associated, and where the ecphory proceeds at the point of division only in one direction. This singularity often depends on the circumstance that up to that moment no simultaneous association has taken place. For instance, if I study separately the first and second parts of the above-mentioned piece of music without hearing, reading, or playing them together, the dichotomy is not simultaneously associated, and therefore liable, not to a simultaneous, but only to an alternating, ecphory. The deliberate creation of simultaneous associations, however, changes the alternating into a simultaneously associated dichotomy. Numerous cases, however, exist, where such a transformation for one reason or another is impossible. Generally, the difficulty follows on the inability of the organism to carry out simultaneously the reactions of both lines of excitations. In that case the alternating dichotomy becomes permanent. On hearing or reading, for instance, the end of the first stanza of Fitzgerald's famous translation of the *Rubáiyát* of Omar Khayyam now in the first and now in the second version, I receive the impression of the following alternating form :—

The Sultan's Turret < in a Noose of Light.
with a Shaft of Light.

Now, it is impossible to transform this alternating dichotomy into a simultaneous associated one, either by simultaneous hearing or by engraphic influences, such as those of the above-mentioned two-part piece of music. And wherever, for some reason or other, a simultaneous association of the branches is impossible, the dichotomy, or as the case may be, trichotomy, remains permanently an alternating one. To the deeper understanding of the nature of alternating dichotomy, acquaintance with the conception of homophony is essential. Here I should simply like to note that at the division-point of each dichotomy, the complex of engrams borders on two or more succeeding complexes instead of one. In the above-quoted poem, for example, the word turret borders on " in " as well as on " with." As this is clearly a case of a dichotomy which only allows an alternate ecphory, we are left to wonder whether the engram " turret " will act ecphorically on " in " or on " with." Little doubt may be indulged, if of the two associations one is closer and, therefore, stronger ecphorically than the other. But often merely a variation in frequency of the repetition will give one branch of an alternative the dominance over the other. Besides this, conflicting side-influences may operate in such a manner that the choice falls now this way, now the other. We shall dwell on this more fully in Chapters XII and XIII.

So far we have taken into account only the association of engrams which present themselves as a legacy of excitations produced by original stimuli. For the sake of simplicity, we have written as if the simultaneous excitation-complex, which at its disappearance leaves a corresponding simultaneous engram-complex behind, consisted simply of original excitations. But this is an arbitrary simplification. The simultaneous excitation-complex usually contains, besides numerous original excitations of all kinds, mnemic excitations; and these as well as the original excitations enter into the constitution of the corresponding simultaneous engram-complex. Therefore, in addition to the original excitations, all the mnemic excitations ecphorised at the moment also belong to each simultaneous excitation-complex and manifest the same engraphic activity.

CHAPTER V

THE LOCALISATION OF ENGRAMS

So far we have made no attempt to deal with the nature
of the change which the irritable substance undergoes
between the emergence and subsidence of the excitation,
and which, with specific modification of the substance,
remains fixed in the engram. All we can say is that
the change in the irritable substance is most certainly
a *material* change. In limiting ourselves to a determination of the orderly connections between stimulus and
reaction, and in rejecting the lure of molecular mechanistic
hypotheses to penetrate into the " real nature " of the
excitation, we had no wish to rid ourselves of the obliga-
tion to enquire whether, within the same individual, the
irritable substance possesses in all its parts the same
properties ; but this question having long ago been
decided in the negative, we can now pass on to consider
the allied problem as to the way in which the irritable
substance, according to its heterogeneous properties,
distributes itself in the individual.

Long ago, and from widely differing starting-points,
the solution of this problem was attempted by physiologists. Here the problem will occupy us only in so far
as it concerns the relation of the irritable substance to
the engraphic effect of stimulation ; that is, so far as it
touches the localisation of mnemic phenomena in the
individual. By approaching the problem of localisation
from the mnemic side, we shall be able to show it in a
special light, and at the same time deepen our insight
into the nature of mnemic phenomena.

8

INTRODUCTORY CONSIDERATIONS ON THE LOCALISATION
OF INHERITED ENGRAMS

A Planarian is a worm standing rather low in the scale
of animal evolution, yet possessing a differentiated central
nervous system—a brain and longitudinal nerves, two
eyes, a complicated intestine, and a genital system. If
one cuts the animal into sections at random, each section
from whatever part of the body is able, if it be not too
minute, to regenerate itself into a complete worm, with
all its morphological and physiological peculiarities, and,
of course, with all its so-called instincts. Sections cut
from any portion of the body of Hydra, with the exception of the tentacles, regenerate the whole animal ; but
the size of the pieces must not be less than $\frac{1}{4}$ to $\frac{1}{2}$ mm.
in diameter, that is, about $\frac{1}{200}$ of an entire Hydra.
Segments cut from any part of the roots of many plants,
as, for instance, Scorzonera, Leontodon, etc., are capable
of building up the whole plant-individual, just as any
segment of a Begonia leaf, placed on moist soil, will
develop into a complete plant.   Infusoria also, such as
Stentor, can be cut into many pieces, and if these are not
too small, and if they contain some portion of the nucleus,
a complete, though reduced, Stentor will grow out of each
piece.   In adopting the view that the majority of the
inherited dispositions are engrams, we are justified in
thinking that the different sections of Planarian, Scorzonera, Begonia, Stentor, possess in its entirety the inherited
engram-store of the complete individual.   These segments
cut almost anywhere and anyhow are capable of a full
development, just as are the germ-products of the respective organisms.

In this connection it would be well to make more
explicit the idea that the germ-products and sections
cut from the bodies of certain animals and plants contain
the entire inherited engram-stock. This possession does
not imply the capacity to ecphorise the engrams at all
times and under all circumstances, for quite definite
external and internal conditions—or, as we would say,

a specific energetic condition—are essential to the ecphory. We are quite justified, therefore, in claiming that the germ-cells, like the body-segments mentioned above, possess also those engrams which are ecphorised only in the fully developed animal or plant, where alone the potentialities for it exist.

But from the fact that sections of certain organisms, cut at random, are in possession of the entire inherited engram-stock, we infer that in these forms, at least, the engram inheritance is not localised in special areas of the organism, but belongs everywhere to the irritable substance of the organism.

There is a point in the division of the organism beyond which further division becomes impossible without touching the vitality of the section, and thereby its capacity for regeneration. It is obvious that a section which is too minute for the absorption of nourishment from without, and which is hardly able to answer the demands made on it in the continuation of its life-processes, will not be able to furnish the working capital for the purposes of regeneration. The above-quoted experiments, however, do not help us much in determining the actual minimum size of those sections which, despite the mutilation, still retain the entire inherited engram-stock.

But observations on the propagation of the organisms prove that the entire inherited engram-stock may be possessed by single cells, namely, the germ-cells. The fact, however, that one can cut up indiscriminately an infusorian like Stentor into various parts, each of which, if it has but a small portion of the nucleus, will regenerate an entire Stentor, argues strongly in favour of the view that at least in this and similar cases the possession of the entire inherited engram-stock belongs to a still smaller biological unit than we get in the cell. With the problem whether within each cell the engraphic change localises itself predominantly or exclusively in the nuclear substance and its equivalents, and whether consequently we have to conceive of the nuclear substances as being the bearers of the engram—to which conclusion a good many data point—I shall not greatly concern myself, as the problem is hardly ripe yet for discussion.

It may be well to state here the assured results of our preceding observations. First, each germ-cell, or its equivalent, which initiated each individuality phase, possesses the entire inherited engram-stock. Most probably neither the cell nor even the nucleus of the cell is the smallest unit able to possess it. For the sake of brevity, we shall call the smallest unit able to contain the entire inherited engram-stock the " mnemic protomer " ; whether it be the cell, or whether it be a more minute morphological unit, we shall leave future research to decide.

Secondly, we find that segments taken at random from parts of a multicellular organism, whether plant or animal, show themselves in numerous cases to be possessed of the entire inherited engram-stock. But in these cases also we are not yet in a position to determine the morphological limits of the smallest mnemic units or protomers, that is, the minimum segments of irritable substance which still retain possession of this inherited engram-stock. We cannot in these experiments depend on extremely minute organic particles, because, compared with the specially adapted germ-cells, they are placed at a decided disadvantage for the double task of maintaining the normal life-processes and of satisfying the abnormal demands of regeneration. Consequently, the question whether, under certain circumstances, a unicellular segment of a *fully developed* multicellular organism can regenerate the whole, and whether it therefore possesses the entire inherited engram-stock still remains unanswered. Evidence in the affirmative, however, can be adduced in many cases from the phenomena of germ-development, especially that of the segmentation of the germ-cells.

Further discussion of the problems connected with the restriction of the regenerating capacity may well be deferred until we are better acquainted with the nature of homophony and the working of the developmental processes.

In Chapter XI of this book we shall again take up

the thread dropped here and shall have to concern ourselves with the question whether the restriction of the regenerating capacity, which is in a certain relation with the processes of development, points to a definite localisation of the inherited engram-stock or not.

LOCALISATION OF THE INDIVIDUALLY ACQUIRED ENGRAMS.

At the conclusion of the previous part we left it an open question whether each cell or each protomer of the growing, as well as of the fully developed, organism possessed the entire inherited engram-stock. We begin this section, however, with the statement that certainly not every cell, not every mnemic protomer of the individuals qualified pre-eminently to acquire engrams, is in full possession of the entire stock of engrams acquired during the individual organic life.

We may affirm this with emphasis because we observe that although the germ-cells are in full possession of the engrams inherited by the organism from its ancestors, only an exceedingly small number, if any, of the engrams acquired in the individual life become manifest in the next individuality-phase. Among the higher animals neither father nor mother is able to transmit to the offspring in sufficient strength for manifestation the countless engrams which during the individual life have been acquired. Ability and power developed during individual existence are not transmitted. We have seen, however, in a previous chapter (p. 57-74) that the transmission of individually acquired engrams from one generation to another can in favourable cases be traced, especially where impressions have been repeated through various generations; but frequently the methods of observation at our disposal render the proof of such a transmission almost impossible. From the facts as we have them we may argue to the probability of a transmission of individually acquired engrams to the irritable substance of the germ-cells, although with greatly weakened effect, and through these to the progeny.

The engraphic action of a stimulus varies greatly in relation to the different parts of the same organism. Compare, for example, the engraphic action of single, momentary, weak stimuli on the nervous substance of the higher Vertebrata with the action of the same stimuli on the germ-cells. The latter action seems so slight as to be inappreciable. But, as we have already seen, stimuli, in some cases, can be proved to act engraphically on the irritable substance of the germ-cells. We are, therefore, by no means justified in assuming straight away from the negative results of certain experiments the absence of all engraphic action.

A new light is thrown on the problem by the important discovery of Tower (*Evolution of Leptinotarsa*, Washington, 1906) that the germ-cells of some insect organisms pass through a period of extraordinarily increased susceptibility to stimuli. This sensitive quality, which is probably not limited to the germ-cells of insects, but is far more generally spread, accounts to a certain extent for the capriciousness in the occurrence of hereditarily acquired variations ; for the engraphic action of specific external stimuli on the germ-cells during their period of increased susceptibility would undoubtedly affect the variations. (See *The Problem of the Inheritance of Acquired Characters*, pp. 107–114.)

For the present, we leave the problem and state simply this fundamental fact, that the irritable substance of the germ-cells is in full possession of the inherited engram-stock, and is thereby enabled to react with undiminished force in the growing and fully developed organism. Of the individually acquired engrams of the organism, however, the irritable substance of the germ-cells ' has but few, and these of a vanishing order, so that hardly any of the engrams acquired by the parental organism appear in the later products, that is, in the growing and fully developed organism.

Apart from the transmission of the greatly weakened individual engrams to the irritable substance of the germ-cells, are there any other data which tell in favour of a wide and varied distribution of engrams over the irritable substance of the organism ? It is wise in deciding this question to turn to those organisms which are especially sensitive to engraphic stimuli, and which manifest the change of state generated thereby by unmistakable reactions. First of these are Man and the higher Vertebrata. In the second place come many of the Insects, among whom some of the Hymenoptera, Bees, Wasps, and Ants are the most important. Finally, there are several Cephalopodes.

A strictly definite localisation of the individually acquired engrams—the memory-images of the physiologists and the psychologists—has been accepted by a great number of scientific workers, and has been located for Man and the higher Vertebrata in the cerebral cortex. The evidence for this lies in the observation which has been made over and over again that, in almost all the pathological affections of the human Memory which confront us in manifold forms, the only constant organic alteration is a somewhat diffuse process of degeneration in the cerebral cortex. In one case at least we are in a position to define the region more precisely, so as to be able to say with assurance that when a right-handed man is suddenly deprived of his memory of words (amnesic aphasia), a cerebral lesion has taken place where the area of the left island of Reil borders the frontal and temporal lobes. Formerly, many physiologists and pathologists went much further in the localisation of memory-images. The visual memory-images were, for instance, in a definite place behind the fissure parieto-occipitalis. The further development of regional demarcation meant that, for the memory-images of landscapes, persons, numbers, letter-signs, etc., there had to be a distinct and separate area. Finally, each letter or number sign, each single visual impression, was regarded as having its own special cerebral area or cell. In similar fashion, the centre for auditory memory-images, and especially for the memory of the sound of words, was located in a certain part of the first left temporal lobe. Throughout, one figured the cell as a kind of drawer in which the memory of the sound of a definite word was stored, a naïve conception entirely superseded among brain-specialists, but surviving in some cases in the wider circle of biologists and medical men.

We seem, therefore, to be placed in the dilemma of having either to reject altogether a localisation theory which imagines that each single engram can be stored up in a cerebral cell—or in a comparatively small complex of cerebral cells—as in a separate drawer, or to admit that in the human organism a special interdependence exists between definite regions of the cerebral cortex and the ecphory, or, as perhaps we ought to say, the possibility of the ecphory of distinct individually-acquired engrams. The latter admission implies, however, the recognition of a certain localisation, although it need not be the kind which makes each nerve-cell of the brain a repository for a specific engram.

In our preceding investigations we have repeatedly emphasised the fact that of the innermost nature of the process of excitation, as of the " nature " of any other energetic process, we have no real knowledge. Our hypotheses are dependent on similes for their intelligibility. But while perforce we must be content with our ignorance of the real nature of the excitation, we can well concern ourselves with the principles that govern its initiation, progress, cessation and after-effects. Here at once we discover something very important for the problems occupying us now, namely, the fact that the process passes through the organism—most markedly through those which are equipped with a well differentiated nervous system—not in a vague, diffuse manner, but along definite and fairly well isolated routes.

In this way the original synchronous excitation may be regarded as already localised ; and as the engraphic change of the irritable substance depends directly on the synchronous excitation, a certain localisation of the individually-acquired engrams within the irritable substance of an organism is implied from the beginning. If the isolation of the routes traversed by the excitation were perfect, we should have a right to expect a perfectly well defined localisation. Much experience, however, has taught us that the isolation of these routes corresponds simply to functional requirements, and is by no means absolute. By " routes " I do not mean only the nerve-fibres, but the whole tract through which the synchronous excitation flows from its start until its cessation, whether through nerve-cells, nerve-fibres, the grey matter of the brain, or through other forms of irritable substance. The whole tract of irritable substance covered by the excitation may be described as the " primary area proper " of a definite excitation. To the overflow of the excitation beyond the usual boundaries of the area proper we may trace the so-called reflex spasms, which can be liberated by ordinary stimuli during a heightened irritability of the central nervous system, such as is induced by strychnine-poisoning, tetanus, and hydrophobia, or by an increase of the strength of stimulation during the normal irritability of the nerves. These spasms have also been called " disorderly reflexes "—a description not altogether exact, as Pflüger has shown that the overflow of the excitation in the central organ does follow a certain order. It manifests itself first in a contraction of those muscles of which the motor nerves are on the same side of the spinal cord, and at the same level as those which in ordinary reflex action respond by contraction to the stimulation of a definite place on the skin. With the greater overflow, the nerve-complexes of the other side, but only those which correspond with the affected nerves of the primary side, are also affected, but in somewhat less measure. Later, a still greater overflow means that the nerve-complexes of the higher levels are influenced.

A relationship similar to that between the reflex spasms and the ordinary reflexes exists between the automatic movements and the so-called " co-movements." While, for instance, it is easy to keep one arm quiet during *moderate* movements of the other arm, control of the disengaged arm during violent movements, such as fencing,

has to be gradually learnt. But a man, whose irritability has been heightened by emotional influences or
by intoxication, will make such co-movements on the
slightest innervation, moving, for example, his left arm
during feeble movements of the right. Other evidence
can be adduced to show that the laws governing the
reflex spasms are valid also for the overflow of the excitations in the case of automatic movements.

In the sensory area, the so-called irradiations of visual
and tactile excitations are also based on an overflow of
the excitation beyond its primary area proper. It tells
of a particularly imperfect isolation of the "lines," or,
as we may call them, the conduit, if, when the outer ear
passage near the tympanic membrane is touched, a tick-
ling is felt in the larynx; it is well to remember that
both regions are supplied with vagus fibres.

We see from these examples that the isolation of nervous
conductors is far from being absolute. A relative isolation may be inferred when during normal irritability,
and with very weak stimuli, the overflow of the excitation
beyond the area proper does not become manifest. But
as soon as the stimulation exceeds a certain measure or
the irritability passes beyond the normal, the overflow of
the excitation becomes apparent. We may infer from this
that non-manifestation does not mean non-existence.

It is adherent in the nature of the process of excitation
that each excitation must first have attained a certain
strength, what may be called a threshold value, before
it becomes manifest to us by reactions. In our consideration of the summation of stimuli, we saw (p. 33) that
an extremely weak stimulus might very well generate an
excitation without the latter necessarily manifesting itself
to us.

The action of an excitation appears to be confined,
as a rule, to a definite primary area proper, which varies
according to the stimulus. How this comes about is
entirely unknown to us. Especially are we ignorant of
the action of the excitation in regard to the peripheral
nerves and to the grey matter of the central nerve-organ,

which is without the isolating structure of the white matter. The action of the excitation is not, however, limited to the primary area proper. It affects the remainder of the irritable substance of the organism, spreading at first over adjoining, thence over more distant, lines of the irritable substance, until at last it permeates the whole body. Observations on reflex spasms, on certain co-movements, and on sensory radiations, convince us that this overflow of the excitation beyond its natural primary area proper, although it varies from case to case, takes place in a quite definite order, the excitation decreasing in strength proportionately to the distance of its secondary sphere of action from the primary area proper. In this manner the excitation finally spreads throughout the whole irritable substance of the organism, in gradually decreasing strength indeed, but still in sufficient vigour to affect those parts of the irritable substance which are at the greatest distance from the area proper of the respective excitation, or which are only indirectly connected with it. Later, we shall explain why we feel compelled to adopt this view.

We have now reached the point from which we can obtain an insight into the phenomena of mnemic localisation. It may be well to restate what seem to us the two fundamental suppositions from which it is allowable to infer the existence of a certain mnemic localisation within the organism.

The first supposition concerns the engraphic action of the excitation, that is, the specific change which remains in the irritable substance after the lapse of the synchronous stimulation. The engraphic effect is in a definite relation to the strength of the synchronous excitation. Very weak excitations *seem* to leave behind no engraphic effect. But the case is really otherwise. For an engraphic effect becomes manifest in the frequent repetition of weak excitations, which proves that each factor must have had an engraphic effect proportionate to its strength. The second supposition was that within the more highly developed organisms, especially Vertebrata with a specifically differentiated nervous system, the original excitation does not affect the whole irritable substance of the organism equally, but that it reaches the climax of its strength in the specific section which we have described as the primary area proper of the excitation. From there it radiates with decreasing force, following the definite paths into more and more distant areas of the irritable substance, exercising a scarcely appreciable influence on the most distant ones, and excluded entirely, perhaps, only from those which by too specific a formation remain altogether outside the sphere of its influence.

It follows from these suppositions that every excitation taking place in the organism in sufficient strength will—with the possible exception just mentioned—engraphically influence each cell or mnemic protomer, as we have called it, in a degree varying in strength only according to the position of the protomer within the organism. For example, a protomer located in those parts which comprise the area proper of the gustatory excitations will be strongly influenced engraphically by gustatory stimuli, but not at all strongly by other kinds.

When, therefore, at any given moment, not merely a single stimulus, but as is normally the case, an entire complex of numerous photic, auditory, tactile and other stimuli acts upon the organism, this complex of simultaneous stimuli will, as such, influence every cell or mnemic protomer ; but the influence will vary proportionately to the relative positions of the protomers.

To make the point still more clear, it may be permissible to use a simile. But in referring specially to phonographic reproductions, I should like it to be distinctly understood that I do not in the least intend to suggest thereby any analogy whatever between the genesis of an engraphic change of the organic substance and the production of a phonogram. An organic engram stands in much the same relation to a phonogram as does a horse pulling a carriage to a locomotive propelling one. The results under certain circumstances are similar ; but the ways and means by which they are achieved are fundamentally different. But as it is perfectly legitimate to compare the work done by an engine with that done by a horse, perhaps I may be permitted, without fear of misconception, to emphasise the idea of the topographical peculiarities of the action of complex influences on the organic substance by referring to the topographical peculiarities of the action of complex acoustic vibrations, as illustrated in the making of certain phonographic records.

Let us imagine that in an opera house of the usual construction a great number of very similar phonographic recording machines are distributed in different parts of the building, among the boxes, the stalls, the dress and upper circles, on and behind the stage, and also in the orchestra between the seats of the players. In the separate reproductions of the various records made during the playing of the orchestra it will be found that no two of the records are alike, despite the similarity of the machines. According to the location of the machines, it will be possible to distinguish differences of clearness and power in the reproduction of the music. Among the instruments distributed in the orchestra itself, those in the vicinity of the basses will reproduce the renderings of the bass parts out of all proportion to the designed effect of the total production. The phonographs placed between the 'cellos will in their reproduction give us the impression that during the performance the 'cellos played the leading part, and that the rest of the instruments provided merely a pianissimo accompaniment. So, with the records made by the other machines, there would be differences of emphasis according to their position.

The nature of mnemic reception and reproduction is, of course, vastly different from that of phonographic records, yet the results due to mere position and to the related reception of complex influences are similar in both the phonograph and the mnemic protomer. In the latter case, however, we are concerned not simply with the effect of acoustic influences, but also with photic, thermal, and electric influences, that is, with stimuli belonging to all possible kinds of energies.

The strongest engrams which a mnemic protomer receives are, naturally, from those excitations of a simultaneous complex in whose primary area proper it is located. From the other simultaneous excitations of the organism it receives more or less diminished vibrations, which, of course, are stored engraphically in their somewhat weakened character.

Again, within the area proper of an excitation, its strength probably varies greatly according to its position in the area. As yet definite data are not available. We are quite justified in saying that the area proper of a certain visual excitation extends over the retina, the optic nerves, the chiasma, the external geniculate body and thalamus, the upper corpora quadrigemina and the connections with the eye-muscle nerves, and includes certain cortical areas of the occipital lobe of the cerebrum. Still, we have only very few data to decide whether qualitative or quantitative differences of the respective excitation-processes may be or must be recognised within this area proper. We need not at this time attempt to prove from merely personal observations the probability that within the area proper of an excitation there are local differences of intensity. We shall begin with certain definite assumptions and show that our observations find an adequate explanation on the basis of these assumptions.

First, we shall assume that the strength of an excitation within its area proper always reaches its maximum in the irritable substance of the cerebral cortex ; and we shall find that this assumption throws new light on numerous groups of facts.

Again, by assuming that the cortex of the cerebrum in the Vertebrata gradually evolved into a kind of " multiplicator " of the excitations, we can best understand the exclusive position which, according to the findings of comparative anatomy, of physiology, and of pathology, it occupies in relation both to consciousness and to the individually acquired engram-stock. For it is to those excitations which have entered into the cerebral cortex and have reached their maximum strength there that, from the point of view of introspection, conscious sensations correspond. And in regard to the individually acquired engram-stock, we find that in the cerebral cortex, where within their area proper the excitations reach their maximum strength, there also are left the most pronounced and most easily ecphorable engrams. As, in accordance with the afferent system of its sensory organs, the excitations of a sensory area reach the highest degree of their development in a definite region of the cerebral cortex, so the most precise engrams from this sensory area will also be found in this region. Relative to their distance from this region, the engrams show decreasing strength, while the engrams from other sensory areas may increase in definiteness ; just as in the reproduction of the phonographic records derived from different places in the orchestra we had the predominance of one or the other instrument and the relative subservience of the rest.

Our assumption adequately explains the correspondence which, in the comparative study of the Vertebrata, we find between the development of the cortex of the cerebrum on the one hand, and the increase in stimulus-receptivity and of engraphic power on the other. The perfecting of the latter factors determines essentially what we are accustomed to describe as increase in intelligence. Among the warm-blooded animals, the individual acquisition of engrams and their full use play a very important part. The entire removal of the cortex of the cerebrum—this multiplicator of excitations and principal retainer of even fugitive impressions—leads to a notable damaging of the individuality, which is the more marked the higher up the Scale of Being it occurs. Schrader experimented with pigeons and falcons and Goltz with a dog. The cerebrums of the creatures were removed. Their subsequent behaviour proves the truth of our statement.

From the same experiments we gather that in warm-blooded animals, the individually acquired memory is predominantly, though by no means exclusively, localised in the cerebrum. Although after the operation the above animals no longer recognised either their own kind, or their keepers, or their enemies, their hearing and vision were practically unimpaired and they were still able to fly and to run. As the latter faculties are by no means inherited, they must be considered as reactions, which prove the existence of individually acquired engrams in places other than the cerebrum.

In the cases cited above the individually acquired engrams, which on ecphory manifest themselves in the complicated reactions of flying and running, are localised in subcortical portions of the central nervous system in consequence of the frequent recurrence of these excitations ; and their engraphic fixation is sufficiently strong to allow of ecphory even in the absence of the cerebrum. As to cerebral " localisation of symptoms " which has been proved beyond doubt and has led to the great triumphs of modern brain surgery, two possible explanations offer themselves. Either an actual localisation of the *engrams* themselves takes place, or the " localisation of symptoms " is only a result of an interdependence between certain definite parts of the cerebral cortex and the possibility of the *ecphory* of specific groups of individually acquired engrams. Reference to this subject may be found on page 120.

Should future research demonstrate the fact of a specific localisation of engrams, such a localisation could at the most be but graduated, and in no case absolute, as has so often been assumed. Such a graduated localisation could be equally well explained by the above simile of the phonographic machines. It may be that it does actually exist to a certain degree, and that together with a localisation of ecphory it furnishes the complex phenomenon which confronts us in the cerebral " localisation of symptoms."

A more detailed explanation of these problems will be given in a later consideration of the Mneme. At this point I should like to show by quotation how C. von Monokow in his recently published book on *The Localisa-*

tion of Brain Functions faces this problem. " Before us lies the difficult problem of determining the exact location of the numberless stored up impressions, those engram-complexes which manifest themselves as occasion demands (mnestic processes). But the nearer we approach the problem, the less sure we are that location can be definitely determined " (p. 22). " The capacity to distinguish auditory impressions according to their nature and intimate æsthetic significance, and the auditory engrams built up thereon, have their proper working areas in the entire cortex, although the parts lying in the periphery of the so-called Heschl's convolutions (first temporal convolution, sphere of hearing) are specially important " (p. 25). " The working areas for the later acquired engram-complexes (Semon), that is, what we describe as ' perceptions,' ' presentations,' ' memory-images,' etc., must, although differently distributed, extend far beyond the proper somatic cortical areas over the entire brain surface like a wide-spread fibrous tent " (p. 27). " A certain local element, however, is essential to all functions, even the highest, namely, that which serves as physiological basis for the immediate realisation, or, as Semon would say, the ecphory of various acts " (p. 27).

Whether excitations can be conducted from the body surface centripetally to the central nervous system and thence centrifugally over the entire irritable substance of the individual, in strength sufficient to furnish in the remote extremities recognisable engrams, is a question exceedingly difficult to answer. In connection with this problem the germ-cells will probably furnish the best field for experiment and observation. The experimental proof can be educed only by exposing the first generation to the influence of a stimulus which reaches the germ-cells only by the indirect way along which the excitation is conducted. Should the generation developed from these germ-cells then show itself changed in the above direction without ever having been directly exposed to the particular stimulus, it is evident that the engraphic stimulus must have reached the germ-cells of the parent

generation in a like indirect way, namely, along the path
on which the excitation generated by the stimulus was
conducted.

The conditions required are fulfilled by the experiments
already mentioned which Miss v. Chauvin made on the
Mexican newt, the Axolotl (Siredon), which is often bred
in Europe and kept in aquaria for amusement. These
Mexican newts are distinguished from their European
relations, the tritons and salamanders, by the fact that
at the end of their embryonic development they do not,
like other newts, lose their gills and make for land, but
under normal conditions they retain their gills and remain
in the water until they are sexually mature. They propagate, therefore, as fully equipped aquatic forms, that
is apparently as larvæ. This is the rule. In Mexico,
however, natural influences similar to those experimental
conditions to which Miss v. Chauvin exposed her material,
seem to have acted on local varieties of the Axolotl ; for
these creatures, under natural conditions, breed varieties
with changed instincts.

The material, however, on which Miss v. Chauvin
experimented and to which we refer here, consisted of
a breed which in no stage of its natural development
showed any tendency to pass from gill to lung respiration, and so to fit itself for land habitation. In animals
once sexually matured this transformation is impossible.

But Miss v. Chauvin was able, by applying specific
stimuli at a certain critical stage of development, to force
the larvæ to lung-respiration. The gills degenerated,
the larvæ left the water, and finally passed by a perfect
metamorphosis into the gill-less land-newt (Amblystoma).
The method by which such changes of instinct and such
radical morphological alterations were effected consisted
of the enforced cessation of gill function and the stimulated working of the lungs instead. This was somewhat
easily done by keeping the animals during the specific
time either in insufficiently aerated water, or by giving
them but a scanty supply of water. Contact with atmospheric air suffices to complete the metamorphosis.

The newts coerced in this manner were kept alive until as land-newts they matured sexually and propagated. They deposited their eggs in the water, and the emerging larvæ passed through the ordinary stages of aquatic development until they had reached the point where the beginning of the metamorphosis becomes possible. The animals were then a length of 14 to 16 cm. To obtain the metamorphosis of their parents, it was necessary to place them under conditions unfavourable to gill-respiration, but for the offspring this procedure was not necessary. Although Miss v. Chauvin kept many such larvæ in well aerated water, they frequently came to the surface to breathe and stayed there for hours—behaviour which the Axolotl is wont to show only at an advanced age and in water deficient in air.

Although further external coercion was withheld, the subsequent course of the metamorphosis which Miss v. Chauvin so induced in these animals was in kind essentially different from and in speed far more rapid than that which took place in the offspring of non-metamorphosed Axolotls of the same breed. Miss v. Chauvin, therefore, felt justified in concluding " that this strongly marked inclination to continue development had been transmitted to these individuals by inheritance."

To me such a conclusion admits of no question, but I may also maintain that in this case there is an overwhelming probability that the engraphic influence has been transmitted to the germ-cells of the parent generation by conduction, and that a direct stimulation of the germ-cells by the respective stimuli is impossible. For the germ-cells are embedded deep in the interior of the body, where, unlike the cells of the external skin, they are not exposed to changes due to the medium in which the animal may live. Further, they are sheltered altogether from the direct influence of all those stimuli, contact with which is certainly involved during the transition from aquatic to terrestrial life.

It may be added that the germ-cells of terrestrial Vertebrata are already surrounded by a moist medium.

They lie in the abdominal cavity, and are thus always flooded by the serous fluid. It seems to me, therefore, altogether improbable that the osmotic condition of the germ-cells should be affected by the fact that their bearer lives as an Axolotl in water, or as an Amblystoma on land ; for the latter, like all land-newts, invariably tries to protect itself against too great a dryness of the medium.

Indisputable facts exclude the possibility that, in the case of aquatic Amphybia, water might penetrate regularly through the oviduct to the germ-cells. Kammerer, who at first thought that this possibility was a reasonable one, felt the force of my argument and abandoned his original position.

Much more inconceivable is such direct physical influence in some of Kammerer's experiments with Salamanders, especially where an hereditary influence on the colouring was obtained by the action of light and humidity, a stronger colouring of yellow in the offspring being induced by keeping the parents on yellow earth. One can quite understand that the comparatively small excess of moisture to which the animal living on yellow earth was exposed, in comparison with the one living on black earth, might produce an effect on the skin immediately exposed to the outside air ; but that this very small difference in moisture should exercise through the bodily tissues a determinating influence on the germ-cells embedded in the permanently moist lymph space of the abdominal cavity is altogether incredible.

In a still more definite way the argument applies to the action of light, for the influence of light even on the skin is indirect, requiring the mediation of the eye. By blinding the animal in both eyes, it no longer reacts to the different colour of its environment by change of skin-colouring.

Many other cases of experimental research might be cited to prove that the direct influence of a physical stimulus penetrating to the germ-cells is impossible.

Nearly all animals kept in captivity gradually grow tamer. Przibram, experimenting with the praying mantis

(*Mantis religiosa*), noticed an increasing tameness in each generation bred in captivity with complete exclusion of selection. Where in this case is the physical stimulus affecting the germ-cells directly? In Chapter VIII of my book, *The Problem of the Inheritance of Acquired Characters*, readers will find a compilation of relevant material.

It cannot be denied, however, that in many cases physical and chemical stimuli may penetrate directly -through the tissues of the body to the germ-cells. For instance, in chilling a plant or a cold-blooded animal, the germ-cells are directly affected by the drop in temperature. Chemical matter introduced into the tissues of the body can directly affect the germ-cells, etc. According to Weismann and his adherents, such stimuli not only act differently on the body proper, the " Soma," and on the germ-cells, but they also display *corresponding* effects in both. Entering by specific receptors, and making use everywhere of specialised conductors, they effect quite definite morphological and dynamic changes in the Soma. Still, they are supposed to be able to effect in the germ-cells, quite independently and without the intervention of such contrivances, a corresponding change in the respective determinants of the germ-plasm. Detto has applied the term " parallel induction " to these hypothetical corresponding influences on the deter-minants " of the germ-plasm, and on the soma with its complicated contrivance for the reception and trans-formation of the stimulus. But in spite of this sponsor-ship he observes in the main a critical attitude towards the hypothesis. Our conception of an influencing of the germ-cells through the soma by conduction Detto calls " somatic induction."

The assumption a priori that all influencing of the germ-plasm by the soma must be excluded led Weismann to the theory of parallel induction. He asserts of the germ-plasm that " its properties, chiefly its molecular structure, do not depend on the individual in which it is by chance embedded, for this, so to speak, is only the nutrient soil at the expense of which it is merely growing, but that its structure is determined from the very beginning." This conception of the physiological isolation of the germ-plasm from the soma is not borne out by anatomical facts, for histology has ascertained beyond a doubt that there is a continuous organic connection between the germ-cells and the soma, and that there does not exist any isolating structure between the two.

As regards the physiological foundation of the theory of parallel induction, I have examined it more minutely in *The Problem of the Inheritance of Acquired Characters*, and need not here do more than demonstrate, by means of a single example, that as far as specific stimulations are concerned, fundamental physiological difficulties prevent our acceptance of the theory. Przibram and Sumner independently discovered that the fur of rats and mice, kept at unusually high temperatures, grows thinner, while the peripheral organs, such as the ears, feet, tail, external genital organs, increase in size. The reverse takes place in animals kept at unusually low temperatures. Under certain circumstances the changes become hereditary, reappearing in offspring bred, born, and reared at mean temperatures. But how do these experiments affect the physiological aspect of the problem ?

Variations of temperature, if not too extreme, act on mammals principally through their skin ; the power of the animal to generate heat tends to maintain the internal organs at an equable temperature. Consequently nearly all morphological reactions due to temperature variations can be reduced to skin reactions. By continued exposure to heat, the peripherally free parts like ears, tails, hands, feet, etc., increase in size, but at the same time a thinning of the hair takes place. These are in the main specific reactions of the only organ directly affected by heat, namely, the skin. The starting-point of these changes is probably the extraordinary development of the sweat glands and their excretory ducts ; and this results in an increase of the superficies of the skin, and the consequent partial shifting of the hair follicles with their sebaceous glands. Comparative anatomy teaches us that the sweat glands are most developed on the soles of the feet and on the palms of the hands, and that the greater development of the sweat glands is in many animals, including man, accompanied by an entire absence of hair. By continued exposure to heat these glands increase remarkably in size. The tropical races of many animals are destitute now of hair on their plantar surfaces, but their near relatives in cold climates retain the hair on those parts.

Under the influence of cold the contrary reactions are noticeable, including not only diminution of the size of sweat glands, but also an increase in the growth of hair.

Apart from the more general effects on bodily size and rate of development, we here meet on closer analysis with a number of purely local and specific effects of stimuli. And yet with these facts before us, we are asked to assume that a problematical heating of the entire germ-cells by a comparatively slight increase of the temperature, which affects the germ-plasm directly without the mediation of the localised and differentiated receptors of the skin, has generated an exactly corresponding and exclusive effect also on the skin of the offspring. This specification of the stimulation and especially its localisation on the skin seems to me to dispose of the fallacious conception of parallel induction.

On the other hand, the assumption of somatic induction presents no such difficulties, for it simply regards the individual with its soma and germ-cells as one organic whole. The " Soma " furnishes for the whole organism, including the germ-cells, indispensable contrivances for the reception and transformation of the stimulus into specific excitations, and this explains the homogeneousness of their effect on the parental organism as well as on the offspring. The only supposition is the sufficient susceptibility of the irritable substance of the germ-cells to respond to the excitations transmitted. Tower's discovery of a period of increased susceptibility of the germ-cells promises to bring within closer reach the solution of the many difficulties connected with an hitherto capricious hereditary transmission.

Our investigations into the localisation within the organism of the hereditarily-transmitted and the individu-ally-acquired engrams may be summed up as follows :— The data of regeneration and of experimental embryology teach us that each cell, or rather each mnemic protomer of a developing as well as of a fully developed organism, is in possession of all those engrams which the organism as a whole inherited from its ancestors. Of course, it does not follow that every mnemic protomer is able at all times to allow of the ecphory of these engrams, that is, to reproduce always the corresponding state of excite-ment, for this may require the presence of a quite definite energetic condition.

The engraphic influences which affect the organism *in its individual life* act, it is true, on each single protomer of the body, but according to the mode in which the stimulus enters the organism and to the changes which the resulting excitation may undergo during its conduc-tion, the engraphic influences act in varying strength in the different protomers and according to their local dis-tribution. The most marked differences in the locally varying influences on the protomers of the same individual occur in organisms with a highly differentiated nervous system, where certain portions of that system may become a kind of multipler of the excitations. The protomers in these regions are the most strongly in-fluenced engraphically. How the mnemic localisation phenomena observed in Man and the higher Vertebrata can be explained on this basis has been already dealt with. Our conclusion may be now briefly stated. Each protomer of the body receives most of the engrams acquired by the organism during its individual life, but according to the position of the protomer one group of engrams is received more strongly, and another group less strongly, than by the protomers situated in other parts of the body. Those protomers which in the higher

Vertebrata appear to be chiefly favoured owing to their position are situated in the cortex of the cerebrum.

By a less direct method we can assume from various data of comparative anatomy and physiology that the protomers of the cortical layer of the upper pharyngeal ganglion in insects, especially in the Hymenoptera, and the cortical layer of the cerebral ganglia of the Cephalopodes occupy a similarly favoured position. A single excitation may suffice to produce a strong engram in those protomers which, so to speak, lie in the respective foci of these condensers. The irritable substance of the germ-cells is situated altogether away from these foci. The nervous excitations reach the germ-cells by many roundabout ways, and generally very greatly enfeebled. Frequent repetition in the individual life and through successive generations raises these originally subliminal engraphic effects above the threshold, that is, they become hereditary engrams capable of manifestation.

In my opinion the numerous data of brain-physiology and brain-pathology, as well as the data bearing on the inheritance of acquired characters, may be interpreted in accord with the view here set out on the localisation of individually acquired engrams and on the mode of their transmission to the germ-cells. To analyse in detail from this point of view the enormous accumulation of data concerning cerebral localisation and the phenomena of inheritance would unduly extend the limits of the present volume. But as I think it possible to carry out this task on the basis already established, I hope to deal with the subject more exhaustively in a subsequent work.

CHAPTER VI

ECPHORY OF THE ENGRAM. THE TWO
PRINCIPAL MNEMIC LAWS

By the ecphory of an engram we understand the passage of an engram from a latent to a manifest state, or as we might say, the rousing into action of a disposition created by the original excitation and characterised as a permanent but usually latent change in the organism.

The excitation resulting from the ecphory of an engram we term "*Mnemic excitation*," and we have no reason to assume that in its nature it differs essentially from its predecessor, the original excitation. The differences lie in the originating conditions.

The original excitation-complex is generated and maintained by the action of a stimulus-complex synchronous with the excitations, and described by us as " the original stimulus-complex." The corresponding mnemic excitation-complex may be released by the *partial* recurrence of this stimulus-complex. The ecphoric factor, therefore, consists of the partial or entire repetition of that energetic condition which formerly acted engraphically. The final exposition of the process will be given towards the end of this chapter. At this point it may be well to elucidate the differences between the production of an original and the ecphory of a mnemic excitation by the help of the following diagrams, of which the first illustrates an original, and the second a mnemic, process in the three phases, *e*, *f*, and *g*.

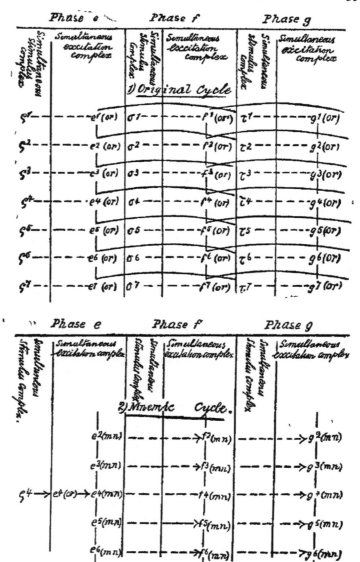

In the original process the stimulus-complex s^{1-7} generates in phase e the original excitation-complex e^{1-7} (or), in phase f the stimuli σ^{1-7} generate the original excitations f^{1-7} (or), in phase g the stimuli τ^{1-7} generate the excitations g^{1-7} (or). Let us assume that of the three successive excitation-complexes—e^{1-7} (or), f^{1-7} (or), g^{1-7} (or) the components with the same indices—e^1, f^1, g^1, or e^2, f^2, g^2, or e^3, f^3, g^3, etc.—are more intimately related with each other than are those with different indices, as for instance, e^1 with f^2 or f^4 with g^5. As we saw on page 95, the engrams generated by the components of like index will form a more coherent association than will those of different index ; that is to say, the successive ecphory of one by the other will be stronger in those of like index. The diagram of the original process suggests this by the horizontally curved lines, whilst the genesis of the simultaneous association is expressed by the vertically straight lines. Objection might be made to the use of these connecting lines in reference to the original excitations, on the ground that the existence of such connections had so far been proved by us only for the *engrams* generated by these excitations. The engrams, however, are simply and solely the products of the original excitations, and for this reason we may refer the peculiarities of their connections to the corresponding properties of the generating original excitations. The validity of this conclusion may be directly established by observation. The introspective method shows most clearly the intimate connection of the original successive components in the identical manner in which this connection appears later in the ecphory of the corresponding engrams. For example, when listening to a piece of music, we perceive the closer connection of the successive excitations due to the operation of the single melodic parts as compared with the succession of harmonies by an immediate process in consciousness ; just as at an operatic performance we note the closer connection of the words or of the music as compared with words and music together. A further illustration is afforded by the ballet. At the sight of two figures dancing simultaneously but separately, the characteristic movements of each dancer are more strongly related in consciousness than are the combined movements of the two.

With the conclusion of each simultaneous phase, the respective excitations seem also at an end, but so far as they have acted engraphically, they have simply entered into a state of latency. When all three phases have run out, then on the presupposition of a strongly engraphic action of all components three engram-complexes remain behind in the following order and connection :—

Simultaneous Engram Complex e	Simultaneous Engram Complex f	Simultaneous Engram Complex g
e^1 (engr) — —	— — f^1 (engr) — —	— — g^1 (engr)
e^2 ,, — —	— — f^2 ,, — —	— — g^2 ,, .
e^3 ,, — —	— — f^3 ,, — —	— — g^3 ,,
e^4 ,, — —	— — f^4 ,, — —	— — g^4 ,,
e^5 ,, — —	— — f^5 ,, — —	— — g^5 ,,
e^6 ,, — —	— — f^6 ,, — —	— — g^6 ,,
e^7 ,, — —	— — f^7 ,, — —	— — g^7 ,,

These three successively associated engram-complexes can be ecphorised from the simultaneous complex e by the appearance either of the original excitations e^{1-7}(or), or of a single component of this complex. In our second diagram on page 139 we selected the single component e^4 (or), to be generated by the stimulus component s^4. It might be asked why I do not simply say that the ecphory results from stimulus s^4, but I prefer the expression used for the following reason : As the successive ecphory shows (see phases f and g in the second diagram on page 139), neither the stimuli, nor a fraction of them, but only the respective corresponding excitations are necessary for the rousing of a mnemic excitation. At the ecphory, as was illustrated in the second diagram of the mnemic process in phase e, we can, after the entry of the stimulus s^4, not only trace the mnemic excitation e^4 (mn), but also the preceding original excitation e^4 (or). This will be set out more fully in the next chapter, when we consider the mnemic homophony. In view of the fact that the engrams e^2, e^3, e^5, e^6, f^{2-6} and g^{2-6} are ecphorised not by the original stimuli, but by the excitations generated by the stimuli, we are fully justified in assuming that engram e^4 (engr) also is not ecphorised directly by the stimulus s^4, but by the original excitation e^4 (or) generated by s^4.

The course of the mnemic process as indicated in our second diagram on page 139 runs as follows :—The stimulus s^4 generates the original excitation e^4 (or), which acts ecphorically on the engram e^4 (mn). But the appearance of the excitation e^4 (or) $+ e^4$ (mn) involves the further ecphory of all or of a part of the engrams simultaneously associated with engram e^4. We assume in our diagram that it acts in sufficient strength only on a part, viz. on the engrams e^2, e^3, c^4, and e^6, but not on engrams e^1 and e^7. The ecphory of the sections f^{2-6} and g^{2-6} follows by successive association on the ecphory of the sections e^{2-6}, in the manner suggested in the diagram. In the course of the mnemic process of the case given, the generation of the original excitation e^4 by the stimulus s^4 produced the same or almost the same effect as the joint action of the stimuli s^{2-6}, σ^{2-6}, τ^{2-6}, in the course of the original process.

Next we have to consider a peculiar feature of the ecphory which we have already suggested in our diagram of the mnemic process (p. 139). The recurrence of but a part of that energetic condition which acted engraphically may ecphorise the whole, or at any rate the larger part, of the corresponding simultaneous engram-complex ; but it need not necessarily do so. In fact, it nearly always ecphorises parts only, and although these may far surpass the ecphorising excitation so far as the number of components is concerned, they hardly ever embrace all the components of the engram-complex. So, referring to the diagram, we may say that the original excitation e^4 (or) generated by s^4, ecphorises the mnemic excitations e^{2-6} (mn), but is not able to ecphorise at the same time the engrams e^1(engr) and e^7(engr).

The reader may refer to the case cited in Chapter IV (page 92). A definite olfactory excitation liberated by the odour of boiling olive oil never fails to ecphorise in me the associated engram " Capri seen from a certain spot at Naples." This excitation, however, is not capable of ecphorising other parts of the simultaneous complex, as, for instance, the engram of the barrel-organ tune. The latter ecphory occurred only when the identical tune casually struck my ear again. To speak in terms of our diagram, where the engram of the introductory chord of the barrel-organ melody might be expressed by e^1 (engr), the ecphory of this engram is possible only by the recurrence of the original excitation e^1 (or).

We can easily convince ourselves that what we call in ourselves and in our fellow-beings good memory is only partially based on the facility and certainty with which the stimuli act engraphically upon the organism.

For almost as important as the possession of numerous and well-established engrams is their *ready* ecphory by way of simultaneous and successive association in all its manifold varieties and combinations. This readiness implies a far more frequent rousing of the engram than an ecphory dependent on the repetition of the original stimulus which formerly had served for the generation of the engram. An instance of the latter case is the playing again of the forgotten melody, or the prompting of the elusive word, which, for some reason or other, " the weak memory " cannot recall. If the melody or word is not then recognised, we may suspect that it has never been fixed engraphically. This supposition is, however, not always beyond question, for in cases where the energetic condition has greatly changed—as, for example, in states of excitement, or during intoxication, or in temporary amnesia—not even the recurrence of the original stimulus suffices for the ecphory of the corresponding engram. In other words, the excited, the intoxicated, or the insane man is not capable of recognising objects well known to him at other times. Very instructive in this respect is the so-called periodic amnesia. The cases of two independent memories, or as it is called " double personality," are especially important to us.

I cite here a famous instance by Macnish (*Philosophy of Sleep*) as quoted by Ribot, which has been confirmed by later observations.

A young American woman lost, after unusually long and profound sleep, the memory of all that she had learnt. She could no longer spell, nor write, nor calculate, nor recognise the objects and persons of her environment. A few months later she again fell into a long and deep sleep. When she awoke she was once more in the full possession of her previous knowledge and of the vivid memories of her earlier life ; but of the intervening experience she had no recollection at all. During more than four years she alternately passed from one state into the other, the passage being marked by long and sound sleep. Of her double personality she had not the slightest consciousness. In the one state she possessed all her original knowledge, in the other only what she acquired during her illness ; in the first state her handwriting was firm and even, but in the second she wrote badly and clumsily, as if altogether unaccustomed to the effort. It sufficed not that persons were introduced to her in either of the two states ; to know them sufficiently, she had to make their acquaintance in both states. And the same held good for all other things

Similar states occur in cases of hysteria. The phenomenon of "alternating memory" may be observed in hypnotised persons, who remember their hypnotic experience only while in the hypnotic state. In the waking state the hypnotic interval is a blank. Alcoholic intoxication may, under certain circumstances, create an energetic condition whose engrams are ecphorable in the next state of intoxication, but not in the intervening state of sobriety. A case cited by Ribot is instructive. An Irish porter, who when drunk had lost a parcel, and when sober could not remember where he had left it, recollected the necessary facts during his next drunken bout. In all these cases during the state of sleep, of hypnotisation, of fever, or of mental disturbance—which we may call state *b*—an energetic condition has been created, so much differing from the state of waking, of soberness, or of absence of disturbance—which we may call state *a*—that the ecphory in state *b* of the engrams acquired in state *a* is more or less defective. Only in cases where by virtue of the experience of years the engrams are deeply fixed and frequently ecphorised may we expect ecphory independent of abnormal or contrasting conditions.

Similar conclusions are drawn by Ribot, who referring to periodic amnesia (op. cit., p. 71) says that the " two physiological states in their alternation involve specific feelings which determine two forms of associations, and consequently two memories."

It is now possible to summarise in a graduated series the influences which produce the simultaneous ecphory of a definite engram. These are :—

1. The *complete* recurrence of the energetic condition which ruled at the generation of the engram. This has the strongest ecphoric effect.

2. The *partial* recurrence of the energetic condition inclusive of the original excitation which generated the engram. This partial recurrence, however, may be altogether ineffective under certain circumstances, as when the energetic condition has been greatly changed, by *intoxication, hypnosis, etc.*

3. The partial recurrence of the energetic condition exclusive of the original excitation which generated the engram. In this case the remaining simultaneously associated engrams act ecphorically with varying strength.

The two kinds of ecphory which we noted in our provisional survey, and which we described as chronogeneous and phasogeneous ecphory, are at bottom but specific cases for which our general definition of the ecphoric

10

influence is valid without qualification or addition. In both instances the entire or partial recurrence of a definite *internal* energetic condition acts ecphorically.

Chronogeneous ecphory takes place, as already noted, in respect of individually acquired, as well as of inherited engrams. Concerning individually acquired engrams, the reader is reminded of the cases analysed on page 49. If we are accustomed to take our first meal daily at eight o'clock, and our second at one o'clock, we have usually no feeling of hunger in the interval. But if, for some reason or other, we get into the way of having a meal at eleven o'clock, an insistent appetite asserts itself regularly and punctually at that time, even when we are quite occupied with other things. So also in regard to our desire for sleep. A little nap taken in the midst of our daily work soon establishes itself as a necessity. At the usual time sleepiness overcomes us as a result of a purely chronogeneous ecphory.

An interesting case of chronogeneous ecphory in the Axolotl is reported by Miss v. Chauvin (op. cit., page 382) For a period of three years and two months the animals were kept during the day on land, and during the night in water. Their development from gill to land newt was thereby delayed, and an intermediate stage maintained.

To quote Miss v. Chauvin's words ·—

One of the animals, for the purpose of its metamorphosis into a land animal, had for some time to give up the water entirely. Only when the exuviation had been effected was it permitted again to make for the water. With the restoration of its liberty, the animal, much to my surprise, went each evening into the water, and each morning on to the land, at those times which previously it had been forced to observe. This behaviour, very striking for an Amblystoma, was kept up without interruption from the 20th of January to the 25th of April. From that date onwards the animal remained concealed in the moss at night also, and only returned into the water when the desire for greater moisture had been generated in it by the process of shedding its skin.

As an instance of the pure chronogeneous ecphory of an inherited engram, we gave the unfolding and closing of the leaves of Mimosa and Acacia while they were subjected for twelve hours to an even, continuous exposure to light. The winter rest of beeches, and the daily and yearly periods of many plants are examples of pure chronogeneous ecphory.

The partial recurrence of the internal energetic condition, we explained in all these cases by the cycle of a definite association of metabolic processes, on the tempo of which the chronometric capacity of the organisms is founded. This chronometer, as we may call it, is of course just as little infallible as a manufactured one, and will gain or lose according as the tempo of the respective metabolic processes is changed by external influences. Under certain circumstances, however, it is very difficult to interfere with this tempo, as the behaviour of the beeches during their winter rest proves. Here, the chronometer is only slightly accelerated by the permanent increase of temperature, although we might reasonably imagine that such increase would very much accelerate the speed of the metabolic process. But probably these winter metabolisms are to a great degree independent of the external temperature.

Phasogeneous ecphory also is, after all, nothing else but the recurrence of a definite internal energetic condition, and numerous facts given in the statistics of development and confirmed by experimental embryology teach us that frequently the partial recurrence of this condition is sufficient. The reader is referred to what already has been stated in my exposition of the factors which liberate the lens formation in embryonic development. Even such great alterations of the internal energetic condition, as are involved, for example, in the experiments by Roux on the eggs of frogs, do not hinder in the untouched half of the developing egg the appearance of phasogeneous ecphory and the reactions of growth which thereupon follow. As it is our purpose to deal fully with phasogeneous ecphory and its peculiarities in the following part, it is not necessary here to enter further into the matter.

The main results which we have reached in this and the two preceding chapters may now be embodied in the following laws, which between them contain the quintessence of mnemic " first principles." They are the two principal mnemic laws.

First principal mnemic law : Law of Engraphy. All simultaneous excitations within an organism form a coherent simultaneous excitation-complex which acts engraphically ; that is, it leaves behind it a connected engram-complex, constituting a coherent unity.

Second principal mnemic law : Law of Ecphory. The partial recurrence of the energetic condition, which had previously acted engraphically, acts ecphorically on a simultaneous engram-complex. Or, more precisely described : the partial recurrence of the excitation-complex, which left behind it a simultaneous engram-complex, acts ecphorically on the latter, whether the recurrence be in the form of original or mnemic excitations.

As already indicated in the course of the last three chapters, the laws of association can be deduced from the above two laws in a simple manner. We therefore add the explanatory proposition : " Association depends on the conjunction of single engrams ; it makes its appearance during their relatively isolated ecphory, and originates simply from the presence of the respective components in the same simultaneous complex." Association, therefore, is always simultaneous association.

CHAPTER VII

MNEMIC EXCITATION AND HOMOPHONY

IN Chapter I we concluded that each original excitation in its emergence, duration, and subsidence depends on the emergence, duration, and subsidence of an elementary-energetic condition regarded as stimulus.

Mnemic excitation is independent of such an elementary-energetic condition. The necessary conditions for the emergence of a mnemic excitation are : first, the existence of an engram whose nature determines the nature and duration of the mnemic excitation ; and secondly, the action of an ecphoric influence.

Each mnemic excitation is, therefore, related to an original one, standing to it much as the reproduction of a picture does to the original. In most cases, however, the mnemic reproduction renders only the strongest lights and shadows, for if the mnemic state of excitation is to equal the original one in vividness, or perhaps surpass it, an especially favourable state of the individual at the time of ecphory is required.

The mnemic state of excitation reproduces the original excitation in all its proper proportions, inclusive of time values. This may adequately be gathered from the study of mnemic successions, which, if no extraneous disturbing element interferes, take place in exactly the same rhythm as the succession of the original excitations. In respect of their intensities and of the tempi of their courses, the mnemic excitations reproduce or represent the original excitations only in their proportional and not in their absolute values. We shall treat this more fully in Chapter XIV, where we discuss the proportional mutability of the mnemic excitations.

Whilst the duration of the main phase of an original excitation corresponds exactly to that of the generating stimulus, the duration of a mnemic excitation is determined not by the duration of a simultaneous stimulus, but by that of a previous stimulus, that is, of the one that acted engraphically. The temporal limitation of the mnemic excitation is therefore, in a sense, predetermined. Much the same qualification applies to the intensity, but not to the vividness of the mnemic excitations.

The mnemic excitation need not necessarily appear as a link in a succession, for when released by simultaneous ecphory, it may also appear as an isolated state, and disappear without having influenced, at least in any manifest way, an ecphoric succession. Readers may be reminded of the image of a landscape, which, on the perception of the smell of oil, arose and quickly faded, but without necessarily having liberated in a perceptible manner the series of successive and related mnemic excitations.

But in this case, also, it may be maintained that the mnemic excitation stands in a certain relationship of temporal duration to the original excitation, for the succession of mnemic excitations is really more or less a matter of chance determinable by various factors ; for example, the later engrams may be much less sharply outlined than their ecphorised predecessor, or the course of the ecphory of the mnemic succession may be disturbed either by new original stimuli or by new associations.

It is of little use, therefore, trying to trace the extended connections of individually acquired engrams, for usually we are distracted by new synchronic impressions and deflected into associated side-tracks. But certain modes of auditory stimuli, the successions of melodic tones or of lines of poetry, produce in us such closely conjoined engraphic connections that, on ecphory, they run throughout an unhindered course more frequently than in any other series of engrams.

Possible disturbances and deflections may therefore cut a mnemic excitation short as compared with the original excitation. But if the mnemic excitations are merely retarded, the retardation takes place with such proportional exactitude for each member in the succession that the rhythm of the original excitations is always maintained.

Mnemic excitation cannot be retained for any length of time as an uninterrupted excitation. Where that seems to be so, it is in reality a case of the repeated ecphory of the one engram. A painter, for instance, may work for hours on a portrait, the original of which is no longer before him. What is perceived by him is an ecphorised engram, a " memory-image." And this mnemic model is not the result of a single, but rather of an oft-repeated, ecphory which later, as the painting more truly resembles the subject, will be exercised by the portrait itself.

In this connection we often meet with a combination which affects the mnemic phenomena in a peculiar manner, and which demands careful analysis. The starting of a mnemic process invariably requires an ecphoric impulse. According to our second mnemic law, this impulse may be the recurrence of either original or mnemic excitations. The reader is referred to the diagram on page 139. Here, the mnemic process follows on the recurrence of an original excitation. In the diagram this excitation e^4(or), which is generated by the stimulus s^4, first ecphorises the mnemic excitation e^4(mn), and this is followed by the ecphory of the mnemic factors of the successive phases. As the diagram shows, in phase e the original e^4(or) and the mnemic excitation e^4(mn) co-exist. But in the later phases f, g, . . . the corresponding original excitations are absent. An illustration may be useful. If the reader hears the first phrase of a proverb, for example, " A bird in the hand——" he will mentally complete it. The original excitations generated by the opening words act as stimuli, and ecphorise the corresponding mnemic excitations which co-exist with them. But during the mental reproduction of the remainder of the proverb mnemic excitations only are involved, the corresponding original excitations being entirely absent.

At present, however, we are less concerned with the purely mnemic course from the sixth word onward than with the simultaneous existence of the original excitations generated by the five stimulating words, and of the mnemic excitations ecphorised by these original excitations e^t(or) and e^t(mn) in phase e of the diagram.

The co-existence of original and mnemic excitations may be admitted, but this admission, as some one may point out to us, does not imply that in their co-operation each maintains undisturbed its independent action. For their action may be a blend resulting in uniformity, or, if slightly different, the one may affect the other, by interference either weakening or strengthening it, but in the conjoint effect showing uniformity, or, lastly, they together may have only the effect of either by itself.

During our investigation of the original synchronous and engraphic stimulation (pp. 90–98) we recognised as characteristic of the synchronous action of stimuli on the organic substance, that the various excitations resulting therefrom do not lose their identity in a diffuse mixture, but co-exist and run their course in juxtaposition. The same may be said of the simultaneous course of a mnemic excitation and of a *new* original excitation related thereto.

This can be strikingly proved by reference to those numerous cases where the new original stimulus, which acts simultaneously with the mnemic excitation, is similar to, but not identical with, the previous original stimulus, which, in its engraphic action, prepared the ground for the mnemic excitation. The results of the incongruity of the mnemic and the new original excitation can be distinctly recognised by us, even in the most trifling details. If after some years we visit a well-loved and familiar scene, we are keenly sensitive even to the slight changes that in the meantime may have taken place.

We note the disappearance of this or that tree, the presence of a new house, or the alteration of an old one. A capable conductor, who knows well the work in hand, and so is able to dispense with the score, notices with astonishing minuteness the omission of this or the premature entry of that part or any slight variant that may be introduced by the soloist. The incongruousness of the mnemic with the simultaneously occurring original process is immediately perceived.

Cases from other sensory areas illustrating the process which ensues when mnemic excitation and the new original excitation are brought, so to speak, into relations of superposition, and where each incongruity causes a reaction of sensitivity, might readily be given, if occasion demanded. Our ordinary daily experience furnishes instances in abundance.

Assuming, however, that the mnemic excitation and the new original excitation coincide so closely that no reaction of perception of difference follows, we may prove by reference to the reaction of recognition that both kinds of excitation co-exist, and that in running their courses they do not blend into a unified whole. In those cases where the mnemic and original excitations are in perfect congruity, the reaction which follows is pure in character ; but in cases of imperfect congruity, the reaction is marked by the perception of difference. In order that the reaction of recognition or of perception of difference may arise as a clear process in consciousness, the mnemic excitation must possess a certain vividness. We may distinguish well-marked differences of state when we compare the initiation of an original excitation with the vague sensation of seeing, hearing, or feeling something over again, accompanied by weak, mnemic excitation, or when we compare either or both of these with precise recognition and strong mnemic co-excitation. Between these different states there are innumerable gradations. For the fundamental problems under investigation, however, it is relatively unimportant whether the reaction of recognition is strong or weak,

By introspection, the simultaneous course in juxtaposition of the mnemic and the new original excitation may be known in two very characteristic reactions, the reaction of recognition, and the reaction of the perception of difference. This phenomenon of the simultaneous course of the mnemic and the new original excitations in juxtaposition plays a most important part in the biology of the organism. It is useful, therefore, to call it by a special name. After long consideration the term " Homophony " has been chosen to signify the state of unison in which (1) a mnemic and a new original excitation, or (2) two mnemic excitations, or (3) two original excitations may find themselves.

The term, of course, is literally accurate only when the excitations belong to the auditory area. To the other excitations—visual, tactile, olfactory, etc.—it can only be applied in a metaphorical sense. But a metaphor which gives wings to our imagination and does not pretend to be an exact scientific description may, in the absence of a term strictly applicable to the facts, fully justify itself in the deepening of a scientific understanding of the subject-matter.

It is, of course, far more difficult to discern the process of Homophony from objective reactions in creatures other than ourselves than from introspection, in which we are aided by the reactions of recognition or of perception of difference. In the case of our fellow-men, the reactions may be made known to us by the agency of speech, and language may be made sufficiently unequivocal to indicate the existence of the mnemic homophony.

But the matter assumes a different aspect when we have to deal with those organisms which cannot express themselves in articulate speech, and which, in spite of their intimate relationship with us so far as structure and vital processes are concerned, are still too far removed from us in other respects to warrant us in invariably interpreting our observations on them in terms of our own sensations. We have consequently to guard against an injudicious reading of our states of consciousness into those of other creatures. In principle, I am adverse to distinctions which set the Genus Homo over against all other organisms, but, in the present state of our knowledge and means of observation, the only safe method in the physiology of stimulus is to consider such reactions as are accessible to direct observation. Inferential and analogical reasoning touching reactions in consciousness must be charily employed. When we are dealing with fundamental evidence, it would be well to avoid analogical reasoning altogether. Such at least has been my aim in this book.

By introspection, we inferred the process of homophony—the co-existence of the mnemic and the new original excitations—from the mode of our recognition and the perception of difference. In a reckless non-scientific mood, we might say that a dog whipped once *recognises* the whip, and manifests this by unmistakable objectively-perceived reactions, thus clearly proving the existence of homophony. This, however, would be altogether wrong. The only thing that is quite certain is the ecphory by a definite stimulus of specific engram-complexes. The sight of the whip acts ecphorically on a complex in which the engram of the sensation of pain plays a prominent part. This is justly inferred from the appearance of the corresponding reactions. It is true that a mnemic process is involved, but it is by no means certain that it is associated with the same feeling of conscious recognition which we ourselves experience. It would be necessary first to prove the identity of these acts in consciousness, before one could infer the presence of homophony in the lower creatures.

Rejecting this method of adducing evidence, let us examine the objectively-demonstrable reactions for those criteria by which may be proved the existence of homophony, the unison of mnemic and new original excitations.

Using objective methods, homophony is more easily proved in those cases where the mnemic excitation and the new original excitation are not perfectly superposed. For then reactions arise which can only be interpreted as reactions against the incongruity of the mnemic and the original excitation. When playing with a dog which takes great delight in recovering objects—fox terriers are best for the purpose—we vigorously throw small stones not easily recognisable when in rapid flight, the dog, with muscles taut and head uplifted, intently watches each movement of our arm and hand. The flinging movement executed and the stone started on its flight, the animal, quickly turning round, rushes off in the direction of the stone. We repeat the action several times. We then make the same movement, but without flinging the stone. At first the dog reacts exactly as before. In the absence of the stone to seize and bring back, the dog redoubles its attention. But after being deceived several times, the animal focuses its attention more accurately, with the result that the structural detail of the original complex becomes thereby completed. The reaction of turning round and rushing off in the direction of the throw now takes place only when the dog sees the stone actually flung ; that is, only with the *perfect* congruity of the homophony of the mnemic and the new original excitations. At the incongruity of movement without the stone-throw, the animal reacts either by an attitude of readiness to go, or, in its excitement, with a false short start which immediately gives way to the previous intense alertness. The different behaviour of the animal can be rightly regarded as reactions which vary according to the congruity or incongruity of the mnemic and the new original excitations.

Another illustration touching the reactions which follow the congruity or incongruity of homophony may be taken from the realm of sport. Some animals, chiefly among the higher mammals, may be allured by certain sounds and tone sequences. In the absence of a special gift for the imitation of animal voices, some sportsmen make use of instruments which mimic the rut cry of the stag or the sex call of the doe, in order to entice the animals within the range of their guns. It has been noted that, *ceteris paribus*, the reactions of the creatures vary

according to the greater or less perfection of the mimicry
of the natural calls. Where the resemblance is not
perfect, the game, contrary to our expectations, is neither
indifferent nor unduly frightened. Rather does it take
an interest in the sounds, reacting to them similarly as
to the genuine calls, thus proving that the mimicry has
acted ecphorically on certain engrams, although only to
the extent of similar and not identical reaction. By
not venturing too near the spot from which the sounds
come, the game shows that it has noticed a difference.
Of course, it is assumed that the game does not otherwise
scent the hunter. If, however, the call instrument is
used by an expert, and the sounds produced are so like
the natural cries that there is little perceptible difference,
the behaviour of the game changes. It then reacts to
the mimicry much in the same way as to the natural
sounds, the more readily the less often it has heard the
genuine calls ; for the younger it is, the less precise are
the engrams of that kind it possesses. But an old and
experienced roebuck, with all its pasha desires in full
vigour, reacts even in case of the most perfect mimicry
to the slight incongruity which still exists at the homophony of the mnemic and the original excitations. It
is timid in its approach, it lurks among the trees, it is
strangely alert, and, as one on the stand can easily observe,
its behaviour is quite different from that which follows
when the genuine calls of the doe reach its ear.

Numerous similar cases of manifestly varied reactions
on the imperfect homophony of mnemic and renewed
original excitations might readily be given. But perhaps
I may be allowed to conclude with an example where
the mnemic excitation involves the operation of inherited
engrams, and not, as in the previously cited cases, of
engrams in the main individually acquired. It is well
known that incubated birds without any experience of
the nest are able, when the time of mating arrives, to
build a nest and to finish it off almost as perfectly as
those members of their species who have already passed
through several periods of mating.

This reactive manifestation of a succession of mnemic excitations, for so we must regard it, is associated only with the mating period, is absent in castrated animals, and terminates with the completion of the nest. It might be thought that the termination depended on the passing of the internal energetic condition into another phase, or on the exhaustion of the disposition through the natural subsidence of the excitations, a condition which is manifested in the cessation of the reactions. Neither of these ideas meets the case. For we have but to remove the completed nest, to elicit at once the same succession of nest-building reactions. And this may be done three or more times. On the other hand, by placing an artificial nest at the disposal of the birds before they begin building, we effectually block the series of reactions. But the nest must be of a certain form, size, and consistency in order to exercise any such influence on the phaseogeneously ecphorised reactions of nest-building. If the form differs greatly from that which is hereditarily peculiar to the respective species of birds, or if the nest is appreciably larger or smaller, or if the material of which it is made is too hard or not sufficiently dry, the bird, after a minute examination of the structure, will either discard it altogether and proceed to the building of a nest, or turning to the thing provided will entirely reconstruct it, removing the unsuitable parts, and replacing the missing ones. And all this is done by creatures that have never seen a nest of any kind and possess no individual experience of the rearing of young. Bees, before they have had experience of the natural comb, manifest a like behaviour towards half-finished artificial combs which the bee-keeper may place at their disposal. For example, they correct the deviations of the artificial comb from the strictly perpendicular.

In all these occurrences, the normal course of the reactions is modified by the original stimulus-complex—here the provision of the artificial nest or comb—in a manner which stands in a definite relationship to the difference between this original stimulus-complex and the final effect of the mnemic excitation, that is, the making of a specific kind of comb or nest. Or, as we may phrase it, as long as the original stimulus-complex of the artificial nest or comb shows appreciable incongruities with the nest normally produced by mnemic reactions, the organism manifests reactions which tend to obliterate incongruity. When congruity has been attained, the specific reactions cease until some interference again demands their exercise.

The objection may be raised that here is no case of congruity or incongruity of homophony, because the mnemic excitation evoked is undoubtedly an unconscious one ; that is, no clear image of the final product of, say, nest-building actions could possibly appear to birds mating and hatching for the first time. It may be admitted that most probably no such clear image arises in consciousness. But for the sure solution of such problems of consciousness, we need criteria which in the nature of things are unavailable. Such problems can only rightly be discussed where the application of the introspective method is possible. But it is valid to meet the objection stated by proving that in ourselves the presence and the evidence of the homophony are independent of the existence of conscious sensations.

In intense mental occupation we are apparently insensible to other impressions. The playing of hackneyed pieces on the piano or violin in the next room does not disturb us. We continue brooding over our problems without deliberately listening to the sounds. But let the player make a mistake or elaborate the theme or so render it as to conflict with our mnemic knowledge of it, and at once the incongruity is followed by the reaction of a start or a smile or a frown, of which for a time we may be quite unconscious. Prolonged duration of the incongruity, however, invariably leads to conscious reaction.

Cases of homophony, in which neither the mnemic nor the original excitations rise into consciousness, occur continually in daily life. We discover a new walk, and on our second or third experience of it we are generally conscious of the homophonies involved. But on further acquaintance with the walk, we are no longer conscious of these homophonies, as when we walk along deeply wrapped in thought or engaged in absorbing conversation. The existence of the homophonies can in the latter cases be demonstrated only by reactions other than conscious ones. This evidence is easily derived from the fact that automatic, unconscious walking is possible only when mnemic and original excitations actually coincide. The ability to reach the destination without the co-operation of consciousness is affected by the appearance of incongruities, as, for example, the blocking of the path or the disturbance of the roadway. Thus, in the life of every human organism, unconscious mnemic homophony plays at least as important a part as conscious homophony, and the question whether or not an homophony becomes manifest in the consciousness of an organism is of relatively minor importance.

We conclude that the presence and action of homophony become manifest to us by special reactions. In experimenting with ourselves in the case of mnemic and original excitations which rise into consciousness, the homophony manifests itself by the sensory reactions of recognition and of perception of difference. Where the excitations do not rise into consciousness, the homophony is known in an indirect way by the appearance or absence of objectively perceptible reactions. The same criterion applies to the demonstration of every homophony in organisms other than one's self. For in these, homophony can only be inferred from the appearance of objectively-perceptible reactions, whose characteristics lie in modifications dependent on the congruity or incongruity of the original state of excitement with a state of excitement that had previously been experienced, either by the same organism or by its ancestors. For the ecphory of this mnemic state of excitement similar conditions must again prevail. With the simultaneous presence of the corresponding original excitation, the mnemic state of excitement can very readily be inferred by the external observer from the reactions arising from a possible incongruity. But the most convincing confirmation of the presence and working of homophony is furnished by those reactions through whose working the incongruity or discord is resolved.

Sensory reactions can only be perceived by introspection. In regard to the quality of reactions other than sensory, we have so far given examples from those reactions resulting from the contraction of muscles. It is clear that it is only by the reaction that we are able to recognise excitations original, or mnemic. But the same excitation may manifest itself by very different reactions. Take, for example, protoplasmic movements, muscular contractions, metabolism, and the phenomena of growth ; the first two are motor reactions, the third are metabolic reactions, and the last are plastic reactions. Now, there is no reason whatever why we should consider excitations manifesting themselves mainly or exclusively by motor reactions as a class different and separate from excitations apparent by plastic or metabolic reactions. We may take the following example :—Heliotropism and heliotaxis in plants and animals are phenomena traceable to the stimulus of light on the organic substance. They can be classified under heads which apply to all organisms. But the reactions by which these stimulations and excitations—say, in plants—are manifested may be either motor, as in amœboid and ciliary movements, or may depend on osmotic processes, such as changes of turgescence, or finally, may be plastic reactions, as in curvatures of growth. No plant-physiologist studying the effect of light on the organic substance of the plant will regard excitations, which manifest themselves by osmotic reactions, as fundamentally different from those which manifest themselves by motor or plastic reactions. What we allow to the original excitations may equally well be claimed for the mnemic excitations. In the previous chapters we acted on this conviction, when, in describing the plastic reactions of the fall and the fresh sprouting of leaves, and the osmotic reactions of the

11

so-called sleeping movements of plants, we regarded them with equally good reason as manifestations of mnemic excitations.

But the moment we recognise in any specific case the presence of excitations, the presence of potential homophony may also be inferred. To educe the evidence for homophony, we have to show, first, that under certain circumstances the conditions exist for the simultaneous rise of mnemic and corresponding original excitations, and secondly, that given these conditions, reactions regularly follow which modify themselves according to the congruity or incongruity of this potential homophony. Among these reactions those which tend to regulate the incongruity are the most striking. There is a large group of plastic reactions which tend to remove any specific incongruity between the normal developing or developed stage and an actual plastic state already existing. These reactions may be described as regulations and as regenerations in the widest sense, that is, inclusive of the conceptions of post-generation, reparation, etc. To justify the inference of homophony from these reactions, first the evidence would have to be adduced that in the given cases the conditions exist for the simultaneous presence of certain mnemic excitations with the new corresponding original excitations, and that at the homophony of these two excitations the reaction under consideration tends to remove any incongruity that may exist.

The evidence required can easily be furnished, but to avoid repetition, I reserve it for the following chapters, which are devoted to the analysis of the mnemic factor in ontogenesis, in regeneration, and in processes of regulation.

So far, in considering homophony, we have regarded the mnemic state of excitement as something uniform in spite of its complexity. The idea equally applies when the mnemic state corresponds to the reproduction of a single preceding excitation. But how if the mnemic state reproduces a frequently repeated excitation ?

There are two methods for the solution of this question. First, by the synthetic method we can note how the mnemic total increases at each repetition. Secondly, by the analytic method we can set out the constituents of a mnemic excitation originated by frequent repetition.

Let us begin with the second method, and endeavour to analyse a mnemic excitation based on repeated engraphic action. We select a case of mnemic excitation introspectively perceivable. Let us try, therefore, to ecphorise the image of the bodily presence of a near but absent relative. We are dealing with a purely mnemic process. At first, the image recalled seems clear and definite, but if it is that of a person with whom we are in constant intercourse, we shall find on closer scrutiny that the ecphorised image is, so to speak, generalised, resembling somewhat those photographs which aim to furnish the general character of a type by the superposition of the pictures of different heads on one and the same plate.

In the case under consideration, the generalisation occurs by the homophonous action of different images of a face which we have seen in many varied states and situations, at one time pale, at another time flushed, now serene, again solemn, once in this light and another time in that. As soon as we inhibit the simultaneous presentation of the multitude of images, and, on the ecphory of the engram, focus only one definite engraphic experience, the cognate mnemic excitation at once predominates over its congeners which faintly sound with it in unison, and we straightway recognise the clear, sharp outline of the face in some specific situation.

So, in the case of persons with whom we are in continual association, it is just this abundance of mnemic excitations usually sounding in unison with each other which, when their features are mnemically produced in us, accounts for the vague outline and generality of aspect. But in the case of people we meet more rarely, our attention during the mnemic reproduction of their faces is usually focused on a particular experience when the face made a special impression on us, and the engraphic results were consequently well marked. By reason of this accentuation, the features sometimes appear to us more strongly delineated than even those of our nearest relatives, seen much more frequently and in the most varying situations.

Where on the ecphory of a frequently recurring engram no predominance of a single component results, that is, of any one of the mnemic excitations sounding in unison with each other, we may observe, so to speak, a growing abstraction of the memory-image, similar, as we have suggested, to the increasing vagueness of the contours on the superposition of a number of exposures not exactly corresponding to each other. The result is—at least with man, probably also with higher animals—the genesis of a kind of abstraction, which I call " Abstraction of Homophony." Mnemic homophony can, without the aid of any other mental process, furnish us with a kind of abstract image of our friend X ; that is, an image robbed of particularity of aspect and situation giving us X, dissociated as it were from a definite moment in time. If the sphere of the ecphorised engrams be further enlarged, abstract images of a higher order arise. We can, for example, summon up pictures of a white man or a negro. I maintain that the primary formation of abstract conceptions is based on such abstract images, and that this abstraction, created in the above-mentioned way by homophony only, is the precursor of the purely logical process. It is no monopoly of the human species, for we find it manifesting itself in different ways among all the higher organised animals.

The fact that, by focusing attention on single homophonic components, we can dissociate almost any one of the number from the rest proves that on the occasion of the homophony there is no perfect blending of the mnemic excitations.

The accuracy of our findings by the analytical method may be tested by the synthetic construction of the results of the frequent repetition of an engraphic action on the basis of the general laws derived from our previous investigations.

In the case of the first ecphory of an engram by the recurrence of the original stimulus, a solution is afforded in the work already done. Let us describe the mnemic excitation at its first ecphory as p_1 (mn), and the original excitation generated by the first repetition of the original stimulus as p_2 (or). Unisonant working follows, or, as we say, homophony takes place ; but there is no blending of these two excitations into one. The result may be expressed as p_1 (mn)$+p_2$ (or). Now, we have already recognised the general law that, where two co-ordinated excitations affect an organism, they are received and fixed in co-ordinate engraphy. It is clear that there can be no exception in the case of the excitations p_1 (mn) and p_2 (or), when respectively they lapse into a state of latency. For if by the recurrence of the original stimulus they are again ecphorised, they must manifest themselves in co-ordination as an homophonous mnemic excitation p_1 (mn)$+p_2$ (mn), and in this form enter into relation with the newly appearing original excitation p_3 (or). Thus there follows the threefold homophony of p_1 (mn)$+p_2$ (mn)$+p_3$ (or). A similar process occurs at succeeding repetitions up to the *n*th power. At the ($n+1$) recurrence we have a mnemic homophony of the mnemic excitations p_1 (mn)$+p_2$ (mn)$+p_3$ (mn) ... p_n (mn), with the original excitation p_{n+1} (or). The process may thus be phrased :—At the ecphory of a combination of engrams, owing its origin to frequently repeated engraphic action, what is given is not a single indissoluble blend of the mnemic excitations—" coalescence," some physiologists call it—but a unisonant chorus in which the single components of an apparently uniform combination of engrams, distinct indeed from each other as to their time of origin, may be individually discerned. Further, we have to remember that in most cases the single components differ considerably from each other ; for it will only rarely happen that an original stimulus at its repetition resembles its predecessor in all particulars, and further, the energetic condition of the organism itself suffers continual change. The original stimulation, therefore, enters into association with various complexes of engrams, and is, therefore, simultaneously and successively differentiated from its predecessor.

Both analytic and synthetic investigations lead us to the same result, that at each ecphory of a combination of engrams which has been created by repeated stimulation, there emerges a unisonant chorus of individual components, each of which is the resultant of a separate stimulation.

With this understanding, we are better able to discern the nature of those bifurcated successions of engrams which can only be ecphorised alternately.

Let us take again the case of the two versions of the line in the *Rubáiyát* of Omar Khayyám, and assume that we have heard both versions recited three times. If we indicate by letters the single engrams generated by the spoken words, and add to each letter-sign the figure index corresponding to the number of its repetition, we obtain by considering the succession of the first nine engrams the following diagram :—

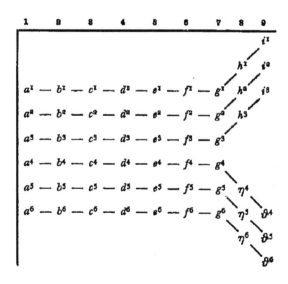

On ecphory, the mnemic excitation in phase 1 consists of the homophony of the excitations a^{1-6}, or in phase 7 of the homophony of the excitations g^{1-6}. The alternative arises in phase 8, when either the engrams h^{1-3} or the engrams η^{4-6} may be ecphorised. But why this alternative? Because, as has been shown at length in the *Mnemic Sensations* (p. 356), a simultaneous manifestation of the branches of a dichotomy which consists of word-engrams is altogether impossible.

Very different results arise where the possibility exists of a simultaneous manifestation of the two branches of the dichotomy, as in the case of a piece of music which begins as a simple melody, but develops into a duet.

Phase 1	2	3	4	5
e —	d —	$e \Big\langle$	$\begin{matrix} g\ —\\ \vert\\ d \end{matrix}$	$\begin{matrix} c\ —\\ \vert\\ e\ — \end{matrix}$

But if the simultaneous manifestation of the two lines of reactions is impossible, the resulting alternative implies either the total suppression of the ecphory of one branch, or a jumping of the ecphory from one branch to the other. In the latter case, where the reactions seem to move in reciprocal succession, what may be called "mixed reactions" result. We are dealing with such a "mixed reaction" when we combine the two alternatives, "in a noose" and "with a shaft" as "The Sultan's Turret in a shaft of light."

Such mixed reactions are not rare in the manifestation of the individually acquired Mneme, nor are they altogether absent from the manifestation of the dichotomic successions of inherited engrams. We shall deal with the matter at greater length in the chapter on the importance of alternative dichotomy in ontogeny. At the same time it should be noted that in most cases of inherited, as well as of individually acquired, alternative dichotomies, the ecphory takes place along either one or the other path. In the case given on page 166, either the homophonous engrams h^{1-3} or η^{4-6} become ecphorised. The emergence of the mnemic alternative depends on the ecphoric predominance of either h^{1-3} or η^{4-6}, and the most diverse factors can turn the scale to this or to that side. In the majority of cases, the predominance of one of the two branches is assured by our experience of the branches being quantitatively unequal. If, for example, we have heard the second version of the Omar Khayyám line more frequently than the first, then, *ceteris paribus*, the ecphory along the path of the second version will predominate. Predominance is also affected by the recentness of the experience, the advantage lying with that path along which the fresher experience has moved. It is for this reason, as we shall learn later on, that reversion to atavistic paths is usually avoided in morphogenetic cases. Further, newly occurring stimuli of various kinds may lend predominance to this or that ecphory, and thereby rob the other side of its apparently established predominance. A reciter may know both versions of the Omar Khayyam poem, but is accustomed to recite the second version. If at the point of bifurcation we prompt him with the word belonging to the first version, we may succeed sometimes, by means of this original excitation, in leading him into the unaccustomed path. Under certain circumstances, deterrent influences affect the ordinary process and divert the course of the ecphory from the more usual channel. The chapter on morphogenetic dichotomies deals with this side of our subject.

It is evidently impossible to elaborate a general formula by whose application we could ascertain beforehand the path by which the mnemic alternative will progress in every individual case. But in many cases, after the event we can discern those influences which at the alternative gave the preponderance to this or to that ecphory.

In conclusion, it may be pointed out that our examination of homophony has given us an insight into the peculiar relation of the repetition of a stimulus to its engraphic action. It might be imagined that by one doubly powerful stimulation we should obtain an engram of effect equal to two ordinary stimulations. But most of us know that in general this is not the case. In learning by heart, for instance, we get on more quickly by superficial scanning oft repeated than by a single intense and concentrated effort. The witchery of repetition in the mnemic domain might be demonstrated by many other examples. It becomes intelligible to us by the conception that the engraphic result of repeated stimulation differs in principle from the result induced by a single, but correspondingly stronger, stimulation.

THE FUNDAMENTAL DIFFERENCE LIES IN THE FACT THAT REPETITION OF A STIMULUS DOES NOT STRENGTHEN AN ALREADY EXISTING ENGRAM, BUT GENERATES A NEW ENGRAM, AND THE MNEMIC EXCITATIONS RESULTING FROM ANY SUBSEQUENT ECPHORY OF THESE ENGRAMS ARE IN HOMOPHONY.

PART III

CHAPTER VIII

EVIDENCE OF THE MNEMIC FACTOR IN ONTO-GENETIC REPRODUCTION

TAKING any organism whatever and surveying its onto-genesis, no special reason seems to exist for regarding the ontogenetic development as due to anything but to the action of original stimuli, producing original ex-citations. Fertilisation, we might say, acts as an original stimulus determining the reaction of the first nucleus and cell-division. The stimulus of position, resulting from the juxtaposition of the first two cleavage-cells, liberates, as an original stimulus, the next segmentation, and so on. At a certain stage of development in Verte-brata, for example, the free end of the optic vesicle touches the ectoderm. The contact acts as an original stimulus, it may be through a specific thigmomorphosis, and this determines a plastic reaction, namely, the lens-invagination of the ectoderm.

All the processes involved can be considered as effects of pure original excitations. Although we are still far from being able to analyse the series of internal changes from the first alteration caused by the stimulus until the final reaction, nothing here seems to point to the action or co-operation of mnemic excitations. For the repetition as such, characteristic of ontogenetic develop-ment throughout the generations, does not require the aid of mnemic principles for its elucidation. The validity of our experience is largely dependent on the axiom that like causes produce like effects ; or, as we may say, given certain premises, certain conclusions follow. On this principle, the repetition of ontogenetic facts can, without any aid from mnemic processes, be explained as we explain recurring natural phenomena, such as the procession of the seasons, the alternations of the tides, and the intermittent eruptions of geysers.

One feature, however, is characteristic of all these repetitions. Much the same conditions must rule, in order to secure the recurrence of the phenomena. In the mechanical world, cases may be devised where the one effect follows either from a sum-total of causes, or from a fraction of this totality. It amounts to the same, whether the opposing forces playing upon a wagon are in the relation of five and four horse-power, or four and three horse-power. The resultant is the same, a pull of one horse-power in one direction. In this instance two factors which already neutralised each other may be eliminated. The resultant of a fraction of causes is equivalent to that of the sum-total only when the eliminated factors cancel one another. But where this is not the case, the effect of a totality of causes is nearly always different from that of a fraction, especially if the latter be selected at random.

There is but one group of phenomena which forms an exception to this rule, namely, mnemic excitations with their concomitant reactions. Our previous investigations have furnished evidence that one essential distinction between original and corresponding mnemic excitations lies in the fact that the former are generated by a definite original stimulus-complex, while the latter may be roused by any one constituent of that complex. To refer once again to our original example : Capri, the barrel-organ, and the oil smell had to be present as original visual, auditory, and olfactory stimuli and to act simultaneously, in order to generate the corresponding original excitation-complex. The ecphory of the corresponding mnemic complex, however, could be induced at any time by the recurrence of any one of these stimuli. Stimuli of warmth, moist air and presence of water induce large broods and premature parturition in *Salamandra atra*, an animal which under normal conditions produces two metamorphosed young ones. With each repetition, the effective strength of the stimuli on the individual increases. In the end, the stimuli may be eliminated entirely, and yet, at gravidation, premature parturition of large numbers will take place. The induced change is manifested also in the next generation. *Mutatis mutandis*, the habitual and inherited parturitions of *Salamandra maculosa* are equally affected, but in an opposite way.

In this last example we have an embryological phenomenon, which the most reliable criterion for these processes, namely, the experimental examination of engraphic action, proves to be undeniably mnemic. The same can be said of the ontogenetic phenomena of the colouring of butterflies described by Standfuss, Fischer, and their adherents ; and also of the rich accumulation of results in experimental breeding, which we owe to Blaringhem, Bordage, Chauvin, Kammerer, Klebs, Pictet, Przibram, Schröder, Sumner, Tower, and many others.

For the great majority of ontogenetic phenomena, an experimental test of all potential engraphic stimulations is impossible. We can, however, by experiment adduce evidence that compels us to regard these phenomena as mnemic. We may eliminate in a fairly arbitrary manner one or other part of the conditions, and yet the course of events will, at first, be altered only in so far as the interference renders impossible certain reactions. A cell that has been removed by the surgical knife cannot of course respond by reaction, but as long as the reacting organs are still there, the course runs on in a comparatively undisturbed manner, in spite of the restriction of certain conditions and the absence of some contributing elements.

Experimental evidence of this kind has already been furnished for the ontogeny of the Metazoan groups. It is obvious that the conditions of a course are greatly altered by the removal of, say, one-half, three-quarters, or seven-eighths of the system in which the course generally completes itself. The alteration of conditions is particularly effective when the course is determined, not by the influence of causes acting externally, but by changes taking place within the system itself. An example of this latter condition is given when by experimental interference we alter the conditions of an embryo during its ontogenetic development. We may take a Ctenophore when in segmentation it has reached the stage of eight cells and divide it into two, four, or eight parts. No regeneration takes place, but the two, four, or eight sections continue their course of development almost as if no such extraordinary change of conditions had taken place. The Ctenophores being pelagic animals, the larvæ, perfect or imperfect, under the unnatural conditions of the aquarium, perish immediately after passing through their metamorphosis. We are, therefore, unable to tell how much longer under more favourable conditions the development of these mutilated part-systems might have continued.

In much the same way, by mutilating the developing eggs of Echinoderms, Annelids, Ascidians, Molluscs, etc., serious changes of the conditions may be effected without any immediate essential alteration of the course of development within the remaining parts of the system. It is true that striking aberrations from the normal course set in *later*; but the point need not engage our attention at the moment, as, in view of its great importance, we shall presently consider it more minutely.

It has been stated that experimental mutilation can be effected in a fairly arbitrary manner without disturbing the rest of the system. But in this respect the range of our freedom has its limits, which vary according to the species to which the organism belongs, and the stage of development it has reached. A fuller discussion of the matter will be found in Chapter XI.

We have already found it characteristic of mnemic phenomena—that is, the manifestations of mnemic excitations by specific reactions—that they require for their ecphory but a fraction, arbitrarily chosen it may be, of the conditions which were required to generate the corresponding original excitations. It is clear that ontogenetic phenomena resemble the mnemic phenomena in so far as in their production fairly large and arbitrary subtractions may also be made from the conditions which normally obtain. It is useful to point out that this is a general characteristic of ontogenetic processes in all kinds of organisms, and at all stages of development. But the kind of alteration we may effect in the conditions, without annihilating or arresting the course of development, varies according to species and stage of development.

In the animal kingdom, the number of classes in which, after experimental interference, the course of development continues for a time as if no such change had been effected, is limited. But with the Hydromedusæ, Amphioxus, Teleostei, and Amphibia, the course is modified almost immediately after the change has set in. The nature of this modification is, however, of such a kind as to furnish a strong argument for the mnemic character of the excitations which manifest themselves in the plastic reactions of ontogenesis. Modification of the course often follows even in those cases where, for a time, the development continues as if no change of condition had set in. This, for example, holds good in regard to the Echinodermata.

In what does this modification of the course consist ? In reference to the elimination by experimental interference of a part of the physical conditions, we used the phrase " undisturbed course." The word " undisturbed " relates only to the reactions of the remaining portion of the system. It cannot, of course, refer to the reactions of the eliminated parts, for it is obvious that, with the excision of parts, the reactions appropriate to them fall away. But as regards the parts that remain, we note that, after some little time, or even in rare cases jointly with the cycle of the usual reactions, new plastic reactions set in, which, however diverse in manifestation, have this in common, that they tend to effect a re-establishment of the conditions disturbed by the interference. Or, as we may phrase it, they finally establish a congruity between the state—at the moment we refer specifically to the morphological state—of the remainder of the system and that state which the whole system would have reached if no interference whatever had taken place.

During the analysis of mnemic homophony, in the preceding chapter, we noted certain reactions which tend to abolish a specific incongruity between two states —the original state of excitement, and the corresponding mnemic state. At the moment, however, we are dealing with morphological states. If, therefore, we wish to establish a direct relation between the above-mentioned ontogenetic observations and the results obtained during the analysis of the mnemic homophony, we shall have to prove—first, that with the occurrence of ontogenetic phenomena, it is valid to infer states of excitement from morphological states; secondly, that conditions exist for the presence of an original state of excitement as well as of a corresponding mnemic state of excitement; and thirdly, that new reactions either partially or entirely effect the removal of incongruities in the homophony of those two states of excitement.

The question, whether states of excitement correspond to the morphological states clearly observable at onto-genesis, is not difficult to meet. But in answering it, we shall take into account the whole body of morpho-logical states, including those of the developed organism on the completion of its ontogenesis. It is evident that the energetic condition of a system, that is, its internal energetic condition, is partly determined by the morpho-logical state. Only partly determined, for besides the morphological state, chemical, thermic, electrical, and other states play, of course, an important part. The various elements of the energetic condition, together with the morphological state, determine the respective organic state of excitement; and the original excitations so generated are joined by mnemic excitations, which, at that moment, are ecphorised in the organism. The morphological state of an organism, therefore, is only in part responsible for the extremely complex state of excitement, which, at a given moment, may develop in the organism. But although the morphological state is only one of several factors, its importance cannot be overrated, for never for a moment does it cease to act. With its changes the state of excitement must also change. A part of the complex state of excitement, therefore, definitely depends on the morphological state of the organism. This we shall define as the morphogeneous part of the excitation-complex.

This distinction of a morphogeneous part from the whole of a simultaneous excitation-complex could hardly be supported by closer analysis, but it facilitates our understanding of the subject, and may, therefore, be allowed to stand as a temporary expedient in the present phase of our investigation. If we consider the morphogeneous part of a simultaneous excitation-complex as the sum-total of the excitations set up by "stimuli of position," we must not forget that the reference to its contents is but summary. On further analysis we shall find that these stimuli of position are resolvable into various classes. For our present purposes, however, the collective definition given will suffice.

To the first of the above three questions, then, we make answer that to the morphological state of a developing or fully developed organism there corresponds a definite part of its state of excitement. This we have summarily described as the morphogeneous part of this state.

The second question asks whether the conditions exist for the presence not only of an original but also of a corresponding mnemic excitation in those cases where the conditions have been changed by experimental interference, and where a modified course of development has followed.

The conditions certainly exist. Two things are required for the rise of a mnemic excitation—an engram and its ecphory. As the engram in this case has to produce an excitation corresponding to the morphogeneous area of excitement, that can only be if the engram is the result of the repeated action of a similar morphogeneous excitation. It has been made clear that, in cases of ontogenetic process, the stimuli of position produce, in each successive developmental stage, excitations which for the individual in question are a singular non-recurring experience. But the same or very similar complexes of stimuli have produced like excitations in the innumerable ancestors of this individual. Our contention is that these influences have acted engraphically, and that the resultant engrams have been transmitted to the offspring. In the nature of things it is impossible to demonstrate this by the direct experimental re-creation of these engrams in the manner, say, of the experiments elaborated by Kammerer, Chauvin, Standfuss, Fischer, Tower, Bordage, and others. Our task is to prove the mnemic nature of definite excitations on the occurrence of specific states (see pp. 65, 66). For the moment we shall regard what has to be proved as proven, and assume that the morphogeneous excitations have acted engraphically in each generation, and that the engrams have been transmitted to offspring. The question then would be whether the conditions exist for the due ecphory in the offspring of these morphogeneous engrams thus hereditarily transmitted.

In each generation the morphological states whose " energetic " action produces the morphogeneous engram-complexes form a continuous succession. The rational inference is that the morphogeneous engram-complexes are successively associated, and that the ecphory of the first in a sequence effects the ecphory of the related series of engrams. Granted, therefore, at the beginning of ontogenesis the ecphory of the first engram—a fact which we shall prove later—the condition is thereby given for the due ecphory of the successive engrams. The mode of this we shall investigate presently.

There is a second operative condition which depends on the ecphory by original stimuli of individual engrams in the engram-succession. This second condition also we shall examine later (p. 183). At the moment let us concern ourselves with those concrete cases, from which we started, of ontogenetic development altered by experiment.

We noted that the removal of parts of the developing organism was followed, generally after some time, but in rare cases immediately, by new plastic reactions in the remainder of the organism. These new reactions, different from those usually given by the corresponding parts of the organism, varied greatly according to the specific case. But they all had this in common, that they ultimately effected a re-establishment of the conditions thus disturbed ; in other words, they established a congruity between the morphological state of the remainder of the organism whose development still continued in spite of the interference, and the morphological state of that stage which the organism itself would have reached if no interference had taken place, a stage through which, of course, its ancestors, unaffected by experiment, naturally passed. This latter state we know from the study of the normal ontogenesis.

Now, we recognised that the morphological state of the organism after operation is a factor determining a corresponding original excitation in the affected organism. But to the morphological state which the organism would have reached in the absence of experimental interference corresponds the *mnemic* morphogeneous state of excitement whose presence so far we have assumed, but for whose release the necessary conditions have now been shown to exist. It is clear that this mnemic morphogeneous state of excitement has not been altered by the experimental interference ; it belongs to the accumulated stock of inherited engrams, which, as we have suggested on page 116, and shall definitely prove in Chapter XI, is allocated in equal measure to each mnemic protomer of an individual, and therefore cannot be destroyed by the removal of morphological sections from the nexus of the whole.

The expression—" the morphological state which the organism *would* have reached if no interference had taken place "—acquires its true significance only when we realize how dependent this state is on the corresponding mnemic excitation actually present in the organism, after as well as before any experimental operation.

Disregarding the two morphological states, one of which cannot of course possess any reality in these cases, and considering only the actually existing states of excitement, we conclude that plastic, regulating reactions, which at the disturbance of development manifest themselves apart from the usual reactions that continue the development, fall under a category of reactions already known to us. We showed in a preceding chapter (p. 155), that by the objective method mnemic homophony can be inferred only from the presence of reactions which are objectively perceptible, and whose characteristic is " that they modify themselves strictly according to the congruity or the incongruity of an original state of excitement with a state of excitement that has already existed in the same organism or in its ancestors, and for the ecphory of which in its aspect as a mnemic excitation the necessary conditions again exist." The strongest evidence for the presence and effectiveness of homophony is furnished by those reactions which tend to remove the incongruity (p. 160).

Our inference from the known facts can be succinctly stated. On experimental or casual disturbance of the ontogeny, reactions arise whose nature and scope are determined by the incongruity existing between a morphogeneous original excitation and an ancestral morphogeneous excitation, that is, one that may be found in the direct ancestral line of the organism. These modifying reactions in the course of time remove the incongruity relating to the excitations. From these reactions we infer homophony, and conclude that simultaneously with the morphogeneous original excitation the ancestral morphogeneous excitation has reappeared as mnemic excitation.

Before passing to the detailed consideration of ontogeny as influenced by this homophony, we may be allowed to revert to a point previously mentioned.

We saw that the morphogeneous engram-complexes are

successively associated, so that the ecphory of the first engram effects in sequence the ecphory of the entire engram-series. But we added at once that there existed a second possibility, in that any one of the individual members of the series might be ecphorised by original stimuli. Let us consider this latter possibility more closely, and from the starting-point of an active mnemic morphogeneous excitation-complex trace the related series of excitations and morphological changes which come into activity in any ontogenetic course. This excitation-complex is manifested in a body of reactions, and the energetic condition thereby created acts as an original stimulus, generating an original excitation-complex which, in the case of an undisturbed ontogenesis, corresponds on the whole to the mnemic excitation-complex from which we started. The process is illustrative of the congruity of the Homophony. It is clear that in this case each of the two homophonous excitation-complexes acts ecphorically on the succeeding associated engram-complex (see diagram I on page 184).

We get an idea of their joint action in the introspective examination of an analogous case. When a well-known tune is played to us on any instrument, mnemic and original excitations together act ecphorically on successive engram-complexes. If suddenly the playing ceases, the mnemic course for a time still runs on. When the latter comes to a stop, a fresh impulse may be derived from a few bars played anew. As regards the tempo of the successions, either the original or mnemic excitations may predominate. But here, too, a congruity of the homophonies will in time become established. In a conductor, for example, who allows his orchestra to carry him along with an accelerated tempo, the original excitations predominate over the ecphorised mnemic excitations. Another conductor, however, whose mnemic excitations may possess relatively greater strength, overcomes the force of the original excitations, and by the restraining influence of his baton subordinates these to the mnemic forces. In each case we see the ecphoric action of both

I.

Phase a.	Phase b.	Phase c.
	a (or) and a (mn) jointly ecphorise the engram-complex b (engr) generating the	b (or) and b (mn) jointly ecphorise the engram-complex c (engr) generating the
mnemic excitation-complex a (mn) ⟶ plastic reactions: morphological state a (z) ⟶ original excitation-complex a (or)	mnemic excitation-complex b (mn) ⟶ plastic reactions: morphological state b (z) ⟶ original excitation-complex b (or)	mnemic excitation-complex c (mn) ⟶ plastic reactions: morphological state c (z) ⟶ original excitation-complex c (or)
homophony between a(mn) and a(or)	homophony between b (mn) and b (or)	homophony between c (mn) and c (or)

II.

Phase a.	Phase b.	Phase c.
	α (or) and a (mn) jointly ecphorise the engram-complex b (engr) generating the	β (or) and b (mn) jointly ecphorise the engram-complex c (engr) generating the
mnemic excitation-complex a (mn) →	mnemic excitation-complex b (mn) →	mnemic excitation-complex c (mn) →
↓	↓	↓
plastic reactions : morphological state α (z) (arisen instead of a (z) as a result of a disturbance)	plastic reactions : morphological state β (z)	plastic reactions : morphological state γ (z)
↓	↓	↓
original excitation-complex α (or)	original excitation-complex β (or)	original excitation-complex γ (or)
↓	↓	↓
eventually plastic reactions tending to remove the incongruity $a: \alpha$	eventually plastic reactions tending to remove the incongruity $b: \beta$	in case the plastic reactions effect the removal of the incongruity between c and γ, ontogeny then progresses normally; that is, the next mnemic excitation d generates the morphological state d (z) and not δ (z)

kinds of excitations. For their action the rule holds good that where, in the homophony, congruity does not exist, it will ultimately be established in one way or another.

During ontogenesis, the tempo of the course of succession is predominantly governed by the tempo of the original stimulus-complexes, which in their turn depend on the tempo required by the plastic reactions. For while the tempo of the mnemic courses may easily be accelerated or retarded, that of the original excitations, depending as it does on plastic reactions, is determined by morphological processes which are influenced by various external, mainly thermal, conditions.

During ontogenetic development the ecphory of an engram results from the joint action of the antecedent mnemic and of the homophonous original excitation-complex. This statement is *not* greatly affected by the fact that the original excitation-complex may be mutilated in consequence of experimental interference. For it has already been enunciated as a general mnemic law that a partial recurrence of a stimulus-complex acts ecphorically on an engram-complex.

We will refer later to specific cases of the ecphory of ontogenetic engrams. At this point, however, it may be well to insert a couple of diagrams, one (I) of which represents the normal ontogenetic course, and the other (II) the course when the ontogeny has·been disturbed by experiment. In this latter diagram only the courses of such excitations as manifest themselves in plastic reactions are considered.

It is obvious that the complicated assemblage of natural phenomena can never be adequately represented by a mere diagram. The utmost we can expect is, by more or less arbitrary distinctions, omissions, and summaries, to simplify the main workings and to present valid generalizations. Our diagrams are the result of this simplifying process.

The division of ontogeny into phases, for example, is a purely arbitrary proceeding, whether the duration of the phases is measured by sidereal time, or by a standard derived from the organic course itself. If, in some definite ontogenetic process, say that of a total symmetrical egg-segmentation, we choose the period required for the completion of a nucleus-division as the time-unit for the phase-division, we cannot be sure of our conclusions, since this period is by no means constant for the organism, but varies according to external and internal conditions. From nucleus to nucleus the duration varies within fairly wide limits. For practical purposes, however, it may be allowable to take the mean time between the nucleus divisions, and apply it as a standard for the phase-division of the segmentation of the organism, so long as the arbitrariness of this break in continuity is borne in mind. We need not give to the phase-division a deeper significance than, let us say, to the division of a melody into bars.

In a piece of polyphonic music a good many different successions may within the bar move in very diverse and distinct tempos, and the continuity of the single component tones may be broken within the bars themselves as well as between any two bars.

In our diagrams I and II the complicated successions range themselves in their totality with apparent exactitude into divisional phases. This, however, must be regarded as an arbitrary simplification. In concrete cases, such an orderly and regular arrangement is practically impossible. That excitation-complex a acts ecphorically on engram-complex b, is, of course, but a summary mode of expression. With regard to the connection of the engram-complexes with each other, the reader is referred once more to the general exposition on page 95, and to the diagram on page 97. What is said there regarding the intimate and the distant connections of the single components of the simultaneous and successive engram-complexes is valid also for the connection between the components of the ontogenetic morphogeneous engram-complexes. Thus, in a simplified diagram after the manner of the one on page 97, the composition of the morphogeneous engram-complex during a symmetrical egg-segmentation would appear as below.

In this diagram we see that the connection of the engrams presents dichotomies subject to simultaneous

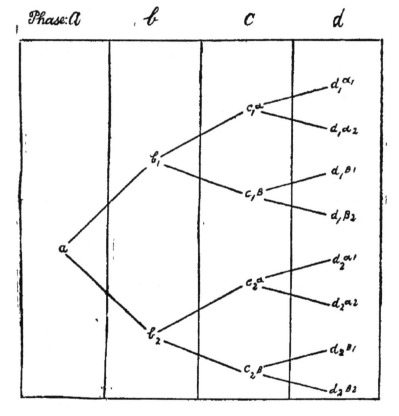

ecphory, the *successive connections* of the engram-complexes being in the case given more closely related than are the simultaneous connections. This follows from the fact that in ontogenesis the simultaneous complexes are less coherent than those of a lineal succession.

This peculiarity may be thus explained. The ecphory of certain components of a *simultaneous* engram-complex may be either accelerated or retarded by diverse occurrences, and consequently may take place in an earlier or later phase than that of other components in the simultaneous association. This is implied in the established fact that the developmental maximum of the organ ordinarily fluctuates in the single " stages " within certain relatively narrow limits. The composition of the simultaneous complexes at each recurrence in the succeeding generations varies within a definite margin. It follows, therefore, that this fact should be mnemically expressed in a blurring of the ecphoric strength of the simultaneous associations. On the other hand, the ecphoric force of the successive associations, by reason of their practical identity each time they recur, increases with every new recurrence, thereby far surpassing in effectiveness the less coherent simultaneous associations.

We may compare the ontogenetic course in this respect with the reproduction of a piece of music, where each separate part is perfectly performed, but where the harmonic working of the parts is subject to slight vacillations, which are yet insufficient to affect the general success of the performance. People of limited executive ability do this sort of thing on the piano when the rhythm of the bass varies from that of the treble, or when, in accompanying their own singing, voice and accompaniment take relatively independent tempi.

When the deviations during ontogenetic development, as also in musical reproduction, pass a certain point, readjustments are effected by various reactions which operate when the incongruity between the original and the mnemic excitations exceeds a certain limit.

I should like to call attention to one more fact. It is the attainment of a definite state and not the mere number of developmental steps which acts on a certain engram as a successive ecphory. As pointed out in Chapter III (p. 75), the beginning of gastrulation in the Echinoderms does not depend simply on the number of the preceding cell-divisions, but follows primarily on the specific reduction of the size of the single cells. With complete ova, the gastrulations begin after a relatively great number of divisions; but with ovum-fragments or with isolated blastomeres, the necessary number of preceding divisions is less, proportionate to the size of the cells. If two developing germs are forced to unite, as they were by Driesch, into a single new individual of double size, then before gastrulation sets in, the number of divisions is necessarily greater than in the case of ordinary complete ova.

There is still one more point whose consideration may obviate possible error. On page 188, we gave a diagram representing the composition of the morphogeneous *engram-* or *excitation-complexes* during symmetrical egg-segmentation. If we now elaborated a second diagram, giving not the connections of the engrams or excitations, but the successive connections of the *cells*, it might be inferred from the concurrences of these diagrammatic representations that, in each phase, one engram or excitation-component corresponded to one definite cell in such a way that we might think of the component as localised in this cell. But the inappropriateness of this notion has already been indicated in the chapter which dealt with the radiation of the excitations over the whole organism (p. 123). Further, the idea could only be validly conceivable if each cell in regard to stimulus-conduction were isolated from its neighbour, which is certainly not the case. It is therefore impossible to say that each morphogeneous excitation-complex runs its course within the organism according to a strict morphological localisation, and that one excitation-component runs off in this cell, and another in that. So definite an allocation of excitation-complexes to specific areas cannot be accepted, for every mnemic protomer in the organism is influenced by the morphogeneous excitation-complex as the latter runs its course.

CHAPTER IX

THE INITIAL ONTOGENETIC ENGRAM AND THE ONTOGENETIC COURSE OF DEVELOPMENT

THE evolution of a series of organisms presents itself as a continuous line which passes through phases of time and space. To each phase in time an individual corresponds. The individual may be regarded as a phase in space. While the continuity in time is an altogether uninterrupted one, the continuity in space may be broken, since at the beginning of each phase of individuality a separation in space usually takes place. This separation is the rule in sexual propagation, but it may not occur in asexual propagation, or, if it does, only comparatively late. In spite of this break in continuity, the evolution proper represents, without exception, a continuous line, whose interruptions are of a secondary nature ; that is, they occur at a point already passed through by the leading developmental line.

This break in continuity, however, is of special importance for our present consideration, because thereby a mnemic separation between the parental and the filial organism is effected. It is only on the completion of this separation that the possibility arises of the filial organism acquiring engrams in which the parental organism has no share. By such a separation it acquires its own mnemic individuality.

But although the filial organism may detach itself from the parental organism, it does not follow that in the majority of cases the new ontogenetic cycle begins straight away. Ignoring the male germs, which from other and external causes may be unable to commence the ontogenetic cycle, and considering only the more favourably disposed female germs, we find that these, after the maturation changes, are in most cases unable to start the new cycle of development without the aid of an external impulse. In the absence of this impulse, the ovum ordinarily remains for a time in a state of rest, and then gradually perishes.

This maturation stage, as is usual in descriptive and experimental embryology, may be regarded as the starting-point of the ontogenesis. We note that in most cases a specific external stimulus is required to effect the ecphory of what we may call the initial ontogenetic engram, and to arouse the mnemic excitation *a* (see the diagram on page 188).

The stimulus that normally acts ecphorically on the initial ontogenetic engram is connected with the process of fertilisation. Interesting and important as the matter is in itself, we will not now examine to which of the numerous energetic influences generated by this process this ecphory is due.

But it is particularly instructive and strongly indicative of the mnemic nature of the excitation initiating the ontogenesis, that the liberating stimulus may be one of many different classes of stimuli, some of which are able to induce a parthenogenetic development, that is, without fertilization by the male element. The reader is referred to what was said on pages 45, 70, on vicarious ecphory. Loeb, who dealt with this problem in a series of excellent experiments, sees the first decisive step in ontogenetic development in the formation of the membrane of the egg.

He effected membrane-formation by the specific action of formic, acetic, propionic, butyric, and other fatty acids. Mineral acids, such as hydrochloric acid, were also effectual. He also found that saponin, solanine, digitalin, the bile salts, the specific fat-dissolving carbohydrates such as amylene, benzol, toluol, and chloroform, ether and the alcohols, the presence of free oxygen, and, under certain circumstances, a mere raising of temperature, would cause the formation of the membrane. The same end was attained by the injection either of blood from animals belonging to a different family, or of extracts from organs belonging to animals of different species. In a great number of these cases it happened, however, that the development thus started ran off abnormally and came prematurely to a standstill. This was most probably caused by an injurious substance produced during the course of the abnormal development. Loeb discovered two ways of counteracting the effect of this poisonous substance. He treated the egg with a hypertonic solution in the presence of free oxygen, whereby the poison was rendered innocuous by oxidation ; or he withdrew the oxygen, and consequently suppressed the oxidation-processes, by means of cyanide of potassium. According to Loeb, it is the cytolytic action in the cortical layer of the egg due to the various acids mentioned—the carbohydrates, the alkalis, the different extracts of organs, and the lysin contained in the sperm of animals of the same species—which accounts for the actual formation of the membrane, and consequently for the abnormal development of the organism, although under certain circumstances the segmentation of the egg may take place without membrane formation. The merely mechanical factors also act, according to Loeb, by means of cytolysis or cell-degeneration. Formerly, Loeb objected to the definition of these factors as stimuli, but recently he himself has classed them amongst the formative stimuli.

At this point I may perhaps be allowed a digression. Loeb, in the introduction and preface to his latest summary on artificial parthenogenesis, writes as follows ·—" The fact that the incitement of the development of the egg suggests processes of 'stimulation' is responsible for the devotion of so much thought to this problem. I found out during my researches on tropism and on the physiology of brain, nerve, and muscle, that no decisive progress could be made until the nature of the process of stimulation had been elucidated. In spite of more than a century of research and experiment we are still much in the dark, and this may be ascribed to the fact that we cannot, at will, directly observe what takes place in the nerve and its terminals during stimulation. In the egg we can see the actual processes at work. What is still more important, we can confirm our conclusions by evidence derived from like simultaneous experiments on a very great number of

13

individuals. This suggested to me the idea that the study of the artificial incitement to development might supply the missing analogies for the successful analysis of the processes in muscle, nerve, and other cells."

If now we ask the question whether Loeb by this method succeeded in penetrating deeper into the nature of the process of excitation, we shall have to reply in the negative, even if we ignore, as we do, the purely hypothetical element in his theoretical results. Apart from the statement that we are able to observe directly with the eye the processes of stimulation in the egg—which statement is much too wide and, therefore, misleading—neither the discovery that the formation of the membrane is, as a rule, the first visible reaction of the initiated development, nor the equally valuable demonstration that this membrane-formation is induced by a superficial cytolysis of the egg, affords us any real insight into the " nature " of this formative stimulation, that is, into the chain of the concurrent chemical and physical processes. Further, we have to note that the formation of the membrane which, according to Loeb, is the first definitely essential process in the incitement to development, may under certain circumstances not take place, and yet the eggs may nevertheless develop. If Loeb, in spite of his apparent failure to understand the nature of the stimulation-process in this specially selected instance, means to suggest the entire obliteration of the words stimulation and excitation from the vocabulary of physiology, we can only say that at the present stage of our knowledge in the realm of muscle- nerve- and sense-physiology such a procedure must lead to utter confusion.

Without doubt, excitation is at bottom a physico-chemical process and nothing else, and the engram simply a residual physico-chemical modification. But as we are still lacking any real insight into the physics and chemistry of these processes, it would be the greatest mistake to discard the serviceable definitions of stimulus-physiology and to deceive ourselves about the distance which still separates us from the goal of a purely physico-chemical interpretation. For such self-delusion, followed by the inevitable disillusion, would only serve the purposes of the vitalists.

While in cases of experimentally induced parthenogenesis we know the stimuli acting ecphorically on the initial ontogenetic engram, we are still in ignorance of the ecphoric stimuli in those comparatively few cases where parthenogenesis appears as a normal phenomenon, as, for instance, with some of the Rotifera, Crustacea, and Insects, and abnormally with the Starfishes. It may be that in some cases the external stimulus is of a chemical or mechanical nature, and that this acts during the passage of the eggs from the abdominal fluid into the air or into the water. But in other cases, as, for example, with the parthenogenetic viviparous Aphides, the intervention of such an external stimulus is impossible, as segmentation follows immediately upon the maturation of the ovum. Here, the probability is that the processes of maturation themselves act ecphorically on the initial ontogenetic engram immediately following.

In the asexual development of ferns generated from spores, the moistening of the spores acts ecphorically on the initial ontogenetic engram.

When the initial ontogenetic engram is ecphorised by a stimulus of any kind, the further course of the ontogenesis proceeds in the main according to the principles enunciated in Chapter VIII. The course, however, is affected by external conditions, which play now an active, now a somewhat passive, part.

The temperature at the time of development plays a passive but yet a very important part. It determines the tempo of the entire metabolism, and consequently of the plastic reactions ; on it depends the tempo of the entry of the original excitations, and thereby, as we explained on page 183, the tempo, but not the rhythm, of the entire cycle of both original and mnemic excitations. By lowering the temperature we are able to retard the ontogenetic course in a most extraordinary way. Whether we can bring it to a complete standstill without permanently injuring the organism has been made doubtful by the recent investigations of O. Schultze on eggs of *Rana fusca*. However that may be, on the return to normal conditions—in this instance normal temperature—the course of development progresses as usual, without requiring any fresh external stimulus to set it going again. The amount of light, the nature of the medium, and the supply of food play a similar, but usually a less important, rôle in ontogenesis. Each of these factors, however, may under certain circumstances acquire in some specific phase of the ontogeny a greater importance, as when the ecphory of certain engrams fails to take place along the habitual path of successive association unless specific external stimuli, acting as ecphoric stimuli, intervene.

For example, specific changes in the skin, gills, and tails of many newt larvæ appear only when the young animal is given a chance to get into direct touch with the atmospheric air. By preventing this contact, by excluding the larvæ from the air by means of a wire netting placed beneath the surface of the water, the modifications are inhibited, but the animals survive as larvæ, continue to grow, and finally become sexually mature. The absence in such cases of an ecphory dependent on specific external stimuli does not, therefore, mean that the development is definitely arrested, but only that certain portions of the mnemic excitation-complexes remain quiescent until ecphorised by stronger original stimuli.

A close investigation of these abnormal cases shows us that this dependence of ecphory on external stimuli generally possesses special biological significance in the way of serviceable adaptations. It is appropriate for the axolotl or the triton to lose its gills and to be transformed into a terrestrial animal when it has the opportunity of reaching dry soil. The problem indicated is fascinating and important, but its discussion would lead us somewhat far afield, as at the moment we are not primarily concerned with the rise and development of useful adaptations. It will be a separate task to consider the Darwinian theory of natural selection in the light of the general views elaborated in this work. At this point I only wish to say that this separate exposition will in no sense be an attack on a theory, which, in recent times, has been so vehemently criticised. At most, some few modifications will be suggested.

Reverting to those cases in which the ecphory of the

morphogeneous engrams does not follow the normal course described on page 184, but demands the action of an external stimulus, we wish to point out that in such instances it is a case of special adaptations, for in most cases we can prove that the necessary external ecphoric stimulus is an integral part of a previous engraphic stimulus which, in the corresponding stages of development, has influenced the ancestors of the organisms in question. Triton larvæ usually lose their gills, if they are allowed to come to the surface of the water and so to gasp for air. It is not altogether necessary for them to get on to dry soil and in that way to expose the gills themselves to the fuller influence of the atmospheric air. Speaking phylogenetically, the entire loss of the gills and the transformations of the skin and the tail must undoubtedly have taken place under a much more direct and intense influence of the atmospheric air and of life on dry soil. Ontogenetically, a mere portion of these stimuli now suffices to induce in the descendants of those primitive tritons the ecphory of engrams originated by those stimuli.

Already it has been mentioned that the absence of ecphories dependent on external stimuli does not imply the unqualified arrest of the development, but simply the inaction of certain portions of the excitation-complexes. We must here ask how this is possible. Does not a simultaneous engram-complex become ecphorised in its totality, or does it still require, under certain circumstances, a specific ecphory for its separate parts? Referring to the general discussion of ecphory on page 78, we note that the recurrence of a portion of an original excitation-complex does not always involve the ecphory of the corresponding engram-complex in its entirety (see diagram, p. 139). In some instances one or other of the engrams of a complex cannot become ecphorised at all along the path of simultaneous or successive association, but only by the recurrence of the corresponding original excitation. The stimulus liberating this recurrence may be an exceedingly weak one. It may be, for example, in regard to a long-lost friend, that neither a description of his person nor a reminder of situations and events in which he played a part suffices to ecphorise his features in our memory; but a slight pencil sketch of his face may bring him before us at once. So as in the case of many salamandrina a casual and short contact with the atmospheric air ecphorises an excitation-complex which manifests itself in such reactions as the resorption of the gills, and alterations in the skin and tail. In the larvæ of many genera, if all contact with the atmospheric air is prevented, the ecphory does not occur.

It may be well, therefore, in order to cover certain exceptional cases, to make the following additions to our diagram on page 184 of the cycles of the normal morphogenesis (Diagram III) :—

III.

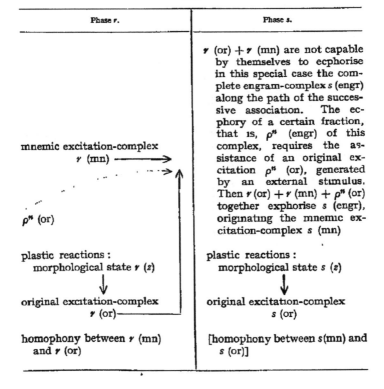

Phase r.	Phase s.
	r (or) $+ r$ (mn) are not capable by themselves to ecphorise in this special case the complete engram-complex s (engr) along the path of the successive association. The ecphory of a certain fraction, that is, ρ^n (engr) of this complex, requires the assistance of an original excitation ρ^n (or), generated by an external stimulus. Then r (or) $+ r$ (mn) $+ \rho^n$ (or) together exphorise s (engr), originating the mnemic excitation-complex s (mn)
mnemic excitation-complex r (mn) ⟶	
ρ^n (or)	
plastic reactions : morphological state r (z)	plastic reactions : morphological state s (z)
original excitation-complex r (or)	original excitation-complex s (or)
homophony between r (mn) and r (or)	[homophony between s(mn) and s (or)]

IV

Phase Γ			Phase S
Morphological state $\Gamma^{1-4}(Z)$, product of the plastic reactions determined by the mnemic excitation complex $\Gamma^{1-4}(mn)$	above: mnemic excitation complex $\Gamma^{1-4}(mn)$ mid. original excitation complex $\Gamma^{1-4}(or)$ below: original excitation $95(or)$ liberated by an external stimulus	Engram complex S^{1-5} (Engr)	above: mnemic excitation complex S^{1-5} (mn) below: original excitation complex S^{1-5} (or)

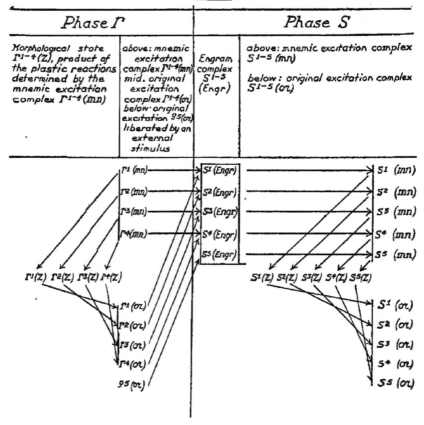

In the preceding diagram (IV) is illustrated more fully the ecphory of an engram-complex s (engr)—for convenience and simplicity limited to s^1 (engr) s^2 (engr) s^3 (engr) s^4 (engr) and s^5 (engr)—by the serial morphogeneous excitations r^{1-4}, and by the excitation c^5, which is liberated by an external stimulus. For detailed explanation the reader is referred to page 96, where is discussed the intimate connection between the single components of successive engram-complexes, and to page 140, where certain ecphoric peculiarities are dealt with. Diagram II (p. 185) should also be consulted.

A superficial study of the latter diagram might perhaps raise the suspicion that the investigations in this book, as far as their application to ontogeny is concerned, had led to nothing more novel than a restatement of processes already well known. Some may think that the processes of evolution directly observable have been understood quite as profoundly and analysed quite as keenly by previous workers, without the results being obscured or confused by mere theoretical formularising. Of theories which merely paraphrase we already possess an abundance. A close study of the diagram in question will, I think, immediately disabuse the mind of this suspicion.

The introduction of mnemic terminology into the diagram and the consequent inclusion of ontogenetic relations under mnemic laws give these relationships a far wider meaning than those which are based on ordinary original stimulations possess. As the diagrams show, the ontogenetic connections are made—at any rate at those points where they cross—by the ecphory of engrams and engram-complexes. But these ecphories, compared with the ordinary original stimulations, have this peculiarity, that a complete engram-complex may be ecphorised by a mere portion of the excitation-complex. For instance, if in our diagram IV, on page 199, the sign c^5 (or) signifies in newt larvæ an original excitation generated by contact with external air, in certain forms the engram-component s^5 (engr) may be ecphorised without the appearance of c^5 (or), either by simultaneous association through the ecphory of s^{1-4}

(engr), or, later, by other ecphoric influences. In some cases, however, ecphory depends entirely on the entry of the original excitation c^5 (or). In the case of Salamandra, the ecphory of the engram s^5 (engr), though often somewhat belated, nearly always takes place without the appearance of the original excitation c^5 (or). But with Siredon, the ecphory is equally certain to remain latent until c^5 (or) appears.

The diagram, it is true, shows but *one* series of relations during a specific ontogenetic process, but that is sufficient for the realisation of what the process means. The process may run out and reach the same goal, even if several components have remained inactive. The reader is referred to page 78, where the various possibilities of lens-development are discussed ; especially is he asked to note those numerous cases where lens-formation takes place even on the elimination of that stimulus of contact which has been supposed to be the sole determining factor. In any consideration of these ontogenetic processes, we must, therefore, take into account the many possibilities of relationship which permit of collateral ways leading to the same end. The mnemic conception of ontogenesis allows us to do this in the fullest way possible.

Another equally important advantage is derived from the application of the mnemic principle to the connections between the ontogenetic cycles. We see the entire ontogenetic course unfold itself, in the presence and by the power of mnemic homophony as a necessary implication of the connections shown in the four diagrams, I–IV, on pages 184, 185, 198, 199. The idea of homophony offers a path by which we may penetrate more deeply than has hitherto been possible into the meaning of the somewhat bewildering phenomena of regeneration and regulation.

I do not claim to have solved the deeper riddles of biology These still remain. I think, however that I am justified in assuming that in this book I have offered something more than a mere paraphrase of the problems discussed therein.

CHAPTER X

MORPHOGENEOUS MNEMIC EXCITATIONS IN THE FULLY DEVELOPED ORGANISM

AT the outset it would be well to make quite clear what we mean by " fully developed " organism. Is an individual to be regarded as developed when it has reached sexual maturity, or only when it has attained its full growth ? The latter criterion is obviously inapplicable to many forms of plant life where the growth is practically unlimited. Further, in the case of many other organisms of limited growth it would be difficult to apply this test. For in many organisms a growth in thickness proceeds for years after the arrest of the growth in height, and ceases only when the other organs have long since passed their highest point of development. In man, for example, the cessation of vertical growth is followed by an increase in volume of the bones, muscles, and other organs. The criterion of the production of mature germ-cells is equally impracticable, so far as the indication of full organic development is concerned. We need but think of those numerous cases of so-called pædogenesis, where morphologically undeveloped forms such as the larvæ of Cecidamyia reach sexual maturity and produce young, in order to be convinced that the criterion of sexual maturity cannot be regarded as absolute.

Embryologists usually consider an organism fully developed when most of its organs have so far matured that any changes arising indicate simply a mere increase in volume and not a further differentiation of function. This definition is useful for descriptive purposes. But phrases like "*most* of its organs" and "mere increase in volume without further differentiation" express clearly the conventional character of this division of the life-cycle of an organism. The definition, like all those based on separate characteristics, such as the attainment of sexual maturity, of full growth, etc., is inadequate.

As long as the individual lives, physiological and morphological changes continually appear, and although we may be justified in summarily dividing the life-cycle into two parts, one in which the course of the morphological changes is intense and rapid, and the other wherein the tempo is remarkably retarded, we have to remember that there exists no sharp boundary between the two divisions. The transition from the one to the other is gradual and almost imperceptible.

If we examine the course of movement in this transition period, by reference to the diagram on page 184, we find that the only real difference is in the increased duration of the separate phases. The tempo of the plastic reactions within each phase is more rapid than the transition from one phase to another, the ecphory of new engram-complexes. The length of the time-periods gradually increases. After reaching a morphological state $t(z)$, the mnemic excitation t (mn) as well as the original excitation t (or) remain homophonically active, until at last the ecphory of the new morphogeneous engram (u) takes place. In organisms of limited growth a time ultimately arrives when a fresh ecphory of new morphogeneous engrams is no longer possible, for the *last* link in the succession of inherited morphogeneous engrams has been ecphorised. We may call this engram w (engr). Its ecphory rouses mnemic excitation w (mn), the plastic reactions of which establish the morphological state $w(z)$. In this state and in the original excitation w (or) determined by it, the organism will remain until it dies. The organism is now morphogeneously stationary in the phase w, within which it passes only through cyclical changes.

A question here arises. At the beginning of phase w, immediately after the morphological state $w(z)$ has been reached, the ordinary homophony holds good between the mnemic excitation w (mn) and the original excitation w (or). The latter excitation lasts, of course, as long as the morphological state w (z) lasts. Can the same thing be said of the mnemic excitation w (mn)? It might be assumed that when the entire morphogeneous succession of mnemic excitations had been completed, the last link would gradually disappear. But the assumption is a fallacious one, for the presence of the original excitation w (or) must act ecphorically on the mnemic excitation w (mn). The surest evidence for the permanence of the homophony $H \dfrac{w \ (or)}{w \ (mn)}$ is adduced by the continuance of reactions peculiar to this homophony. In perfect homophony these reactions naturally do not appear, but in imperfect homophony they are fairly constant, though with varying results according to the species. These reactions, now so familiar to us, either remove the incongruity or diminish it. If on the establishment of homophony it is a case of the re-building up of parts which have been experimentally removed or otherwise lost, the reactions are usually described as regeneration. Many biologists apply the term " regeneration " only to fully developed organisms. Corresponding phenomena in earlier developmental stages are labelled with other terms. The point is that they regard as fully developed those states where the tempo of the ontogenetic development has indeed become very much retarded, but where the succession of morphogeneous engrams has not yet been finally completed. The expression " fully developed state " is in this connection used in a very loose and arbitrary manner.

For this reason, and also because no real necessity seems to exist for distinguishing the processes of regeneration in the different ontogenetic phases, we refrain from giving a separate definition, and content ourselves by describing all these reactions as regeneration.

In the next chapter we shall deal more fully with the restriction of the generative capacity in the latter stages of life. For the moment it suffices to point out that the undoubted presence of the generative capacity in the latest stages of existence must, in spite of all restrictions, be regarded as a reaction proving the efficacy of the morphogeneous mnemic homophony, and, consequently, the existence of a morphogeneous mnemic excitation in all the stages of life.

We mentioned a state which one might feel justified in terming "fully developed," in so far as no new ecphory of inherited morphogeneous engrams occurs after it has been reached. But this state does not involve the cessation of every morphogeneous course. The course which then begins, or, as it may be, continues, is a cyclic one with regularly recurring phases, which manifest a certain dependence on the periodicity of sidereal phenomena, diurnal recurrences, and seasonal changes, and even, as in the case of the Palolo worm, on the phases of the moon. The periodic maturation of male and female germ-products, which is generally accompanied by morphogenetic processes manifested in the appearance of various secondary sexual characters, belongs to this category. Plants also show us similar cyclic morphogenetic processes in connection with the diurnal period, and especially with the annual period. That these cycles are not exclusively induced and regulated by the periodic change of the external conditions, but that an equal share in these adjustments belongs to mnemic processes, may easily be proved by the fact that the organic periodicity continues for some time after the periodic change of the external conditions has been eliminated by the cultivation of the respective organisms under artificial conditions.

On page 54 we show how the genesis of "chronogeneous" ecphory must be conceived. Under normal circumstances the ecphoric action of the periodically changing external conditions is added to this chrono·geneous ecphory. In certain plants, difficult or impossible to force, the latter factor acts far more powerfully than the former, but in others the case is reversed.

Further exposition is here unnecessary. Still, it has been useful to refer again briefly to those cyclic processes which frequently warp ontogeny proper and survive it in organisms of limited growth, in regard to which it might be perhaps permissible to speak of a " fully developed " state.

CHAPTER XI

ENGRAM LOCALISATION AND REGENERATION

DEALING with the localisation of inherited engrams, (p. 116), we concluded that the entire inherited engram-stock of each individuality-phase, whether this is initiated sexually or parthenogenetically, is to be found within the limits of a cell. It is most probable that the engram-stock may be encompassed by something smaller than the cell or even the nucleus of the cell. We called the most minute morphological unit encircling it a mnemic protomer, but made no attempt at any precise morphological delineation of this unit. We also found that in the later course of an individuality-phase, when the plant or animal has become multi-cellular, fragments cut from any part of the organism seem in many cases to be in possession of the entire inherited engram-stock.

But at the beginning of Chapter V we saw that the regenerative faculty, even in forms especially capable of regeneration, such as Planaria and Hydra, diminishes towards the end of the ontogenesis as compared with its strength at the beginning. In Planaria this diminution of regenerative power is evinced by the fact that portions from the extremities of either front or sides, devoid of nervous structure, cannot regenerate the entire individual, although sections from the rest of the body may do so. In Hydra, any section of more than $\frac{1}{6}$ mm. diameter may regenerate the entire Hydra, but sections of the tentacles, however large, lack regenerative power. The restriction of the regenerative faculty observed in these two cases is very slight, but in other forms it is more pronounced. Many of the higher animals such as the warm-blooded Vertebrata, possess, even when fully developed, only a very limited capacity for the regeneration of entire organs, although regeneration of tissue may still take place in them to a great extent.

This raises the question whether this restrictive power of regeneration and regulation is based on any specific change in the localisation of the mnemic properties of the organism, or whether it can be traced to changes which occur during the ontogenesis.

The discussion of the problem of the localisation of the inherited Mneme is reserved for a sequel to this book, where it will be treated on broad general lines. Here it is only necessary to show that facts, even those representative of the most striking restrictions of the capacity for regeneration and regulation during ontogenesis, do not clash with our conception that each living cell, nay, each mnemic protomer, from whatever part of the developing or fully developed organism it may have been taken, is in possession of the entire inherited engram-stock.

We may at once rule out those cases of restricted regeneration and regulation, where the regeneration is tardily effected by part of an organism, but where, nevertheless, regeneration does occur. In regard to those cases, there can be no doubt that the fragment of the organism has been in possession of the whole body of inherited engrams ; otherwise, it would not have been able to replace the entire organism with all its morphological and physiological properties. Very belated regulations and regenerations occur frequently with fragments of eggs or in the early developmental stages of Echinoderms and Amphibia, while with corresponding fragments of Medusæ, Amphioxus, or Teleostei, regulative adjustment is immediate. In this connection should be mentioned cases of regeneration in fully developed animals, such as those observed by Przibram among the Crustacea—*Portunus, Porcellana, Galathea*, etc.—where an imperfectly regenerated third maxilliped was replaced after each shedding by an increasingly improved new formation.

These cases indisputably prove the presence of the entire inherited engram-stock in the parts capable of regulation.

They are of special interest in view of the problems with which at the moment we are concerned, in so far as they show how, even in the presence of the whole body of inherited engrams, interference and disturbances may so affect the morphogenetic adjusting processes that the regeneration and regulation become perfected only after great delay. If by reason of still greater obstacles, regulation or regeneration does not follow, it would be a hasty inference to say that this was due to mnemic deficiency

If we define the processes of regeneration and regulation as the sum total of plastic reactions which at homophony effect the removal of incongruity, then the entire absence, or the imperfection, of the regenerative process may as probably be caused by a retardation or incapacitation of the plastic reactions as by the absence of homophony through a deficiency of the corresponding engram-complexes.

Take the case of a pair of Weaver birds in captivity, who give no evidence of their weaving capacity. It is clear that we cannot infer the extinction or congenital absence of this capacity unless we are sure that the birds have all the needful material for nest-weaving at their disposal, and that the necessary preliminary conditions, such as sufficient feeding, absence of disturbance, and suitable space, have also been fulfilled.

Absence of regeneration and regulation implies in most cases simply the absence or insufficiency of definite material for the neoplastic activity of the organism. In other cases, the decrease of the regenerative capacity coincides with the decrease of the neoplastic capacities of the organism in general, that is, with a decrease of plastic capacity in which mnemic processes do not come into play at all. Neither do these cases indicate a deficiency of inherited engrams, or, as we may put it, they cannot be quoted as furnishing evidence for a localisation of the inherited engram-stock. After examining them, we shall

14

have to see whether anything at all remains that cannot be explained without the assumption of such localisation.

As we have seen, the absence or insufficiency of definite building material, which in certain circumstances can prevent regeneration or regulation, makes itself chiefly felt in the initial stages of the various individuality phases. For we note that the material for its life journey which an organism receives from its parent is most frequently so well packed and arranged that everything is close at hand for the later processes of differentiation. A master-builder would never dream of mixing up all his materials indiscriminately before he began to build. Boveri acutely observes that "the development is simplified, if already in the ovum the different substances are so allocated that each primitive organ directly receives just those materials which are most serviceable for the process of its further differentiation." Boveri discovered in the ovum of the sea-urchin *Strongylocentrotus lividus* a directly visible stratification of the egg-plasm in at least three separate zones. Granted normal development, one of them serves for the formation of the mesenchyma, the second for the formation of the archenteron, the other becomes the ectoderm. An equally distinct allocation of material can be discerned in the eggs of Annelida, such as Nereis, Myzostoma, and Lanice ; and of Mollusca, such as Dentalium, Patella, and Ilyanassa. In them we can see, in normal development, different material used definitely for plastic reactions and the like. The removal of certain parts is, at the early stages of development, often equivalent to the elimination of specific material which is present nowhere else in the organism and which is essential for bodily growth. We need not be surprised, therefore, that such a removal either makes definite plastic reactions impossible, or delays them until the metabolic processes of the organism have reproduced the necessary material. In many instances, however, it is only the fully developed maternal organism that is capable of the reproduction of this material. For example, in the snail Ilyanassa, the formation of the mesoderm, according to Crampton, depends on the so-called vitelline lobe. If one separates this lobe from the egg· before segmentation begins or soon after, the mesoderm is not formed. In all these cases we see not so much a localisation of dispositions as a *localisation of the necessary material* for these dispositions—Wilson's "cytoplasmic localisation." It is not a case of the *localisation of the directing forces, that is, of the inherited engram-stock*. We are supported in this view by H. Driesch, who, in respect of a special case occurring in Echinoidea, writes : " When animals at their eighth and sixteenth cleavage stages fail to gastrulate—for Boveri's researches permit us to state this—this apparently results from a certain lack in their material means, and not, as I previously assumed, from some deficiency in their regulating capacity."

It is not at all difficult in a great number of cases, described by some as " the restriction of the prospective potentiality," to trace the decrease of the regenerating and regulating capacity of the parts to a localisation of the material used in the building up of the body. In many cases this localisation, which may consist of a specific plasmatic distribution or stratification, cannot be ocularly demonstrated, but this does not at all justify us in denying its actuality, and in ascribing the decrease of the capacity for regulation simply to a localisation of the inherited engrams. We are inclined to agree with Boveri, when he says :—" We can with assurance say that this stratification exists in all echinoderm-eggs of the same cleavage type, although we are not able to see a trace of it. This naturally suggests the idea that in the egg of Strongylocentrotus, a still finer stratification exists than those three zones which we are able to distinguish."

That this applies, *mutatis mutandis*, also to the Ctenophora seems to me indisputable, if we are to judge by the experimental data already to hand, although the ocular evidence of such stratification has not yet been given. A happy chance may reveal it to us some day. In any case, even if the localisation of what we have called the building material is questioned, no reason exists for assuming that the lack of the regulating capacity in these forms points to a regional allocation of the inherited engram-stock.

We have already noted that the majority of those cases where defective or insufficient building material is undoubtedly responsible for the lack of the power of regeneration or regulation occur mostly in the very early stages of ontogenesis. But similar cases are found during the intermediate stages of development, and also among fully matured organisms, where one expects not merely the regeneration of one part or organ by the whole, but the regeneration of the whole creature by a part. In the case of Hydra, it has been found that a dissevered tentacle is unable to regenerate the entire animal. Here the case may be one of the lack in the tentacle of certain constructive materials essential for the building up of the entire animal. The isolated tentacle, unfitted to absorb nutrition, is unable to produce the material necessary for regeneration. But in the great majority of relevant cases it is only a question of the regeneration of a small part or a single organ (limb, eye, etc.), by an organism otherwise intact. In those cases the failure to regenerate can hardly be traced to the lack of definite building material. For it is hardly conceivable that an organ, otherwise uninjured and with its functions in perfect working order, should not be able to produce the material necessary for the purpose of regeneration.

The problem then may be stated thus. In all Metazoa, the regenerative capacity, varying of course according to the species, undoubtedly decreases with the advancing age of the individual. This decrease cannot be traced to the lack of definite building material. Are we justified in inferring from this mere decrease of regenerative power a regional allocation of the inherited engram-stock, an allocation which becomes increasingly specific as ontogenesis advances ? I think we can answer this question decidedly in the negative, even although we are not yet in a position to enumerate all the factors which make during the course of the individual life for the diminution of the regenerating capacity. For the decrease of the regenerating capacity of a specific organ is not in any definite relation either to the development of the organ or to the differentiation of its tissues. The researches by Barfurth have shown us that one tadpole was able to regenerate only extremities—limbs and tail—that had just begun to emerge, while other individuals of the same species with greater regenerative power were able to replace more highly differentiated extremities. Spallanzani found that even young frogs and toads were capable of re-growing limbs that had been removed. But these were exceptional cases. It is clear that the power of regenerating the extremities is exhausted in individuals of the same species at different times, and that this follows without any constant regard to the differentiation of the tissues in the organ specifically concerned. A trout-embryo is able before absorption of the vitelline sac to regenerate the already well-developed and differentiated tail with anus and the so-called urethra; but a little later, when the vitelline sac has been absorbed, it is no longer capable of doing so.

With the Anura, the power to regenerate extremities ceases in the fully developed state; but with the Urodela, this capacity is retained by the sexually mature and fully grown animal. Among the more highly differentiated forms of the Salamandrina we meet with a considerable restriction of this capacity. Formerly, it was thought that in the fully developed *Salamandrina perspecillata*, the power of regeneration was entirely absent. But this is not so. Kammerer discovered (*Z. f. Ph.*, vol. xix, 1905)[1] that the larvæ and young ones of this species required a much longer time for the regeneration of the legs and tails than all the other Urodele larvæ examined for this purpose; and that in the adult *Salamandrina perspicillata* the regeneration proceeded with extraordinary slowness, but that regeneration did take place.

Taking the Urodela, whose regenerating capacity is well developed, and comparing the behaviour of individuals

[1] *Zentralblatt für Physiologie.*

at different ages, we generally find a retardation of the
regenerative processes commensurate with the age. In
order to furnish reliable data, I made a number of experiments, the detailed results of which need not here
be given.   It is sufficient for our present purposes to note
that larvæ of *Triton alpestris*, 25 to 32 mm. in length,
and in possession of fully developed extremities, required
on the average four weeks for the regeneration of an arm
with the distinct formation of all the four fingers ; while
fully developed animals, kept under the same conditions,
required on the average seven and a half weeks to reach
the same stage.   To re-establish the normal relativity
of size took five weeks with the larvæ, and four to five
months with the fully developed animals.   Kammerer in
his recently published essay sets out similar results.
The essay is of special value to us because it comprehensively deals with the dependence of the regenerating
capacity of Amphibia larvæ on age, developmental stage,
and specific size.   He also notes that " the Urodela
regenerate bodily parts capable of regeneration more
slowly in the adult state than in the larval stage."

We thus have a factor retarding the processes of regeneration, whose power increases with advancing age.
We shall not at the moment examine the nature of this
factor, but content ourselves with the assertion that it
has nothing to do with a mnemic defect.   But we may
ask whether this factor, which so often retards the process
of regeneration, is identical with that which in other
forms counteracts it entirely and causes it to disappear ?
Restricting our observations to the group of Siredon,
Triton, Salamandrina, and Anura, the question may
without hesitation be answered in the affirmative.   And
if, on further survey, we meet with similar instances in
other animal groups, we shall not hesitate to draw the
same conclusion, without thereby committing ourselves
to the position that the obstruction and entire inhibition
of regeneration must always and under all conditions be
traced to one and the same fundamental cause.

It is not our present task to discover the causes of

the decrease of the regenerative capacity during the individual life. We have only to prove that the decrease does not depend on a regional distribution of the inherited engrams. But I should like to say that, in my view, the decrease of the power of regeneration does seem to rest partly on a gradual decrease of the capacity to fulfil the larger neoplastic functions, as may be observed in the course of the individual life, particularly in organisms of limited growth. The more highly organised and the more complex the organism, the more this becomes apparent. It reaches its extreme manifestation in the remarkable fact that in the genus Homo the female becomes incapable, towards the middle of her normal individual life, of fulfilling any longer one of the cardinal functions of the organism, namely, the production of germ-cells. In like manner pathological neoplastic re-actions, such as tumours, are impeded concomitantly with advancing age until they finally cease altogether. It is well known that a senile carcinoma grows very slowly.

It may be that some will point to the fact that the presence of a central nervous system and the undisturbed transmission of nervous energy are necessary to certain regenerative processes, and thereby infer, since certain inherited engrams are deposited in the central nervous system during the course of ontogenesis, that on the re-moval of these organs the engrams also disappear, and with them the possibility of specific processes of regeneration.

This position is based on a false conception of the place the central nervous system occupies in relation to the plastic reactions of the other tissues. In the first place, experiments bearing on this problem seem to have definitely established that in the early developmental stages all the organs develop independently of the already existing central nervous system, and that they display, where necessary, regenerative capacity. The reader is referred to the experiments by Loeb, Raffaele, Harrison, Barfurth, and Rubin, and to the interesting work on anencephalous amyelous frog larvæ, by Schaper, which is confirmed by Goldstein. Even the muscular system

develops and regenerates in these early stages independently of the central nervous system and the spinal
ganglia, as experiments by Harrison, Schaper, and Goldstein demonstrate. In the later stages of development
certain modifications are effected, as Rubin (*Archiv. f.
Entwicklungsmech,* vol. xvi, p. 71, 1903), clearly has shown.
He points out that "the elimination of the nervous
system in *Siredon pisciformis* does not prevent the timely
start and the first stage of regeneration," but that, "later,
the defective innervation, or the fact of the missing
function, expresses itself in an increasing retardation of
regenerative processes until ultimately the power to
regenerate ceases." We must add to this that the arrest
of regeneration in later stages, on the elimination of
nervous influence, expresses itself not simply in the size
of the regenerated limbs and organs, but also in the
fact that the various tissues are affected in very different
degrees. Rubin discovered that "the elimination of
the influence of the nervous system was most apparent
in the muscular system. Here regeneration stopped
completely between the tenth and the twelfth day, before
the formation of specific muscular substance had even
begun." In order to appreciate the significance of this,
we have to ask how the muscular apparatus, on elimination
of all nervous influence, behaves in an organ which is
not stimulated to regenerate by some further interference ? The answer is that the muscular apparatus becomes
atrophied. Whether this is merely an atrophy of muscular
power—a view which might be very well defended in
spite of conflicting arguments—or whether in the atrophy
the lack of the "trophic" action of the nervous system
also plays a part, is a question the answer to which would
lead us too far away from our main argument, and, as
far as the present problems are concerned, is of no fundamental importance. The fact itself, however, suffices
to explain why a paralysed muscular apparatus is in-
capacitated from regeneration. It is simply because its
energetic condition has been radically changed by the
severance of its nerves, and an abnormal state created.

If anything is remarkable here, it is surely not the cessation of regeneration, but the fact that, as Rubin notes, regeneration can be observed at all in the initial stages in such a muscular apparatus.

According to Rubin's investigations, in the other tissues of a regeneration-stump, where the nervous influence was eliminated by the cutting through of the nerves, regenerative phemonena ceased, although relatively later than in the muscular apparatus. The growth of the skin, however, continued until the whole regeneration-cone was covered, but further growth in thickness did not take place. The growth of the connective tissue was but slight. A very much restricted regeneration of the cartilage commenced when regeneration of the muscular apparatus had already ceased. In the vascular system, the capillary vessels formed during the first ten days were enlarged and became filled with blood. There was no further formation of vascular capillaries.

In this case, that which gradually impaired the regenerative power of the remaining tissues was not the absence of the nervous influence, but most probably the general disturbance of the energetic condition caused by the cessation of muscular regeneration.

The impossibility of muscular regeneration precludes at the outset the removal of the incongruity in the homophony, which in these cases would occur only if the complicated regenerative processes could be carried out by the harmonious co-operation of all parts. The reactions tending towards the removal of the incongruity cease on account of the incompleteness of the co-operation. That the absence of nervous influence does not seriously affect the regeneration of slight defects in this or that tissue is proved by numerous observations and experiments. Wounds of various kinds heal as well in limbs that are deprived of nervous influence as in those with nerves intact. In bone fractures, for example, an equally perfect regeneration takes place in paralysed as in non-paralysed extremities.

I may briefly mention the well-known experiments

by Herbst on Crustacea, which demonstrated that regeneration of the eye takes place only when the optic
ganglia of the amputated eye are allowed to remain.
It appears to me that more has been read into these
highly interesting experiments than is actually contained
in them. Embryology teaches us that, at the development of the paired, composite eyes of the Crustacea, the
eye proper and the ganglion opticum emanate from a
common ectodermal growth. It follows that to extirpate
the coherent whole, both the eye and the ganglion opticum
must be removed. It is quite unimportant that this
latter part of the optic organ establishes in some forms
by secondary processes of growth a somewhat separate
position, thus presenting itself to the untrained observer
as something independent. It is now one of the best
known data of regeneration that an organ is regenerated
the more readily if parts of it are left behind in the
organism, than if the whole is radically removed. In
the latter case, in forms with only a moderate power
of regeneration, no regeneration whatever takes place.
Thus, according to Philippeaux, the Urodela, whose
regenerative capacity is comparatively great, regenerate
their extremities only if parts at least of the scapula or
of the pelvis have been allowed to remain in the body.
Minor defects in the eye may be remedied by regeneration,
but the Urodela are unable to regenerate the whole ball.
Throughout, the general rule holds good that the regenerative capacity, especially of the higher animals, becomes
more and more restricted as their life proceeds. That
the Crustacea are able to regenerate even a part of the
optic organ is an imposing performance compared with
those possible to other highly organised animals. That
they cannot regenerate the radically extirpated eye, that
is, the eye with the ganglion opticum ontogenetically
belonging to it, only proves that their regenerating
capacity has its limits ; it does not prove that the ganglion,
which is, of course, connected with the central nervous
system, exerts any specific formative influence. This is
especially important, as during these experiments the

central nervous system proper—the brain—was left intact and in function. Herbst has proved that a great number of Crustacea can regenerate the organ if the eye is not radically extirpated, that is, if the ganglion opticum is allowed to remain ; but that they never do so if both eye and ganglion opticum are removed. In this case of incapacity to regenerate the eye, Herbst noted that an antennæ-like organ sometimes sprouted from the seat of amputation.

Similar "heteromorphoses" have been not seldom observed in Crustacea and Arthropoda. In such cases a limb may be replaced by one less differentiated. This is typical where the segment and the new formation are in close proximity. In other cases, the replacing formations are in their arrangement more intricately involved. At some future time I shall try to show in a continuation of the *Mneme* that these apparently enigmatic phemonena are also open to explanation, and that they conform to general laws. The discussion of the subject here would lead us too far away from our main purpose, but I should like to make clear that, so far as these cases are concerned, I as little deny a definite influence of the nervous system as in those instances where the tempo of the regeneration is strikingly retarded by the cutting of the nerves. The point is that these cases do not prove that the nervous system exercises any "specific formative" influence.

Przibram, in the second volume of his *Experimentalzoologie*, gives an exhaustive account of the data relevant to regeneration. It is interesting to note that on page 224 he presents a conclusion which closely harmonises with my own. Here are his words :—" If we keep in view the fact that, on the one hand, regeneration is accomplished only by parts capable of growth, and that, on the other hand, the regenerated parts develop out of the growing tissues themselves, it is obvious that the favourable influence of the nerves must be regarded as simply stimulating growth, and not as a specific formative force. Among the mammals, as is well known, the promotion of growth by the influence of the nerves is a common occurrence. Also during the heterochely of the Crustacea it occurs in a noteworthy manner."

In this present chapter I have tried to show first, that the restrictions of the faculty of regeneration, which appear in the course of ontogenesis, are not to be explained by a regional allocation of the inherited engram-stock ; and that, secondly, the facts of regeneration, from which many authors infer a specific creative or formative influence by parts of the nervous system, may be interpreted quite differently.

We feel, therefore, justified in assuming that each cell, nay, each mnemic protomer, is in possession of the entire inherited engram-stock of the respective organism. On the other hand, in order to avoid misunderstanding, I wish to reiterate that I regard the *ecphory* of each inherited, as well as of each individually acquired, engram as localised, that is, as bound up with specific conditions of environment.

The reaction of pecking at grains and other small objects, which newly hatched chickens manifest, must be understood as evidence of the ecphory of an inherited engram. But this ecphory is possible only where vision is unimpaired. There must be at least one intact eye with its nervous connections. The photic stimulus of the grain liberates in the irritable substance of the retina an excitation which, by conduction, releases in other parts of the central nervous system another excitation which acts ecphorically in its own specific area. But this *localisation of the ecphory*—the existence of an area proper of an *ecphoric* stimulation, whence it radiates through the remainder of the organism—has nothing to do with a regional allocation of the inherited engrams. The predominating position in ecphory of the "area proper" is explained quite simply by the fact that the state required for the ecphory of the energetic condition is *here* first realised, and this state cannot become realised at all if the area proper is either missing or badly damaged.

CHAPTER XII

ENGRAM DICHOTOMY IN ONTOGENESIS

HERE and there in our considerations (pp. III, 166, 188) we have been confronted with the fact that the engram-successions, which usually are characterised by an unbroken, unilinear, and non-reversible arrangement, may occasionally split into dichotomies. Engram dichotomies may be divided into two classes, namely, those whose branches can be ecphorised simultaneously, and those whose branches can only be ecphorised alternatively. The former are of frequent occurrence in ontogenetic engram-successions (see p. 187, on the grouping of engrams during egg-segmentation), but it is with the latter in their relation to ontogenetic engram-lines that we are just now chiefly concerned. The reader will remember that we set out in diagrammatic form the structure of an alternative dichotomy, taking as our illustration the two versions of the line from the *Rubáiyát* of Omar Khayyam—

The Sultan's Turret ⟨ in a Noose of Light.
with a Shaft of Light.

In its essential points this diagram is valid for all alternative dichotomies, including those that determine plastic reactions. We refrain at this point from enquiring into the *modes of genesis* of alternative dichotomies in ontogenesis. We shall here content ourselves with the examination of those cases in which the choice of alternative is prompted by external influences, and defer until the next chapter the analysis of those dichotomies which are generated by cross-breeding.

Take first the case of the honey bee, *Apis mellifica*. It is well known that in regard to the females there are two possibilities in the development of the fertilised bee-ovum. Either a sexually mature queen emerges, or an imperfect female worker. These forms differ strikingly from each other in their structure and in their instincts. In the worker the genital organs are not fully developed, but compensation is given in a number of positive characteristics, among which are the gathering apparatus, the pollen baskets and bristles on the hind legs, and the wax pockets on the medial abdominal keel. In the queen, however, we find, with a full development of the genital organs, an absence of the characteristics just mentioned. Further, there is a reduced development of the trunk, of the masticatory organs, of the salivary glands, and of the wings. The shape of the sting differs from that of the worker. The queen is also deficient in the instincts connected with the rearing of offspring, the building, feeding, and food-gathering instincts. She has become simply an egg-laying machine. That is, the physical and dynamical qualities, which we find united in the female solitary bee, have in the case of social bees been apportioned to two forms of female, the queen and the worker, sharply distinguished according to the perfect or imperfect development of the genital organs.

If now we note the ontogenesis of these two forms, we find that each fertilised egg is capable, according to circumstances, of producing either a queen or a worker. It has long been known that a grub belonging to a queen-cell, if fed on worker's, that is, unmasticated food, will develop into a worker ; and vice versa, a worker-grub, if fed on queen's food, will develop into a queen. The point is that the kind of food determines the nature of the reproductive system.

It takes from three to four days for the egg of the honey-bee to hatch. On the emergence of the grub, it is fed by the workers for six days. Then follows the sealing of the cells by the nursing workers, the spinning of a chrysalis-case by the grub, a longer or shorter period of rest and pupation, and finally, the emergence of the imago. Klein has demonstrated experimentally, and v. Buttel-Reepen has confirmed his conclusions that, if a grub is fed during the first thirty-six hours of its development with worker's food, and then afterwards with queen's food (we shall refer later to the specific chemical composition of the foods), the short and early period of feeding on worker's food does not produce any marked change, that is, there is no ecphory of the " worker-engram," but the development is typical of that of a queen. It turns out differently, however, if the time in which the grub is fed with worker's food is increased by one or two days. We then get a queen with unmistakable signs of worker-characteristics. Finally, grubs which have been four and a half days in workers' cells and fed during that time on worker's food, being then exposed to different conditions, and submitted to the influence of queen's food for the short remaining time of the larval stage, show marked characteristics of both worker and queen.

Klein took worker-grubs of twelve to thirty-six hours' old, fed them for two days with queen's food, and for the succeeding day or day and a half with worker's food, with the result that he obtained workers slightly modified by queen-characteristics.

These experiments show that the ecphory of either of the two engram-branches is influenced by the external stimuli of nutrition. The accompanying diagram may serve to illustrate the case.

It is assumed in the diagram that the dichotomy commencing in phase four of the respective engram-complexes is of such a kind that the possibility of transition from one branch to the other remains until phase 9, and is only excluded from phase 10 onwards. Such an oscillation of the ecphory between two branches or even the simultaneous ecphory of parts of both branches manifests itself in *mixed reactions.* In the case of the honey-bee, we obtain under such conditions "transition-animals," that is, queen-bees with characters of workers, or workers with characters of queens. The reader is referred to the writings of Klein and v. Buttel-Reepen, in which the experiments on bees are fully described and illustrated. Similar mixed forms are possible in the case of ants also, as presently we shall see.

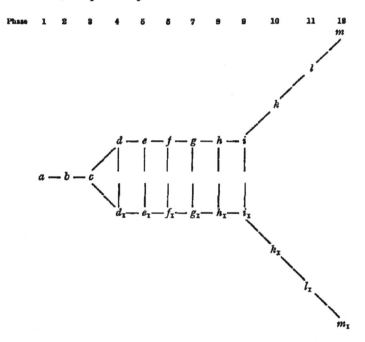

Something should be said on the nature of the stimulation, which determines the initiation of the alternative. In the case of the honey-bee, the result depends entirely on the quality of the food supplied. There can be no doubt that the stimuli in question are chemical. According to Planta, the queen's food as compared with that of the worker's is, on the average, 5 per cent. richer in albumen and 7 per cent. richer in fat, but 11 per cent.

poorer in sugar substance. It is not difficult to imagine, however, that these quantitative variations are not the sole determining factor, but that an admixture of specific ingredients, inclusive perhaps of certain excretive products of the nursing-bees, represents the ecphoric stimulus for this or that dichotomy of the engram.

In the case of the ant where, according to Janet and Wheeler, a qualitative apportionment of the nourishment is hardly possible, it is most probable that the dichotomy depends entirely on the admixture of such specific ingredients. Ants are similar to bees in this respect. Regarding them, we are not as yet in possession of such complete experimental data as in the case of bees. We have to rely more on inferences from comparative observations and experiments. These, however, are in perfect harmony with the experiments obtained with bees.

In 1874, Forel, dealing with various species of ants, described forms intermediate between females and workers. Since then, Wasmann has given a sufficient explanation of the appearance in overwhelming numbers in certain nests of the so-called pseudogynes, which are intermediate forms.

He has proved by observations extending over many years that in these cases the appearance of the pseudogynes is casually connected with the presence of certain ant-guests, the Lomechusa, Xenodus, and Atemeles. These beetles, tolerated by both the Formica and the Myrmica, decimate the eggs and larvæ of their hosts. A sudden and appreciable reduction in the development of the worker generation takes place. The ants thereupon try to remedy the deficiency by rearing into workers all the remaining larvæ of the immediately preceding generation originally destined for queens. Viehmeyer was able to confirm this fact by a control-experiment. He placed in a non-infected nest a queen which, living in a colony infested with Lomechusa, had produced pseudogynes for four years. From that hour the pseudogynes disappeared from the progeny of this female, only pure full females and pure workers being produced.

There is one difficulty of which mention should be

15

made. With bees and ants, as also with termites, these cases always refer to that one branch of the dichotomy which leads to the development of individuals restricted as to their generative capacity. Are we to be allowed to regard this branch as a succession of *inherited* engrams, despite the fact that the individuals in which the engrams are aroused into activity appear to be excluded from the reproductive group of the species ? The answer would have to be in the negative for all those cases where we had to assume that the dimorphism or polymorphism had become developed only *after* the sterility of the branch had set in.

But Herbert Spencer has already made out a strong case in favour of the assumption that the *reversed* temporal relation has ruled for the main forkings of the branches.

The point is illustrated very clearly by reference to the honey-bees, where, as already mentioned, most of the distinctive anatomical characteristics of the queen and of the workers are in the case of the more simply organised humble-bees united in the one individual. The same thing holds good in regard to the instincts. Buttel-Reepen, referring to the difference in instinct between the queen and worker forms, says that " *the main change takes place in the queen*, who sinks down from her high position as universal provider, loses all her peculiar instincts, and becomes simply an egg-laying machine. *The workers, however, retain nearly all the instincts of their previous female nature*, such as the building, feeding or gathering instincts, etc , and lose only the sexual instinct, in place of which they gain what has been called the instinct of attachment to the hive-mother, which involves the specific nutrition of the latter." Of course, it cannot be denied that, besides the retention of already existing characteristics, new organic properties and instincts have also been acquired in the presumably sterile branch. But this offers no insuperable difficulty to our conception, since the worker caste is by no means entirely excluded from the reproductive circle of the species. As early as 1874 Forel reported cases of egg-laying by ant-workers, and his observations have since been confirmed by Lubbock, Wasmann, Viehmeyer, Tanner, Reichenbach, Wheeler, Miss Fielde, and others. Silvestri found the same thing among the workers of the termites, and observations by Grassi prove that the termite soldiers lay eggs. Escherich, who has studied most closely the biology of the termites, has no doubt that further positive evidence of the kind indicated will accumulate as soon as these problems are definitely attacked. Finally, we have to note in regard to bees that among the workers absolute sterility is found only in one species of honeybee, *Apis mellifica*, and even of this species it is said that among the Egyptian variety (*Apis mellifica fasciata*) egg-laying workers are frequently found with the queen in the hive. Among other varieties of honey-bee, whose workers do not normally produce eggs, the absence of a queen and of a brood capable of reproduction means that eggs which develop parthenogenetically are laid by the workers. From all this it follows that among the social insects the workers are not entirely excluded from the reproductive circle, and that even in the extreme case of the honey-bee, where the specialisation of the worker seems complete, the exclusion, especially with certain varieties, is by no means absolute.

Up to now we have considered alternative dichotomies where both branches are equivalent, in that both under the normal conditions of life reach ecphory either in this or in that individual of the species in question. In these cases the ecphory of this or that branch depends simply on the presence or the absence of a definite original stimulus.

Such dichotomies may be defined as being in equilibrium, and may be contrasted with those where the branches are not equivalent. In the latter case the ecphory normally takes place almost exclusively in the one succession branch, while in the other branch ecphory is realised by but a few individuals of the species, and then only under special conditions, which may be furnished by human agency.

The reader is referred to the example on page 168, where the dichotomy of successions of individually acquired engrams was explained by the example of a poem learned by heart in two versions. When there is quite a distinct break between the learning of the one version and the other, and when for some reason or other we prefer to use only the second version, this branch becomes in time the main path into which the ecphory naturally turns at the point of bifurcation. The other branch is still there, but a specially strong impulse is required to force the ecphory into its path. To these two succession-branches of individually acquired engrams correspond, in the case of inherited successions, the branch that was ordinarily used by our remote ancestors, and the branch that gradually was preferred by later generations. These dichotomous branches may fitly be described as "atavistic" and "recent." The former may be obsolete, but the point is that it still exists.

A word on Atavism or Reversion may not be out of place. It must at once be admitted that it is difficult, even impossible in many cases, to decide whether this or that ontogenetic abnormity—a word to be understood in its widest meaning—should be regarded as atavistic or not. The difficulty is especially great in cases where the ancestral line of the form is not at all or insufficiently known, or where we are entirely ignorant of that part of the line supposed to have possessed the presumably atavistic peculiarity as a normal characteristic. The inference that this abnormity is of an atavistic nature, and that consequently the unknown ancestor of the form showing the abnormity must have possessed this morphological character, is very often quite fallacious and hardly ever demonstrable. Critical caution is fully justified, but it betrays itself as prejudice when it represents the idea itself as a mere notion, vulnerable, problematical, and antiquated.

For an example, we may take the hornless cattle of Galloway and Suffolk. Although they have been without horns during the last hundred or hundred and fifty years, they are undoubtedly descended from a horned stock. Occasionally calves are born with loosely attached horns. The phenomenon may rightly be regarded as a case of atavism. The conclusion is equally valid in the case of the hornless South Down sheep, of whom male lambs with small horns are occasionally born. Sometimes the horns grow to their full size, but often they are simply attached in a loose way to the skin, from which in some cases they drop off altogether.

Many other examples of undoubted atavism might be given, but to be absolutely sure of our ground, it is essential that the ancestors whose characteristics reappear in this atavistic form should be known to have existed. A merely hypothetical construction is insufficient, but even where hypothesis is used, the case may be adequately strengthened to the point of conviction by arguments from comparative anatomy, from embryology, and from general biology.

We regard the reappearance of horns in a stock of cattle or sheep that has been hornless for generations as an instance of the emergence of a character which for some reason or other has died down, but not out. Surely it is permissible to speak of such cases as illustrative of the dichotomy of engram-successions.

In the accompanying diagram, k, l, m, n signify the engram-complexes in their aspect as the sum-total of all the inherited engrams extant during the respective phase, minus the engrams connected with the horn development during the critical period when it is a question of horns or no horns. The engrams of horn development we denote by the engram succession α, β, γ, δ. We then obtain the following diagram :—

(Atavistic Branch)

$$(l + \alpha) - (m + \beta) - (n + \gamma) - o + \delta) -$$

$$k$$

$$\underline{\qquad\qquad} m \underline{\qquad} n \underline{\qquad} o \underline{\quad} -$$

(Recent Branch)

A strongly pronounced dichotomy of the engram-successions can be seen to exist. If now a plastic or motor acquisition is refashioned, moulded into something new and not simply discarded, the diagram shows it in this way :—

$$\begin{array}{c} {}^{\nearrow}(l + a) - (m + \beta) - (n + \gamma) - (o + \delta) - \\ k \\ {}_{\searrow}(l + a_{\mathrm{x}}) - (m + \beta_{\mathrm{x}}) - (n + \gamma_{\mathrm{x}}) - (o + \delta_{\mathrm{x}}) - \end{array}$$

A series of special cases may be regarded as definite examples of the first-mentioned group, where we are concerned with the reappearance of characters which in the later generations have not usually attained development. There are cases in which such an arrested development affects not merely a few, but the great majority of the components of the engram-complexes, so that at a certain stage an almost complete arrest of development takes place. Apart from mere increase in bulk and one or two unimportant alterations, the organism remains permanently at this stage, and becomes sexually mature in this state. This phenomenon is called Neoteny. As we possess in this group significant and well-authenticated examples of atavism and of its experimental generation, it may be well to deal with it a little more fully.

We have already noted (p. 130) that the female and male of the Mexican salamander, *Amblystoma tigrinum*, usually become sexually mature in their larval (Axolotl) stage and remain permanently in this state, but from observations made in 1865 by Dumeril in the Paris Jardin d'Acclimatisation, we know that young salamanders go on land occasionally, lose their external gills, develop into true salamanders of the Genus Amblystoma, and are able to propagate in this state. The facts were fully elucidated by the thoroughgoing experimental researches of Miss M. von Chauvin, on the strength of which Weismann recognised the maturation in the axolotl-stage as a case of typical neoteny. Interpreting this neoteny in the light of our theory of engram-successions, we may construct the following diagram :—

Phase	1	2	6	3	4	5	7
Engram-complex	a —	b —	c —	d —	e —	f —	g —

Phase	8	9	10	11	12	13	14
Engram-complex	h —	i —	k —	l —	m —	n —	o —

Phase	15	16	17	18	19	20	—
Engram-complex	p —	q —	q_1 —	q_2 —	q_3 —	q_4 —	—

Let the letters signify the sum-total of the ontogenetic engram-complexes until the close of the transformation into the land species in phase 16 ; then only the engram-complexes q_1, q_2, q_3, q_4, in which the changes are quite unimportant, are successively associated with the engram-complex q. In order that this entire engram line may be ecphorised and so manifest itself in corresponding plastic and motor reactions, a special external impulse is required in the course of phase 10 (p. 131). This may be given in the lack of oxygen in the water inhabited by the larvæ, so that they are compelled to breathe not only with their gills, but also with their lungs. Or if this does not suffice, the removal of the animals from the water to damp moss or mud is usually effective. In the absence of either of these external impulses, no ecphory of the engram-complex l takes place at phase 10, and the state symbolised in the engram-complex k becomes altogether or approximately permanent. In the following diagram, this permanency is indicated in the fact that the annotations k_1, k_2, k_3, k_4, etc., denote simply the significant changes which occur after the ecphory of the engram-complex k.

In phase 10 the diagrammatic indication of the existent dichotomy is given by $k \Big\langle \begin{smallmatrix} l-\\ k_{\mathrm{I}}- \end{smallmatrix}$

But according to Miss von Chauvin's investigations, even when the animal in its development has entered on one branch of the dichotomy, the ecphory may, on the action of appropriate original stimuli, pass during the phases 11 to 17 from the neotenic to the atavistic branch. The process is indicated by the connecting lines between l and k_{I}, k_{2}, k_{3}, k_{4}, k_{5}, k_{6}, k_{7}. The comparative length of the lines may be taken to indicate that in these later stages the development passes from the neotenic to the atavistic branch, with difficulty increasing proportionately with age. The possibility of the movement from one line to the other ceases when the animals attain sexual maturity, a point we assume for both branches in phase 18, and marked by the affix $+\gamma$. In the atavistic line the index of the sexual maturity engram-complex is $q_{a+\gamma}$; in the neotenic branch the index is $k_{8+\gamma}$. According to Miss von Chauvin's observations, it would be possible to connect engram-complex $k_{\mathrm{2}}-k_{\mathrm{7}}$ with m, $k_{\mathrm{3}}-k_{\mathrm{7}}$ with n, and perhaps $k_{\mathrm{4}}-k_{\mathrm{7}}$ with o, just as l is connected with $k_{\mathrm{I}}-k_{\mathrm{7}}$. For although the ecphory may have gone some way along the atavistic branch, manifesting itself in a series of reactions, it is still possible in the case of the amblystoma for it to cross over again to the neotenic branch; although the process grows more and more difficult the further the ecphory has moved from the engram-complex l.

The reader should refer to the extremely interesting observations by Miss Marie von Chauvin in her original work of 1885, and read them in conjunction with the diagrams on page 224 of this book. In the atavistic branch we assume that the transformation into the terrestrial type is completed at phase 16, after the ecphory of the engram-complex q and on the initiation of the relative reactions. This terrestrial type not only differs from the aquatic type in the absence of gills and in the

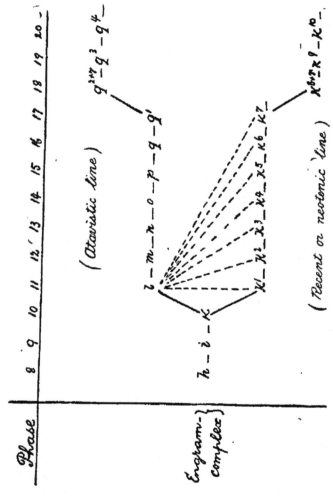

great development of the lungs, but also in the absence of the crests on back and tail, in the transformation of the rudder tail into a rounded tail, in the shape of the head and legs, and in the histological nature and pattern of the skin. When all these distinctive changes have been finally effected, a return to the neotenic form is altogether impossible.

Very interesting is the fact, observed by Miss von Chauvin, that sexual maturity is not attained so long as the ecphory of the engram-complexes is kept, so to speak, in the balance between the atavistic and neotenic branches, when neither the engram-complexes q–q_x–q_2 on the one side, nor the engram-complex k_8 on the other side, become ecphorised. Apparently the engram-component, the ecphory of which manifests itself by the appearance of sexual maturity, is associated with the engram-complexes at the ends of both the succession branches, and can only become ecphorised with either of these. Its ecphory is thus inhibited, if the course of the succession is in any way arrested.

It has been mentioned that Miss von Chauvin succeeded in obtaining, not only at phase II, but also at later phases, a passing of the ecphory from the atavistic to the neotenic branch—say from engram-complex n to k_2.

This change is first manifested by the arrest of the atavistic course of development, and then by the regression of the plastic and motor reactions which belong to the engram-complexes l, m, n, and which have already occurred. The stump-like gills are restored to their full size ; the crests, the shrivelling of which had already begun, stiffen and erect themselves ; the rudder tail forms itself anew and exercises its function, which had practically ceased during the atavistic course of development. After the ecphory of the engram-complex k_2, the incongruities arising in the homophony between the now dominating mnemic excitation-complex k_2 and the overpowered, but still-existent, original excitation-complex n slowly disappear.

In Amblystoma a relatively strong external influence is required to turn the course of ecphory from the neotenic to the atavistic branch. Without such an influence, the course of development in the majority of individuals whose parents belong to the neotenic branch follows simply in the same branch. But in those Salmandrinæ where a neotenic engram line has never developed the course takes place in the usual succession of engrams, and the engrams of the metamorphosis ($l-q$ in the diagram on page 233) are generally ecphorised, even when the external stimuli, which, as original stimuli, on the ancestors generated the engrams of the metamorphic phases, fall away. Thus the larvæ of *Salamandra maculosa* accomplish their metamorphosis—although late—even if they are kept in water rich in oxygen, and prevented by a wire netting from coming into contact with atmospheric air. The metamorphosed animals would become asphyxiated if they were not then allowed to emerge from the water (see von Chauvin, op. cit., 1885, p. 385). The force of the successive association is here stronger than the presence or absence of external stimuli. With the Tritons, however, an original—not a mnemic—neoteny may under special circumstances be produced, so that these newts are able to reach sexual maturity while they are still in the gill stage. By breeding the offspring of such individuals, it might be possible in the course of time to transform the original neoteny into a mnemic one ; but as the experiment has not yet been tried, we do not feel justified in assuming the result. Miss von Chauvin's observation, however, is a matter of fact (see p. 131), i.e. the offspring of those Amblystoma, which have grown sexually mature in the atavistic branch, turn into the atavistic branch under less external pressure, and pass much more quickly through the atavistic succession-line than do the offspring of neotenic parents. The freshening up of the atavistic engram line in the parents thus effects an easier ecphorability of this engram-succession in the progeny.

Quite recently a case has been experimentally discovered, which is remarkable for the fact that the branching off into the atavistic line, effected by external influences on the parents, exercises a particularly striking effect on the progeny in so far as, if not in the first generation, then all the more in the later generations, characteristics recur which had disappeared completely from the generation on which the experiments were made.

It is well known that most frogs and toads make for the water when they intend to generate their kind. While in the water, the male clasps the female, and during many hours of hard labour squeezes the eggs from her body by the pressure of the fore-limbs. As the eggs, small in size but great in number, pass out, they are fertilised by the male. The eggs are covered with a glutinous layer which immediately swells up in the water and forms a clear, round, somewhat elastic globe, slippery to the touch. The eggs, united into masses or into long bead-like strings, remain lying in the water without any further attention from the parents. After some time the larvæ emerge, provided with a rudder-like tail. They pass the tadpole period of their life in water.

A remarkable advance in parental care is shown by a European species of toad, *Alytes obstetricans*. With the Obstetric Toad, the fertilisation and deposition of the eggs take place on land. The number laid is far smaller than with other Batrachians, but the eggs are relatively large and light in colour, and contain more yolk. The male assists in the process, not only by squeezing the eggs out of the female, but also by pulling and pressing them with his hind legs. In the absence of water, the glutinous envelopes of the eggs do not swell up nor lose any of their stickiness. On the contrary, they adhere to the hind legs of the male, and, in consequence of his continual movement, the egg-strings are gradually wound about his legs. A few hours later the viscous envelope hardens and shrinks and loses its stickiness, but the spawn-strings remain closely adherent to the legs of the male. If the spawn-strings do not adhere at once, the animal tries by repeated twisting round to give them the right position. The eggs safely deposited, the male Alytes burrows into the damp earth until the larvæ emerge.

By external influences, Kammerer in a simple manner induced the Obstetric Toad to return to the more original

propagation habits of ordinary toads and frogs. He kept
the animals in a room at high temperature (25°–30° C.),
until they were induced by the unaccustomed heat to
cool themselves in the water-trough placed at their disposal. Here the male and female found each other, and
the clutching of the female by the male and the fertilisation
and deposition of eggs took place in the water. Under
these circumstances, the glutinous envelope, coming into
contact with the water, at once swelled up and lost its
stickiness. Thus it was rendered impossible for the
male to affix the spawn-strings to his hind legs. After a
number of fruitless attempts on the part of the male, the
egg-strings were left in the water to develop in the ordinary
way.

By the repetition of these experiments during several
mating periods, the animals gradually accustomed themselves to copulate in the water, and to deposit the eggs
without any attempt by the male to twist them round
his legs. Finally, when the coercion of the high temperature was entirely withdrawn, the creatures went through
the whole process of sexual intercourse in water of normal
temperature. The number of eggs, however, increased ;
the eggs themselves became smaller, poorer in yolk and
darker in colour, until at last the resemblance to the eggs
of the common frogs and toads was almost complete.

Now just as this modification of the propagating and
breeding instincts in the parents grows into a settled
norm, so it appears in their progeny. Kept at normal
temperature, the sexually matured offspring of such
parents make for the water at the approach of their first
breeding period, and deposit their strings of numerous
small and dark eggs without attempting to take any
further care of them. In the ontogenetic development
of this generation, and still more in the case of later
generations, reversions into the ontogeny of the more
primitive tailless amphibians take place ; but into that
we shall not here attempt to enter.

We shall concern ourselves simply with the appearance
of a group of characters which, in the fully developed

Alytes obstetricans, seemed to have entirely disappeared.
The males of frogs and toads copulating in water possess,
as secondary sexual characters, peculiar breeding pads,
which enlarge during each breeding season. These pads
are so characteristic that their location and configuration
are very important for purposes of classification. Their
biological value consists in making it possible for the male
to embrace the female in the water, and to this end a
morphologically very pronounced hypertrophy of the
forearm-musculature appears, in consequence of which
the shape of the limbs assumes a very characteristic,
inward curve. These secondary sexual characters are
absent in the normal male Alytes copulating on land.
At any rate, they were entirely absent in the many hundreds
of specimens used by Kammerer in the elaboration of
his experiments. When Kammerer coerced the animals,
in the manner already described, to copulate and to
deposit their eggs in water, no indication of these breeding
pads appeared even when this mode of propagation became
usual. No sign of the pads appeared in the first progeny
bred under those conditions. But in the second progeny,
roughnesses appeared on the thumb and on the thenar
eminence ; and in the third progeny, all the sexually
mature males were furnished with typical, grey-black
coloured pads on the upper side of the thumb and on the
thenar eminence. At the same time there was an ex-
cessive development of the musculature of the forearm,
and with this an inward curvature of the fore-limbs,
which meant that the palmar surface of the hand was
pressed on the ground nearer the median line.

Here we have exceptionally convincing evidence for the
fact that, under the influence of stimulations continued
through four generations, a branch of an engram-succession long obsolete is brought again into use. Primitive
morphogeneous engrams are reawakened, and their ecphory
is manifested in new reactions. Morphologically, the
case is one of the reappearance of an atavistic character ;
viewed as the manifestation of instinct, it is an
instance of the substitution of the neotenic obstetric

instinct by the atavistic one of copulation and the deposition of eggs in water.

In conclusion, the attention of the reader is directed to the fact that, in all cases quoted in this chapter, the course of the ontogenetic alternative depends entirely and without exception on the strength of *external influences*. These are open to close analysis, whether the course of the ontogeny is in the direction of dimorphism or polymorphism, of neoteny or atavism. This fact of the possibility of analysis has been my guiding principle in the selection of illustrative material.

CHAPTER XIII

THE ORIGIN OF ONTOGENETIC ENGRAM-SUCCESSIONS

1. THE ORIGINATION OF DICHOTOMIES BY STIMULATION.

IF by stimulation a new link is added to an already existing succession of engrams $c - d - e$, the addition may be by either of two ways. Either the line is continued so that the hitherto ultimate link e becomes the penultimate link of the unilinear succession $c - d - e - f$,

or a dichotomy is affected, $c - d\Big\langle{}^e_f$, in which the new link

f enters as an alternative to what was previously the ultimate link e. In Chapter IV I have already analysed such dichotomies in the sphere of individually acquired engrams, but without regard to their inheritability.

It is of the very nature of engraphic stimulation that already existing engrams are never remoulded, but remain as they were first imprinted. New engrams are deposited as detached and fresh creations. This characteristic of engraphic action is the essential element in the formation of the large group of alternatives in the sphere of individual acquirements, as also in that of hereditary engraphic action.

As regards individually acquired engrams, the reader is referred to the experimental and other evidence in Chapter XV of *The Mnemic Sensations*. In the case of hereditary engrams, the preservation of the relatively independent engram is seen most clearly in such phenomena of atavism as come under our notice in the second part of the preceding chapter. The old engrams, which had apparently disappeared without leaving any traces, were still in being, and only required a special external impulse to revive them and to reopen the old paths. One of the most convincing examples of a revived engram-stock was given in the reappearance of the breeding pads in the third and fourth generations of the Obstetric Toad, where, as a consequence of external stimuli, the neoteny that had become a norm was suppressed in favour of a return into forsaken ancient tracks.

In other fields, also, reversions or atavisms have been experimentally effected. Under certain circumstances they appear quite regularly as a sequel to regenerative phenomena. Reference may here be made to one particularly clear case, for the exact demonstration of which in a large series of different forms we are indebted to Przibram. On the removal of the third maxilliped of the short-tailed Crayfish, regeneration-formations arise which correspond in every respect to the ambulatory limbs. Only in the case of further "sheddings" does the gradual transformation into a typical maxilliped take place. In the normal ontogenesis of the Crab, such an "ambulatory-limb-like" character does not occur. But maxillipedes resembling the ambulatory limbs occur all through life in the longtailed Crayfishes, the ancestral stock of the short-tailed kind. Analogous atavistic phenomena occur, as Fritz Müller ascertained in 1880, in the regeneration of the claws, and especially of the fifth leg, of Garneela Atyoida. These, however, were cases of temporary regenerative stages which were gradually corrected in later "sheddings."

I wish to emphasize here that, in all the cases hitherto considered, the reversion was in no way caused by cross-breeding, but only upon the ecphory of latent atavistic engrams by external stimuli.

In other reversions, however, the return into old and disused evolutionary tracks is often a consequence of crossing. Recent research in hybridisation has succeeded in showing somewhat more clearly than heretofore certain interrelations in these cross-bred reversions. Yet the basis of the explanations given is always the actual existence of "ancestral factors," which by themselves are incapable of manifestation. In certain cases of crossing, however, special combinations are re-established, which arouse these factors into activity so that they manifest themselves in plastic and motor reactions.

Attention may also be directed to the fact, proved long ago, that reversion to characters, which for generations have been lost or modified, occur also in pure bred forms. Of great importance in this respect are the careful and accurate observations on the spontaneous atavistic reversions of oats to wild oats, made in Svalöf in the nineties. More recently H. Nilsson-Ehle established beyond doubt that these atavisms arise, not in connection with crossings, but as an entirely " spontaneous " alteration.

We reserve for our next chapter the investigation of the question whether these factors arise by stimulation or not. At this point, however, it will be convenient to consider the dichotomies which result from *crossing*.

2. ORIGINATION OF ALTERNATIVE DICHOTOMIES BY CROSS-BREEDING.

If two varieties or species distinguished from each other by a clearly definable character are crossed, as, for example, a white-flowering plant with a red-flowering variety, or a rough-haired with a smooth-haired guinea-pig, or an obstetric toad of a species mating on land with one of a species propagating in water, the question arises— which parental path of development will the progeny follow ? To use the formula of our diagram :—Will the progeny follow the path $d - e$ of $d - f$ at the

dichotomy $d\Big\langle\begin{smallmatrix}e\\f\end{smallmatrix}$, resultant from the crossing ?

In the exposition that follows we are concerned only with the progeny issuing from such a crossing. In the nomenclature of modern science, the first filial generation ⋅s known as the F_1 generation, the second generation (grand-children) as the F2 generation, the third as the F3 generation, and so on.

It is clear that no one can with any certainty predict which of the two paths, $d - e$ or $d - f$, will be followed by the products of the crossing, the F1 generation. Indeed, in keeping with the phenomena of mixed reactions in the domain of higher memory (p. 167), the chances are that the alternative is not decided at all in any hard or exclusive way, but that mixed reactions occur, from which an ecphory of the engrams belonging to both branches may be inferred.

Experience shows that in some cases the one, in other cases the other possibility is realised. If the alternative is adopted in a clear and decided way, in the sense that development follows one path exclusively, then we say, accepting Mendel's terminology, that the structural or functional character resultant on the following of this path " *dominates* " over the character corresponding to the other path. The latter character is termed " recessive."

It frequently happens, however, that neither alternative is exclusively chosen, but a compromise is effected by the co-operation of the diverging paths of development. The result is a mixed reaction, and the appearance of an intermediate character in all the members of the F1 generation. This character, however, need not invariably be an intermediate one. A product peculiar in many ways may result from the mixture, as, for example, the metallic blue of the Andalusian fowl, which regularly appears when the white variety is crossed with the black. In some cases the character is, however, in its most literal sense intermediate, as when a red-flowering variety crossed with a white gives a pink flowering F1 generation, as in the case of Lychnis and the miracle flower, *Mirabilis jalapa*.

There are extreme cases of perfect dominance, where no trace of the recessive character can be found even on the most exacting research, as for example, the dominance of multicolour over white in the flowers of Lathyrus and Matthiola, and of hairiness over smoothness in Matthiola. There are cases of the appearance of an exactly intermediate character. Between these extremes may be found all kinds of transition-states.

If we now ask what determines the choice, complete or partial, we shall have to admit that we really know very little about the matter. The supposition that the phylogenetically older path is more or less dominant over the phylogenetically younger path does not stand close examination, for the younger path is often taken. Nor can we say that, in the crossing of species of which the one possesses a character lacking in the other, this character invariably dominates.

In general, the dominance, that is, the absolute or comparative predominance of one of the hybridisation-alternatives, is a constant phenomenon occurring in nearly *all* the progeny of crossed parents. But irregularities and exceptions are not unknown. The subject needs further elucidation by carefully elaborated experiments. That it is possible under certain conditions to divert the dominance into this or that direction by external influences has been proved by Tschermak's experiments with wheat strains and by those of Vernon, Doncaster, Herbst and Tennent in the cross-breeding of various species of Sea-urchins, and by Tower in that of Colorado Beetles. The researches, especially those of the last three named, give us some insight into the nature of the influences at work. Those of Herbst were the first attempt to analyse closely the character and action of these influences. We are only at the beginning of our understanding of them, and we shall have to leave to further research the task of formulating the results in any definite way.

From what we have said, it follows that in the generation which arises as the first product of a crossing—the F_1 generation—a dichotomous combination of the diverging lines of development has been created. The development in the members of this generation may then follow one of three ways. There is either absolute dominance where the movement is exclusively in one path ; or there is imperfect dominance where the movement is chiefly in one path, but the influence of the other path makes itself

felt ; or there is what may be called intermediate inheritance, where the development progresses with approximately
equal and simultaneous actuation of both engram lines,
so that a mixed reaction results, usually assuming an intermediate character.

As a rule, the separate representatives of the F_1
generation behave exactly alike. This similarity of
behaviour holds good almost without exception in cases
where the F_2 generation may be differentiated according
to Mendelian rules.

Let us follow the course of the crossings in the succeeding
generations, dealing first with the second filial generation—
F_2. To obtain unimpeachable results and to ensure strict
breeding, it is necessary to exclude all foreign elements
in such a manner as to obtain the F_2 generation by the
exclusive use of the products of the first crossing, that
is, the representatives of the F_1 generation. This is the
line which Gregor Mendel followed fifty years ago, and
along which he reached his epoch-making discoveries.

Just as one character in the F_1 generation dominated
over the other so that it alone appeared in each representative, or, in the absence of such dominance, an intermediate
path was entered upon so that every representative of
the F_1 generation became the bearer of an intermediate
character, thus with the F_2 generation certain differences
became pronounced, which on closer scrutiny are merely
the varied manifestations of the identical principles. It
may be well to consider first the case of the complete
or nearly complete dominance of the one character over
the other, taking as our example the classic case given
by Mendel. He crossed two varieties of the edible pea,
Pisum sativum, characterised by a well-marked difference
in the colour of the seed-leaf, one being yellow and the
other green. He found that the yellow dominated over
the green, so that in the F_1 generation the offspring
possessed all yellow-coloured cotyledons. In the F_2
generation, which in this instance had been obtained
from the F_1 generation by self-fertilisation, " along
with the dominant characters the recessive characters

reappeared in their full peculiarity and in an unmistakable average ratio. Of every four plants from this generation, three showed the dominant and one the recessive character." In regard to the third generation raised from the crossing, and also bred from self-fertilisation, Mendel proved that those forms which possessed the recessive character in the preceding generation did not vary in the second generation in regard to this character, which remained constant in succeeding generations. With those of the first generation which possess the dominant character, two of the three remaining parts produce offspring which, just as in the case of the known hybrid forms, bear the dominant and recessive characters in the ratio of three to one. One part only remains constant in the dominant character. If we represent this by a diagram in which *d* denotes the dominant character, and *r* the recessive, we shall have the following arrangement, which will show the typical splitting of a Mendelian hybrid form.

Crossing of *d* with *r* (*d* = dominant, *r* = recessive).

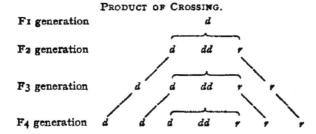

PRODUCT OF CROSSING.

F1 generation		*d*	
F2 generation	*d*	*dd*	*r*
F3 generation	*d*	*d* *dd* *r*	*r*
F4 generation	*d*	*d* *d* *dd* *r* *r*	*r*

In the case of the crossing of characters where the one does not dominate over the other, but where the F1 generation presents an intermediate character, as with the Andalusian fowl, the modification of the theory is only apparent. We may take in illustration the miracle flower, *Mirabilis jalapa*. By crossing a white-flowering specimen with a red, we obtain an F1 generation, in which the offspring bear pink flowers. This generation, when selfed or inbred, produces a generation—F2—in which one-half bear pink flowers, one-quarter pure white flowers, and the remainder red. Each of these two latter groups breeds true, producing when selfed only pure white or pure red flowers. The pink flowers, when self-fertilised, produce in the F3 generation the same proportion of one-quarter true breeding white flowers, one-quarter true breeding red flowers, and one-half pink flowers. The last, when inbred, produce flowers in exactly the same proportion as the pink flowers of the F2 generation. If we denote the white-flowering specimens by *a*, the red-flowering by *b*, and the intermediate pink by *ab*, we obtain the following scheme :—

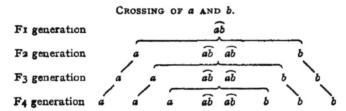

CROSSING OF *a* AND *b*.

F1 generation		$\widehat{ab}$		
F2 generation	*a*	$\widehat{ab}$ $\widehat{ab}$	*b*	
F3 generation	*a* *a*	$\widehat{ab}$ $\widehat{ab}$	*b* *b*	
F4 generation	*a* *a* *a*	$\widehat{ab}$ $\widehat{ab}$	*b* *b* *b*	

It is clear that this scheme is practically identical with that on the preceding page, as soon as pure dominants and pure recessives emerge on the self-fertilization of *ab*, instead of giving an intermediate character

How are we to explain the different behaviour of the F2, F3, F4, etc., generations as compared with that of the F1 generation ? The perspicacity of Gregor Mendel succeeded in discovering the lines on which the explanation must proceed. We accept in the main his views, but later we shall have to show why and how far we deviate in at least one instance of fundamental importance from the Mendelian interpretation as generally advanced.

Take the case we have just considered. On referring to the diagram, we note that in the F1 generation the character *ab*, apparently resulting from the mixture of *a* and *b*, appears in each individual. But in the F2 generation the case is altered, and the "intermediate" appearing only · in one-half of the progeny. Of the remainder, one-half, that is one-quarter of the entire generation, shows the character *a*, and the other the character *b*. Throughout the generations *a* and *b* breed true. There is no sign of the character *ab*, we may therefore regard it as eliminated. How to account for this elimination will require more definite consideration later on.

Now, when does this elimination take place? Mendel was aware of the importance of this point. Elimination takes place at the formation of the germ-cells or gametes. If we take a representative of the F1 generation and propagate it by a purely vegetative method, by cuttings, buds, bulbs, etc., the process may as a rule be continued indefinitely without the emergence of Mendelian divisions. Very rarely does the vegetative method allow of the manifestation of Mendelian characters.

In most cases of cross-breeding, however, where an F2 generation results from an F1 generation by the formation of germ-cells or gametes, a segregation of characters regularly takes place in 50 per cent. of the representatives of the F2 generation. The constancy of this occurrence strongly suggests that the different behaviour of the F2 generation should be traced to the germ-cells from which F2 originated. We have, therefore, to assume that in the germ-cells the factors, which later on determine the appearance of the Mendelian characters in the course of the ontogenetic development, are so arranged that in their evolution one only of the two retains its efficiency. Its fellow or competitor either is removed altogether or its action is neutralised. In any case, it is eliminated as a factor.

If we denote the factor that determines the appearance of the character *a* by A, and the one that determines *b* by B, we can then say that from one-half of the gametes of the F1 generation A is eliminated, and from the other half B. The ratios suggest that the principles which govern the calculus of probabilities hold good in the case of this process of elimination. For if we make the safe assumption that the competitors whose fate is determined at the formation of the germ-cells have an equal chance, then according to the laws of probability A will triumph over B in one-half of the cases, and B over A in the other half.

When the germ-cells of an individual of the F1 generation, of a hermaphrodite plant for example, are crossed amongst each other, what happens? As we saw, of fifty female gametes, twenty-five possess the factor A, twenty-five the factor B. The same proportion holds good in regard to the fifty male gametes. Now, according to the law of probabilities, in one-quarter of the cases the male gametes that possess the factor A will unite with female gametes bearing the same factor. The result will be AA. In a second quarter of the cases the male gametes possessing the factor B will unite with females bearing the factor B. The result will be BB. In the third quarter of the cases male gametes with factor A will unite with female-bearing factor B. The result will be AB. And in the remaining quarter, the male gametes with factor B will unite with females bearing factor A. The result will be BA. If we now consider that in the overwhelming majority of cases it is indifferent whether a factor is introduced by the male or the female gamete, it is easy to conclude that AB is equivalent to BA. The generation-products in our examples accordingly arrange themselves in the following mode :—

25 AA   25 AB   25 BA   25 BB

This corresponds to the distribution of the characters in the F2 generation, as already noted :—

a $\overset{\frown}{ab}$ $\overset{\frown}{ba}$ b

Those copulation-products or zygotes which possess only A as an active factor, if mated amongst each other, produce individuals with the character a. Zygotes bearing simply the factor B produce the character b. Hybridisation, at least in relation to the characters here specified, has not permanently affected the copulation-products. They are not hybrids as regards these characters, for they are not cross-mated, but like-mated. They are, according to modern terminology, *homozygotes*.

But where gametes bearing the factor A unite with those bearing the factor B, as in cases denoted by AB and BA, hybridisation takes place, and zygotes, which are hybrids in specific regard to these characters, are defined as *heterozygotes*. The homozygotes AA, mated amongst each other, breed true, and the same is the case with the homozygotes BB. But with the heterozygotes AB and BA, a fresh segregation takes place in the next generation in conformity with the laws of probability. The result is expressed in the formula :—

$$AA \qquad AB \qquad BA \qquad BB$$

This recurs in each new generation. Readers are referred to the diagram on page 247.

If we consider in the same way those cases where crossed antagonistic characters do not give an intermediate character to the hybrids (heterozygotes), but where one character (d) dominates over the other one (r), and if we denote the corresponding factors or determinants by D and R, it is clear that, at the mating of the gametes from the F1 generation, each hundred copulation-products will arrange themselves in the following ratio :—

$$25\,DD \qquad 25\,DR \qquad 25\,RD \qquad 25\,RR$$

As character d dominates over character r, the following formula of character sets out this relation. (Compare the scheme on page 246.)

$$d \qquad\quad d \qquad\quad d \qquad\quad r$$

This means that, of the seventy-five individuals with the dominant character d, only one-third are homozygotes (DD). The remaining two-thirds are heterozygotes (DR and RD). Thus at bottom the proportion of homozygotes and heterozygotes is the same as in those cases where the dominance of one character over the other is not so apparent. The superficial difference is explained by the fact that the dominance of one character over the other prevents us from distinguishing in that generation the homozygotes DD from the heterozygotes DR and RD. It is only by inbreeding the apparent dominants that we are able to distinguish the pure dominants from the impure.

The discovery of these fundamental data and their lucid interpretation we owe to the penetrative genius of Gregor Mendel. His discoveries have been confirmed by subsequent investigations in other and wider fields. It is certain that an explanation of the numerical ratios in hybridisation on any other basis is impossible.

One point only remains in doubt, *a point which does not affect the numerical ratio of Mendelian characters*, but which is of the greatest importance for any ultimate conception of the structure of organic substance. How in the formation of the gametes is the " elimination " of one of the factors effected ? Is it a mechanical separation of the two factors united in the hybridisation, and a distribution of these factors to two different gametes, that is a " segregation " in its most literal sense ? Or is the undoubted elimination of one of the factors effected in some other way ? Is it, perhaps, not expelled, but only put for a time out of action ? Mendel confidently adopted the obvious and simple assumption of a segregation of the factors concerned, and of a distribution of these to two different germ-cells during the process of cell-division. Many workers have followed him in this view, and with the less hesitation in that some of the difficulties, which at first told against it, have in the course of investigation been since removed.

Nevertheless, a number of real difficulties still remain. One objection to the Mendelian assumption lies in the subsequent necessity of regarding each Mendelian factor or determinant as an isolable particle morphologically independent. This consequence appears to me, at any rate, too far-reaching to be valid. That the segregation of the Mendelian factors at the formation of the gametes is a simpler and easier conception than that of a temporary neutralisation of one factor by the other is not a sufficient reason why the theory should be accepted.

Perhaps the "elimination" of one factor by the other depends simply on the advantage of position which under usual conditions, according to the laws of probability, falls in one-half of the cases to the one factor, and in the other half to the other factor. In certain circumstances, however, and according to definite rules, this advantage may be counteracted by external influences in favour now of the one, now of the other factor. Recent experiments, carefully carried out by Tower from quite new points of view, confirm this. By varying the external conditions Tower induced a marked dislocation of the ratios of segregation as compared with the usual Mendelian ratio. Tower's experiments are the first systematic attempt to influence hybridisation by varying the external conditions, and the results obtained are so remarkable that they call for further investigation into this hitherto neglected field, and warn us against hastily making up our minds on the problem of segregation. For it follows from the assumption of an actual segregation that the determining factor in cases of dwarf growth, of sterility, of immunity against rust, of colour-blindness, of cataract, of short fingers, or of specific markings, is a definite isolable particle. Useful as such symbolic ideas may be for purposes of Mendelian research, the materialisation of symbols in the shape of morphologically isolable units appears to me a very dangerous procedure. Other reasons besides the simplicity of the assumption and the ease of its application are requisite before we are justified in accepting segregation, in its literal sense, as a fact.

In passing, however, I should like to point out that the elimination of one of the competitive factors in the formation of the gametes—that is, what is usually described as the Mendelian mode of inheritance—seems to be a process which by no means appears in all cases of cross-breeding. This means that a segregation of the characters in some part of the F2 generation does not necessarily take place after each crossing. As a rule, such segregation does not occur when the two crossed forms differ from each other so much in their constitution that a systematist would classify them, not as different varieties, but as belonging to different species or genera. In crossing different species, contrary to our experience in the crossing of varieties, the general thing is that neither dominants nor uniform intermediate types emerge, but forms, denoted as Pleiotypes, in which appear numerous gradations due to the mingling of the parental types. As species-hybrids are usually sterile, the behaviour of the later generations— F2, F3, etc.—can only be ascertained in exceptional cases. Occasionally, however, fertile species-hybrids have been obtained, which, on inbreeding, showed intermediate characters in the successive generations. Experiments have been made in the crossing of butterflies, of pheasants, and of rabbits with hares. The two silver pheasant species, *Euplocamus nychthemerus* and *E. albocristatus*, were crossed and the hybrids inbred. For five generations the hybrids bred true. Leporides-hybrids, resulting from hares and rabbits, were bred by Conrad in the agricultural experimental station at Jena, up to the sixth generation. Throughout they retained a number of intermediate characters. True breeding species-hybrids from the vegetable kingdom are also known. Research in this direction is, however, only in the initial stages. The cases so far presented need to be subjected to further analysis, and to control-experiments continued through longer lines of generation.

In his latest work Tower reports on cross-breeding experiments made under differing external conditions on *Leptinotarsa decemlineata, L. oblongata, and L. multi-taeniata,* three species of the Colorado Beetle. Left to themselves on an island in the Balsas river, these three forms eventually produced a new hybrid race, which showed an intermediate mixture of all three ancestral types, but in which the *oblongata-decemlineata* characters predominated over the *multitaeniata* characters. This form bred true without segregations and without reversions. From time to time, however, spontaneous variations appeared in the breeds, parallel in every respect to the mutations of *Oenothera lamarckiana* in the breeding experiments of De Vries. Under changed ,external conditions, the same treble crossing resulted in hybrids which showed the intermediate characters of only two of the parental forms, either *decemlineata-oblongata* or *decemlineata-multitaeniata*. These hybrids in the main main bred true, but occasional mutations occurred.

In conclusion, it may be of use to summarise briefly the latter section of this chapter.

The crossing of two individuals which differ from each other in a definite character initiates in the first filial generation (F1) dichotomies of the kind already described. In the ontogeny of this F1 generation, either one path of development dominates more or less completely over the other, or both assert themselves in a kind of compromise which manifests itself in mixed reactions, that is, in the appearance of an intermediate character or its equivalent. How the choice of the dichotomous alternative will fall depends mainly on the specific nature of the competing paths, and, under certain circumstances, also on the action of external forces, as recent researches have shown.

On the formation of the gametes of the F1 generation, the unstable state of the alternative in the F1 generation becomes stable. In the large majority of cases this occurs by the putting out of action of one branch of the dichotomy. The chances of gain or loss are equal for both competing branches, so that, according to the laws of probability, in the one-half of the cases one branch, in the other half the other branch, is neutralised. Though it is possible, under certain circumstances, to dislocate this ratio by external forces, as Tower proved, this ratio is the rule. This explains the numerical relations of the Mendelian (segregating) inheritance in its simple and in its more complicated forms. Extended research has but confirmed the findings of Mendel.

In rare cases neither branch of the dichotomy neutralises the other at the formation of the gametes of the F1 generation, but there is the fixation of a state in which both branches exist juxtaposed. This juxtaposition manifests itself by the constant and exclusive appearance of intermediate characters in the F2 generation, and in succeeding generations. These intermediate hybrid characters breed true. It is possible, therefore, to produce a pure-breeding hybrid form.

The problem—how in Mendelian inheritance the neutralisation or elimination of one of the two competitive factors is effected in the formation of the gametes—we shall leave in abeyance. Mendel and the greater number of his followers assume that there is a literal segregation, that is, a separation and distribution of the two competing elements over the division-products of the parent cells of the gametes, probably at the reduction-division. But any explanation, simple and effective though it may seem to be, which necessarily leads to the assumption of isolable particles as representative of the characters in the gametes, must be regarded with extreme caution. For this apparent solution of the riddle is simple only as long as we ignore the greatly complicated, but most delicately attuned and harmonious, *co-operation* of those assumed isolable particles.

The problems we have here indicated are in themselves fundamentally important, but it is not necessary, so far as the purpose of this book is concerned, to discuss them exhaustively. Their solution we may safely leave an open question. Of more direct importance to us is the enquiry into the origin of the determinants. The next chapter will be devoted to this problem.

CHAPTER XIV

ENGRAPHIC ORIGIN OF THE DETERMINANTS

IN the foregoing pages I have tried to show that the new potentialities of the germ-cells originate as the products of stimuli or as the residue of excitations, and that they correspond in all their properties with the somatic engrams which have engraved themselves during the life of the individual on the irritable substance of the body. ·The reader is referred to the many examples quoted in the course of the preceding chapters. To these more might be added from those submitted in *The Problem of the Inheritance of Acquired Characters.* When we consider that experimental research-work in this direction has been carried on systematically only during the last few years, the number of examples available is all the more remarkable. Experiments by Chauvin, Kammerer, Standfuss, Fischer, Schröder, Pictet, Tower, Summer, Przibram, Blaringhem, Klebs, Bordage, and many others, have concurrently proved that the new potentialities originate from excitation.

The question arises whether these engrams are produced by the direct action of external stimuli on the germ-cells, or by the conduction of the transformed stimuli through the irritable substance of the soma. Do the engrams result from " parallel induction," or from " somatic induction " ? The question is discussed in Chapter V of this book (pp. 129–136), and more exhaustively in a separate chapter of my essay on *The Problem of the Inheritance of Acquired Characters.* I think that I have there demonstrated the insufficiency of physical and physiological evidence for the general applicability of parallel induction. But whatever position is taken up, or whatever mode of induction is assumed, all agree that it is a matter of induction, and that means, of course, stimulation. No doubt can exist, therefore, as to the engram-nature of these new potentialities. Tower and Kammerer investigated the action of such newly-generated determinants or hereditable engrams and found that, if their bearers were crossed with individuals not possessing them, these determinants or engrams were inherited alternatingly, following the Mendelian mode. They behaved exactly as those inherited engrams with which cross-breeding experiments are usually conducted.

We have already seen (p. 135) that a stimulus affecting the irritable substance of an organism and inducing excitation therein, may in some cases affect also the germ-cells, leaving demonstrable engrams behind, but that in other cases the germ-cells are unaffected. This apparent capriciousness of inheritance may be traced to various causes ; primarily, of course, to the nature and the strength of the stimulus applied. Recently, however, Tower discovered and fully described a second modifying factor which in many cases is of decisive importance. He found in the Colorado Beetle (*Leptinotarsa*) a temporary period of extraordinarily heightened susceptibility of the germ-cells. This we may call the germinal sensitive period. If stimulation takes place during this period, engrams capable of manifestation are generated, but the same stimulation applied at a time when the susceptibility of the germ-cells is normal produces no germinal engraphic effect. It is possible, of course, that in some cases where an engraphic alteration of the germ-cells occurs, other factors may have co-operated to determine the issue. Our investigation, however, of this problem has hitherto only gone a short way.

In this connection it may be well to enquire briefly into the *apparently spontaneous* appearance of new potentialities as manifested in the sudden and more or less isolated appearance of " sports." At the very commencement of his researches into the problem of descent Darwin turned his attention to this phenomenon of mutation or saltatory variation. Later, De Vries, working on *Oenethera lamarckiana,* believed he had discovered the real cause of the origin of new species in apparently spontaneous mutations. Tower's breeding experiments have recently furnished important contributions to the subject. The riddle of the apparent spontaneity—for no thinker would admit the possibility of real spontaneity—will in a number of cases presumably find its solution in the varying sensitivity of the germ-cells. These in certain circumstances become abnormally susceptible to engraphic action. If by chance an especially strong stimulus affects the germ-cells just at their period of heightened susceptibility, the resultant is likely to be a " sport," a mutation, or a saltatory variation. Hybridisations appear to create special predispositions in this direction, as Darwin inferred from the experiences of breeders. Tower's latest experiments seem to confirm this idea. In regard to such hybridisations, the possibility must not be lost sight of that many saltatory variations may be simply the result of new groupings of already existing engrams. They do not represent anything really new, especially when the variation is of a regressive or atavistic nature.

Attention must here be called to a noteworthy peculiarity of many newly formed " mutations." As shown in the preceding chapter, an alternative character $d\!\!<^{e}_{f}$ may be generated by stimulation (p. 240) as well as by crossing (p. 242). In this latter case, dichotomy appears in the heterozygotes of each generation. On crossing these again with either of the two parents of the cross, the heterozygotes distribute themselves in the ratio $1 : 1$ in conformity with the Mendelian law. The same ratio, however, is also revealed by a good many true breeding mutations, if these are crossed with the original form from which they sprang. They behave like heterozygotes. Thus in them an alternative exists which, latent in pure breeding, is manifested on recrossing. In mutations which do not breed true—a case by no means rare—the alternative already manifests itself in in-breeding.

When we speak of the genesis of the determinants by stimulation, that is, by engraphy, we do not thereby wish to convey the idea that the single " determinant " or " gen " always corresponds exactly to one engram. Recent research in heredity has proved in a great number of cases that the determinant, which one was at first inclined to regard as simple, is in reality exceedingly complex. Such complex factors, therefore, are not to be regarded as single engrams, but either as engram-complexes or as co-operating engrams of different origin.

Again, what appears to be a single stimulus is usually a very complex phenomenon. The seemingly simple sunbeam, for instance, that strikes our face is composed, according to the wave-length, of chemical, visual, and thermal rays which, acting on different stimulus receptors, simultaneously originate different kinds of excitations and leave behind different kinds of engrams. The same ray stimulates in various ways the plant on which it impinges, and generates engrams of various kinds. Sumner and Przibram reared young mice and rats in an unusually high temperature, and found that the external skin was the first thing affected. The regulated bodily heat of the animals modified in a great measure the influence of the atmospheric temperature on the rest of the organs of the body. The skin and its glands and, above all, the hair were changed under the abnormal conditions. Corresponding hereditable engrams were left behind in the germ-cells, as was shown by the fact that the offspring of these animals, even when reared in a normal temperature, exhibited the induced alterations. Abnormally high temperatures act also on the entire metabolism of the animals, accelerating development, diminishing growth, and producing premature sexual maturity. The excitations producing these reactions leave behind in the germ-cells hereditable engrams which determine the corresponding alterations in the offspring. Thus, the *same* thermal stimulus, acting on the complex organism, causes different kinds of excitations and leaves behind different kinds of engrams. These latter, it is true, are simultaneously associated, but there is the possibility that by properly arranged crossings the association or correlation may be broken up. Cross-breeding has proved itself in many cases to be instrumental in breaking up correlations. Whether in the case just discussed this holds good will have to be ascertained by further investigation.

There are also, however, factors of quite a different origin, engrams which were produced at distinct times in the individual or in the ancestral line, and which, therefore, cannot be defined as engram-complexes according to our meaning. These can determine characters which seem to be throughout of a uniform nature, but regarding which evidence can be adduced—especially from the analysis of crossings—that they arise by the co-operation of different determining factors. It may be well to consider in detail some of the results of recent experimental research, which has disclosed certain characteristics of the hereditary determining factors ; these characteristics correspond in a most striking way with those already seen to belong to individually acquired engrams.

It has previously been pointed out (p. 169) that if a stimulus which has already generated an engram again acts on the individual, it does not reinforce or intensify the existing engram, but creates a new engram similar but distinct, and ecphorable separately. If two or more equivalent but isolated engrams are ecphorised, then homophony of the corresponding mnemic excitations follows. If these homophonous excitations manifest themselves by reactions of feeling, the excitation resulting from the homophony is strengthened not so much in its intensity as in its vividness.

What interests us here especially is the fact that the repetition of the same stimulus generates in an individual a number of qualitatively equivalent engrams, which maintain their separate identity. They are distinct entities, and yet they display a joint homophonous activity.

Nilsson-Ehle has recently demonstrated in his interesting crossing experiments with oats and wheat, that in many cases a character owes its development to the co-operation of a number of qualitatively equal determinants or " units." Thus, his investigations (p. 66) gave "for the brown colour of the ears of wheat, as well as for the black colour of the beard of oats, several units, or at least more than one, which could not be distinguished qualitatively from each other." He further showed (p. 71) that " THE RED COLOUR OF SWEDISH VELVET WHEAT IS DETERMINED BY THREE UNITS, INDEPENDENT OF EACH OTHER AND EACH DIVIDING BY ITSELF, AND THAT EACH OF THESE UNITS IS CAPABLE BY ITSELF OF PRODUCING THE RED COLOUR." . . . " IT CAN BE STATED WITH CERTAINTY THAT THE DIFFERENCES IN THE MANIFESTATION OF THE DIFFERENT UNITS FOR THE RED COLOUR OF THE CORN ARE HARDLY PERCEPTIBLE, AND THAT THERE CAN CERTAINLY BE NO QUESTION WHATEVER OF A QUALITATIVE DIFFERENCE IN THE UNITS, either in those for the black colour of the beard of oats or in those for the colour of the ears of wheat." The same comment is valid for other characteristics, such as the panicle inflorescence, the beard in wheat, and the lingule-character in oats. " NO DIFFERENCE IN THE CHARACTER OF THE LINGULE IS DISCERNIBLE AS RESULTING FROM THE TWO INDEPENDENT LINGULE-UNITS OF THE KIND 0353, AND THEREFORE THE EXTERNAL APPEARANCE GIVES NO CRITERION OF THE PRESENCE OF ONE OR OF THE OTHER UNIT " (p. 89).

Nilsson-Ehle showed in his work the important bearing of this peculiar fact on the theory of descent, and how the appearance of certain saltatory variations, as also the manifestation of inherited *gradations* of certain qualities, might be deduced from it. It is not impossible that many cases of seemingly constant intermediate inheritance might also find their explanation on the same basis of fact. Sufficient evidence in this direction has not been adduced yet, but, so far as the subject of this book is concerned, the important point is that we have now indubitable evidence of the co-existence in the same individual of like determinants, that is, in their manifestation.

NILSSON-EHLE BY HIS CROSS-BREEDING EXPERIMENTS HAS THUS ARRIVED AT EXACTLY THE SAME CONCLUSIONS IN RESPECT TO THE HEREDITARY FACTORS AS I HAVE REACHED BY AN ALTOGETHER DIFFERENT WAY IN RESPECT TO INDIVIDUALLY ACQUIRED ENGRAMS AND THE CO-EXISTENCE OF ISOLATED BUT QUALITATIVELY SIMILAR POTENTIALITIES, EACH OF WHICH ON ECPHORY CAN OF ITSELF PRODUCE THE CORRESPONDING REACTION, BUT THE HOMOPHONOUS CO-OPERATION OF WHICH BRINGS ABOUT UNDER CERTAIN CONDITIONS AN INCREASED EFFECT.

On this, as well as on other points, the method of reasoning adopted in this book and the conclusions reached in no way conflict with the result of researches on variation and hybridisation ; rather are they supplementary. The advances which we owe to these modern branches of scientific research are incalculable. A mathematical precision, hardly to be obtained elsewhere in the domain of biology, distinguishes them and makes their study an æsthetical pleasure. The fact, however, must not be lost sight of that this line of research regards the determining factors either as definite magnitudes, or as symbols *detached* from the characters. The symbols are used not only as such, but also as if they possessed the marvellous capacity to behave at all times and in all places in the manner prescribed.

In proceeding thus in regard to variation and hybridisation research has followed the only right method. It has thereby very nearly reached a solution of the problem presented.

The limitations of this method, however, which is fully justified in its own proper field, must be borne in mind, otherwise our conclusions might overstep the right limits of this kind of research. We must not ignore, for example, the physiological aspect—how the " determin-

ing factors " fulfil their proper task and function—
or leave out of account the data accumulated by experimental embryology, such as the phenomena of
regeneration and of periodicity, that is, the co-operation
of the determinants.

To my mind the facts do not warrant the inference
that the determinants are isolable particles of matter ;
such inference would only be valid on the supposition
that in no other way can " segregation " be explained.
The question, however, is in our present state of knowledge
too difficult to be handled here. Although personally I
take an entirely different view from that just mentioned,
I prefer to leave the matter open.

The isolability of the structure, known as the determining factor, is a subject worth discussing. One conclusion,
however, accepted by many biologists is quite unwarrant-
able : that a lack of correlation of these structures amongst
themselves has been proved, and that we have therefore
a right to assume that the determining factors were
lying about in the germ-plasm in a disconnected and
unorderly way.

The biologists referred to were led to this position by the
fact that they were able to split up character-correlations
established by cross-breeding, and to separate characters
which were apparently indissolubly united.

Against this we may set the fact that correlations
exist, the segregation of which by crossing has so far
not been accomplished. The reader is reminded of the
strange phenomenon of gametic union. Further, cases
exist where two factors cannot be made to unite by
crossing. They seem to repel each other. It appears,
however, not improbable that such cases of spurious
allelomorphism may yet be explained. Nilsson-Ehle,
for instance, showed quite recently that, under certain
circumstances, one of the factors may act as a check,
and so neutralise the action of several quite independent
factors. In that way factors are correlatively united,
and the relation may be determined by factors acting
independently and in no sort of special unity. But

even if we assume that it is possible by cross-breeding to separate the various factors from each other, this does not at all prove that in the antecedent state there was a complete lack of correlation among these elements. Latterly the analyses of those engaged in hybridisation research have been frequently compared with chemical analyses, a comparison against which many objections might be raised. Allowing, however, the comparison, we may note that, in any chemical combination, an orderly arrangement of the respective units and a definite union under the image of more or less closely coherent, subordinated complexes is assumed. We may think, for instance, of the six carbon atoms in the Benzene ring, and of the subsidiary attachments of the six hydrogen atoms. Nobody dreams of asserting that the possibility of separation implies a non-orderly juxtaposition of the chemical units.

The segregations brought about by hybridisation are, in my opinion, essentially different from the separations of chemical analysis. But granted that I may be entirely mistaken in this view, it by no means follows that a differently graduated relation, an established contiguity of the genetic determinants, such as is generally assumed in this very chemical parallel, does not exist. The existence of such contiguity seems to me to be proved by the physiological data of development, of regeneration, of regulation, and of periodicity.

We also find individually acquired engrams in a well-established contiguity, which on ecphory manifests itself in the phenomena of simultaneous and successive association. The simultaneous engram-complexes form, it is true, a coherent unity, but we can nevertheless produce from the single components of these complexes entirely new combinations. In Chapter IX of *The Mnemic Sensations* I have defined these processes as " the association of the components of different engram layers." The manner in which, in the individual life, the components of engram-complexes are used over again for the creation of new complexes is markedly different from the process involved in the re-combination of the components during hybridisation. But the "tertium comparationis" is contained in the fact that in both cases a severance of the original associations and a new combination of the components are possible, and that it would be illicit in both cases to infer from this fact that no established contiguity of the components had ever existed.

The connection of the hereditarily transmitted "factors," their co-operation, the localisation of their action in time and place, are problems of such a nature as to be incapable of solution by the methods of Mendelian research alone.

We may quote Tower's just observation, "To say that together they direct the development of one part after another in orderly succession puts upon these determiners a burden of great responsibility—almost involving intelligence—and makes necessary some co-ordinating mechanism behind it all."

If we acknowledge the engraphic origin of the determinants—a position proved by experiment in many cases—and if we use the two principal mnemic laws as keys to all the processes determined by the ecphory of engrams, then by grouping the accumulated data on hereditary and on individually acquired engrams under common heads, we obtain some idea of the "co-ordinating mechanism" of which Tower speaks, and we do this without leaving strictly physiological ground and without having to ascribe anything like intelligence to the determinants. Our procedure of deducing the orderly arrangement in time and space of ontogenetic processes from a law of a more general order thus furnishes the necessary supplement to the methods of Mendelian research, which has primarily altogether different aims. A bridge is thereby thrown across from the study of variation and hybridisation to that of experimental embryology, and it is made clear that the action of the determinants is in accord with purely physiological laws. The methods of this procedure are markedly mechanistic, and its results render the assistance of any vitalistic principle entirely superfluous.

CHAPTER XV

THE PROPORTIONAL VARIABLENESS OF MNEMIC EXCITATIONS

IN the chapter on mnemic homophony we explained that the mnemic state of excitement is a repetition of the original state in all its proportional values. But let us here emphasise that it is so in its *proportional* values only, not in its absolute values. According to the energetic condition at the time of the repetition, the mnemic excitation or succession of excitations may be less or more vivid than the creative, original excitation. Moveover, from the same cause or from the influence of new original stimuli, the mnemic repetition may take place in a tempo slower or quicker than that of the original excitation, but the ratio of the time periods, that is, the original rhythm, will be uniformly maintained.

If a change in the internal or external energetic condition at the time of the reproduction causes a proportional change of the mnemic excitations, this change may affect all values which can manifest themselves by reactions differing in quantity.

We have the power, as we well know, to give what size we like to a mental image when projecting it spatially. The engram of any form can be ecphorised either greatly magnified or greatly reduced, according to the nature of ecphoric influences, of homophonous original excitations, or of co-operating associations. An example of this may be seen in the case of a sculptor or painter who is able to reproduce an original percept in different dimensions, but with perfect fidelity to the proportions. Most people unconsciously write smaller between narrow lines than between wide lines, yet, proportionately, the letters are a correctly reduced copy of the usual and characteristic hand of the writer. Proportional variation in size of handwriting may also occur, mainly as motor reaction, when writing with the eyes shut.

In like manner a succession of mnemic excitations may proceed more quickly or slowly than the original excitations, without disturbing the original proportions between the members of the succession. Under the influence of a conductor beating time, or 'of a fellow singer, or of a pianoforte accompaniment, or of emotions heightened by the stimulus of alcohol, a piece of music may be sung, consciously or unconsciously, in a much livelier tempo than previously.

These two examples, the changed size of handwriting and the altered tempo of a piece of music, are characterised by the fact that, while the proportional alterations of the mnemic processes *may* be accompanied by reactions in consciousness, this does not necessarily follow. Nor is it solely the peculiarity of engrams acquired during individual life that their mnemic excitation is affected by the energetic condition ruling at the time of ecphory, the alteration still maintaining the original relative proportions, for we meet with a like peculiarity in the case of inherited engrams, and this in a very striking manner.

Just as the tempo of a piece of music may be changed by any of the above mentioned influences, so the tempo of the ontogenetic courses may be retarded or accelerated by lowering or raising the temperature without any alteration of the proportions of the rhythm, which is often extraordinarily complicated. For example, the tempo of the morphogenetic processes in the egg of the frog is more than four times quicker if they are initiated at a temperature of $24°C$ instead of $10°C$. But in both instances the rhythm of the processes is identical. Again, if in a developing organism the quantity of material at its disposal for plastic processes is reduced, or if the production of fresh material is hindered, the entire plastic structure is built up in proportionately reduced dimensions, and the resulting organism is relatively smaller than the normal type. Conversely, if the quantity of the building material is increased or the abnormal production of fresh material is induced, everything is developed in proportionate enlarged dimensions. The organism becomes enlarged as a whole, but in proportion strictly corresponding to the normal type. It is experimentally easy to obtain a decrease in building material by severing the egg of the animal during the process of segmentation. Medusæ, Echinodermata, Acraina, etc., provide fit material for observation. Or, during their development, we may deprive the plants and animals of adequate nourishment, or otherwise place them in unfavourable conditions of life, and the result will be a decrease of material for the building up of the body.

On the other hand, an increase in material may be obtained by taking two ova at the blastula stage of segmentation, and inducing them to blend into one organism as Metschnikoff succeeded in doing with Medusæ, and Driesch with Echinodermata. Or, by cultivating organisms under very favourable conditions of life and by nourishing them richly, we may succeed, especially with plants, in obtaining a proportional enlargement of the whole organism, or of single parts such as flowers or leaves, far beyond the normal dimensions.

Cases might be multiplied without difficulty and extended to the various regions of mnemic operations. They prove that this phenomenon of proportional rhythms is specifically characteristic of all mnemic excitations, and of all successions of such excitations.

In organisms of restricted growth, where the proportions of the parts are definitely determined engraphically, the disturbance of the proportions produces an incongruity of the mnemic homophony, and induces reactions which tend to remove the incongruity. Animal life furnishes the greater number of instances. Let us take, for example, the well-known case studied in detail by Th. H. Morgan.

If, from a Planaria, a segment is cut so small that it contains only the material for the building up of an animal one-fifth the size of the original worm, and if, in the segment an organ, say the pharynx, is left intact, this does not retain its normal size, but as soon as the processes of regeneration begin, it is, so to speak, melted down and rebuilt in proportions proper to the organism as a whole. It is evident that, in the proportionately reduced whole, the original excitations due to the presence of the unreduced pharynx introduce a strong incongruity into the homophony of the mnemic excitations, which correspond to the reduced whole. This incongruity is removed by the reactions involved in the absorption of the old, and the reconstruction of a new pharynx. This remarkable phenomenon, one of the most marvellous instances of regulation we know, ranges itself, on the theory of the proportional variableness of mnemic excitations, amongst that large group of reactions which tend to remove incongruities in the mnemic homophony.

We may now state comprehensively that the engram determines, not the absolute quantity of the mnemic excitation resulting from its ecphory, but only its quality and its ratio to other mnemic excitations associated with it.

In *The Mnemic Sensations* I have investigated in detail what determines the absolute values of the mnemic excitations aroused at each step in the ecphory of a succession of engrams, at least, as far as the excitations manifest themselves by reaction in sensation. I have reached the conclusion that, in consequence of the engraphic fixing of certain *additional* characters, the reproduction normally occurs as to space, time, and intensity, in the same values as in those of the original sensations, but the proportional increase or diminution of these values has to overcome a certain, however slight, inertia. The reader is referred to Chapter XIII of the above-mentioned book for further particulars.

In mnemic excitations which manifest themselves by plastic reactions the same principles hold good. In this area, also, the determination of the absolute values depends, in the first place, on the co-operation of certain additional engraphically fixed factors. The number of cell divisions, which have to be made before a definite new developmental phase can enter (see p. 75), appears to be the first thing engraphically determined. Thereby a certain norm for the absolute size of the organs at the various stages of development is given. It is true we have already admitted (p. 77) that this factor is not the only determining one, but that under certain circumstances other factors may play a still more decisive part. This only proves that, in this area too, the resistance against the enlargement or decrease of the normal type can be overcome by various internal and external factors, although only within certain mnemically fixed limits.

The absolute values for the reactions resulting from the mnemic excitation are thus determined in the first place by additional components—engraphically fixed—of hereditary or of individual origin. These become simultaneously ecphorised, and determine according to their nature certain absolute values. In the second place, the absolute values are determined also by original influences, active at the time of the ecphory. As we observed, on the appearance of well-marked incongruities the homophony acts in this instance also as the regulating factor.

PART IV

CHAPTER XVI

RETROSPECT—REJOINDER TO CRITICISMS

So far my purpose has been to furnish evidence of a common physiological foundation for the apparently heterogeneous organic phenomena of reproduction. The two corner-stones of this foundation are, first, the fact of the primary coherence of all simultaneous excitations in the organism ; and second, the fact that the effect of the stimulus does not entirely vanish with the synchronous nor yet with the acoluthic phase, but that after the dying away of the latter, the " engram "—an enduring material change of the irritable substance—remains behind, which, though latent, can be roused to manifestation at any moment in conformity with known laws. As the germ-cells are not separated from the rest of the body by any isolating contrivance, the excitations produced in the irritable substance of the body reach them also, leaving behind, especially during the period when the germ-cells are most sensitive, engrams which later may become manifest.

The above foundation is formally expressed by two correlated mnemic laws—the law of Engraphy and the law of Ecphory.

The First Mnemic Law, or Law of Engraphy.—All simultaneous excitations within an organism form a coherent simultaneous excitation-complex which acts engraphically ; that is, it leaves behind a connected engram-complex constituting a coherent unity.

The Second Mnemic Law, or Law of Ecphory.—The partial recurrence of the energetic condition, which has previously acted engraphically, acts ecphorically on the whole simultaneous éngram-complex ; or, as it may be more explicitly stated : the partial recurrence of the excitation-complex, which left behind the engram-complex, acts ecphorically on this simultaneous engram-complex, whether the recurrence be in the form of an original or of a mnemic excitation.

Association is the nexus of the single components of an engram-complex. The engram-association is a result of engraphy and becomes manifest on ecphory.

A further result of our investigation is the insight gained into the nature of Homophony, or the co-operation of simultaneous and qualitatively similar excitations. When there is practically complete similarity between these simultaneous excitations, there ensues a perfect homophony ; when not so, the homophony is a differentiated one.

In the light of these ideas, I have examined in the third part of this book the action of the mnemic processes in ontogenesis. I hope it has been sufficiently demonstrated that the mnemic laws, without the help of any other theory, do adequately account for the strictly regional and temporal order of the ontogenetic processes, for the entry of each of the innumerable separate occurrences in given places and at given times, for the dependence of all simultaneous processes on each other, and for their occasional independence. Also with equal cogency we can bring the phenomena of hereditary and non-hereditary periodicity within these laws, and further we have the key to a physiological interpretation of the otherwise mysterious processes of regeneration and regulation.

Before I examine the objections which have been raised against the mnemic theory so set out, let me discuss a criticism which is concerned not so much with its truth as with its explanatory value and its fruitfulness for science. Granted the truth of the exposition, " What else is it but another paraphrase of old enigmas ? " I am asked.

It will be well to state the possible objections at further

length, and to reply to them *seriatim* ; they have often occurred to my own mind.

First, the utility of the phrase " engraphic action of stimuli " and of the word " engram " may be called in question, and it may be asserted that the theory does not advance matters at all, in the absence of any explanation of the real nature of the engram and of the engraphic action of stimuli.

I reply that neither science nor philosophy has yet explained the " real nature " of any phenomenon whatever. I claim, however, to have succeeded in discerning some phases of the engraphic action of stimuli in their orderly recurrence, and in reducing them to a minimum of fundamental law, and this too without the aid of any other hypothesis, and based entirely on actual observation, which can be tested at any moment, the only exception to this being engrams not capable of repetition. It may be, I admit, that the nature of the engraphic action of stimuli is not explained, but its explanation has in the " scientific sense " been initiated.

In the first German edition of this book I stated that I had relinquished the attempt " to reduce the engraphic change to a hypothetical dislocation of hypothetical molecules."

This point of view, which was simply the attitude of cautious reserve, has been altogether misunderstood by some of my readers and critics, one of whom has reproached me for giving a metaphysical aspect to the engram-doctrine. No reproach is less justifiable than this. Throughout I have carefully avoided the notion that the engram might be something immaterial or metaphysical. On the contrary, I have conceived and definitely described it as a material alteration. I made the point clear in describing the engram as a change left behind in the irritable substance after the excitation has died down. As the altered state of a *substance*, the engram must necessarily be substantial or material, and it may therefore be quite correctly described as a material alteration.

Moreover, in this book, as well as in *The Mnemic*

Sensations, special attention has been devoted to the specific structural side of engrams, and to their localisation. In *The Mnemic Sensations* (pp. 282 and 373) I have called attention to the existence of a chronogeneous localisation, an important new factor which must be borne in mind in the further analysis of the problems of localisation.

Later, it will be necessary to refer to the question how far it is admissible to associate the problems which have occupied us here with invisible structures whose existence is a matter of pure imagination. Granted that the morphology of engraphic action must remain unknown until the more minute structure of the engram is better understood, is it not of great advantage in dealing with biological problems to replace as far as possible such unknown quantities as memory in the restricted sense, heredity, capacity for regeneration and periodicity, etc., by the function of one single factor—" the mnemic excitation," whose existence becomes the more firmly established the more one studies its multifarious manifestations ? If by close study we find that all the apparently heterogeneous phenomena may be referred to three fundamental principles, namely, the two mnemic laws and the laws of homophony, which in their turn are simply sequels of synchronous stimulation, have we not made a step forward in actual knowledge by this simplification of our conceptions ?

But critics may object that when we describe the phenomena of regeneration and regulation as " reactions for the removal of the incongruity of a homophony," we have not explained the problem, but merely re-stated it in other words, since it is just the way in which the removal of the incongruity is effected which constitutes the essential problem to be solved, and by saying that a reaction appears which removes the incongruity we are guilty of reasoning in a circle.

To this I reply that I am fully conscious of not having made sufficiently clear the processes of regulation in all their essential relations. But, it may be added, their explanation has been raised to an entirely different level by the introduction of a new factor, namely, the conception of Homophony.

This conception helps us to realize the existence of two excitations in the regulating organism—an original excitation produced by the stimulus which thus causes a temporarily abnormal state, and a mnemic excitation which belongs to the normal state of the organism or its ancestors. How the regulating reactions arise and run their course under the joint influence of these two excitations is at present very obscure, and probably will be until the relations between excitation and reaction in general have been far more closely studied and more accurately discerned than at the present stage of our physiological knowledge is possible.

The problem has become amenable to scientific treatment only since the acquisition of this evidence of the action and counter-action of two actually existing excitations in the processes of regulation. It was merely a metaphysical problem so long as one had to speak of regulation as bearing on some imagined future state. The discrediting of conceptions which fail to touch the objects themselves, and their replacement by the idea of the homophony of two material processes, which change from phase to phase, but are always there, suggest at least that the introduction of the mnemic principle is by no means a repetition in a new form, but a conception which renders the problem soluble by physiological methods.

The argument for the autonomy of form-development and of life and the case for Vitalism are founded mainly on the assumed impossibility of attacking the phenomena of heredity, adaptation, and regeneration by the way of mechanical causality alone, and without the assumption of a special teleological principle. Our mode of regarding these problems renders unnecessary vitalistic principles like Entelechy, and gives us a vantage ground from which these problems may be solved in a purely physiological way.

Let us now turn to those attacks which are directed against the correctness of our conception, and especially against the citadel of our position, viz. that all the heterogeneous phenomena of reproduction rest upon a common physiological basis. Of two main objections, the one is directed against the assertion that characters acquired during the individual life are not transmissible, the other against the identity of the laws governing the higher memory and those governing inheritance, though a certain similarity between these laws and the possibility of transmission of acquired characters are both admitted.

The objection that individually acquired engrams are not transmitted to offspring has been met by established facts, some of which are given in the preceding pages. For fuller information and for a critical appreciation of the problem in all its bearings, the reader is referred to my essay, *The Problem of the Inheritance of Acquired Characters*. Modern experimental research has furnished what to me is incontrovertible evidence that the new inheritable acquirements of the organism originate as products of stimulation or induction, in whatever manner the latter may have arisen, and that they have to be regarded as engrams. This conclusion is not to be shaken by the mere assertion that the engraphic alteration of the germ-cells is effected, not by a conduction of the excitations from the rest of the body to the germ-cells (somatic induction), but by external stimuli penetrating directly to the germ-cells, in a manner equivalent to their action on the rest of the body (parallel-induction).

For, as my critics must admit that the engrams of the germ-cells possess exactly the same properties as those of the soma, which are generated by parallel-induction, it makes little difference, so far as the engram theory is concerned, which kind of induction is preferred. But as regards the effect of external stimuli, I think I have made it sufficiently clear in the above-mentioned essay that a great number of physical and a still greater number of physiological facts render impossible the general application of the idea of parallel-induction;

and, therefore, the engram-theory must proceed on the assumption of the somatic induction of the germ-cell. It is on these lines that the theory in the present book has been elaborated.

Those who refuse to accept this line of argument, and who prefer to adhere to the assumption of parallel-induction, an assumption quite inapplicable in many cases, and from the physiological side easily assailable, might be reminded that they also assume a stimulation of the germ-cell, that is, an hereditary engraphy, and that they, therefore, are obliged to build on the foundation of an engram theory. Their objections against the Mneme theory cannot, therefore, be regarded as *fundamental*.

Let us turn to the second objection, which says that, even granted the inheritance of acquired engrams, the case is one of mere analogy with the concurrence of the phenomena of higher memory and heredity, and that it is not the manifestation of a common conformity to the same fundamental laws of what is, in principle, an identity.

That the cerebral process of memory is not identical with the process of growth in embryonic development, and that the latter is not identical with the unconscious movement of the plant—well, " There needs no ghost . . . come from the grave to tell us this."

For the " memory process " is not identical in the strict sense with any other process. I may remember one minute, and five minutes later recall the same visual impression, but the processes are not identical. Every organic process, every phenomenon can of course be identical only with itself, and yet one is justified in stating that an identical principle may be at the root of phenomena non-identical and very different to the outward eye.

A simple water-wheel attached to a lawn-sprinkler or garden-fountain is very much unlike a turbine of modern construction, and the processes of the two are by no means identical when compared in detail ; yet the physicist will tell us that the principle underlying both processes is *identical*, and not merely analogous.

Oscar Hertwig has been quoted as an adherent of the
" analogical " theory. He repeatedly emphasised that
" there exists a ' remote analogy ' between the marvellous
properties of hereditary matter and the no less marvellous
properties of brain matter. That this analogy is no
identity will be patent to the clear thinker." We have,
therefore, often cited O. Hertwig as an opponent of the
theory here developed. It is with peculiar satisfaction I
announce that he can no longer be regarded as such.
For, in the later editions of his book, he expressly recognises
the identity which we affirm. " In my opinion, the
phenomena of the ' Mneme,' that is, of heredity, and
the phenomena of memory fall under the general conception of reproduction, and, thereby, show a certain
identity in their character, a fact I have never disputed
nor do I question now." In the light of this statement,
O. Hertwig, in spite of certain qualifications which he
makes and to which we shall refer later, cannot be claimed
as belonging to those who deny the identity of principle
underlying the phenomena of heredity and of the higher
memory.

As regards the opponents of the possible identity of
the physiological foundations of all organic reproductions,
it would seem that their main difficulty is the diversity
in the *form of expression* of two or more excitations, a
diversity which forbids the idea of conformity to any
single principle. Nobody will deny that motor reactions
are altogether different from those of secretion, and
both again differ from plastic reactions. The nature of
the consequent reaction, whether motor, secretive, or
plastic, is of no more importance as an indication of the
character of a mnemic excitation than it is in the case
of an original excitation.

Plate, indeed, maintains " that the Mneme is a psychical
process, and, consequently, like all psychical phenomena,
absolutely enigmatic. It is, therefore, unsuited for an
explanation of heredity, that is, for any real understanding
of the physiological processes involved in heredity." It
is interesting to compare this statement with one made

by the same author a year earlier, when, quite correctly according to our views, he wrote : " I do not see what difference it makes that the case is one of psychical process in the one realm and of material process in the other ; for, as the former is indissolubly connected with the substance of the nervous system, both are radically affected by changes of the protoplasm, and these can be directly compared with each other." If this is correct, then it is wrong to characterise the mnemic processes and their conformity to fixed laws as psychical. Throughout my argument I have considered the material aspect, a fact Plate adequately recognised in 1908. Further, I have attempted to establish a physiological theory of excitation, and have used the psychical side of phenomena as manifested in sensations, as one out of many characteristic ways in which material excitations are made known to us. My position in regard to the problem of the relation of the excitation to its sense-manifestation is given in the introduction to *The Mnemic Sensations* (p. 4–14). "We see in an excitation and its manifestation by sensation not two separate things, but the one thing looked at from two different points of view." The metaphysical theory of knowledge does not, however, at this moment concern us. Throughout, in dealing with the behaviour of organic substance, I have been concerned exclusively with the *material* processes in the phenomena of the higher memory, of heredity, periodicity, and regulation, and, so far as I know, the existence of material changes in the phenomena of memory is not denied by any scientist.

This is the reason why I adopted a specific terminology —original excitation, engram, mnemic excitation, etc.— which has allowed me to be independent of the question whether the respective material processes manifested themselves in any given case by conscious sensation or not. During the whole of the analytical work, as well as throughout the subsequent synthesis, and especially in formulating the principal mnemic laws, and in fact in every definition offered, I avoided the use of such expressions as memory, remembrance, memory-image, etc.

This was done of set purpose, and my reasons for so doing are set out on page 24. I note, however, on the part of my critics a determination to involve me in the use of the word " memory," a term I carefully avoided both in the analytic and in the synthetic elaboration of my position. The creation of a special terminology embodying the main ideas of the theory has justified itself. Such objections as those of Driesch which really refer to memory, or to " what is usually called memory in all systems of psychology," consequently fall to the ground as inapplicable to the subject actually in question.

Regarding the justification for the simultaneous use of the subjective and so-called objective methods of observation, sufficient has been said on pages 40–44. I think I have there met the objection that Rosenthal raises when he writes : " One can rightly defend the position that the logical inferences from data of states of consciousness can only be applied to data of the same kind and can never throw light on processes which appear to us as ' perceptions ' of processes outside of ' Self.' " If this were indeed true, and if we accepted uncompromisingly the logical consequences of such a position, we should find that between our own sensations and those of our fellow creatures there was no reliable link, and that neither psychological nor physiological research had any right to establish relations between results obtained by introspection and those arrived at by the " perception of processes outside of Self." The practical observance of the intellectual principles involved in such a position would be as impossible in daily life as in scientific research, and as disastrous for experimental as for introspective psychology—departments of science which, by virtue of the principles adopted in this book, and notwithstanding the ban of Rosenthal, can look back on splendid achievements of lasting value.

Let us turn to specific objections against the identity of the physiological foundation of the phenomena of reproduction. To Plate, for example, " the main difference consists in the fact that in memory the recurrence takes place in the same brain which received the original stimulus, while in heredity the recurrence appears in the next generation ; the problem lies in the transmission of stimuli from the soma to the germ-cells." But surely the real difficulty exists only for those who, with Weissmann, deny the possibility of any conduction of excitations to the germ-cells from a body which is in continuous connection with them. But, if we may judge by the statements on pages 328–330 and 344–355 of his book, Plate does not belong to this group of scientists. The objection, therefore, sounds strange as coming from him. Whoever admits somatic induction, that is, a conduction of the excitations of the soma to the germ-cells, must accept the possibility that traces of these excitations may be left behind, and consequently the possibility, where the conducted excitations are sufficiently strong and the germ-cells in their sensitive or receptive condition, of corresponding engrams in both germ-cells and soma.

For the partisans of an exclusive parallel-induction, a difficulty exists so far as they have to assume that stimuli, which directly reach the germ-cells, produce effects in them *without* the interposition of the transforming stimulus-receptors of the soma, and that they leave behind engrams which are of like nature with those which are generated by the interposition of complicated transforming contrivances. From the physiological point of view, this is inconceivable. For it is by the somatic reception that the stimulus is transformed into an excitation with distinct local and specific characteristics, and so enabled to leave behind an engram endowed with local and specific characteristics. It is in this reception of the stimulus on the part of the soma that the influences receive, so to speak, the stamp which, on the induction of the germ-cells, guarantees in the offspring a recurrence of localised and specific characters.

The question, not very pertinent, is sometimes put : " How is it that the germ-cell stores up thousands of engrams, while the ganglion-cell is able to store up only one, or at most a very small number of impressions ? "

The reply is simple. The notion that each ganglion-cell is unable to store up more than a very small number of impressions implies that the engrams are so localised in the brain that each cerebral cell represents, so to speak, a drawer for each single " memory-image." This idea, held at the beginning of brain-physiological-research, was soon relinquished as absolutely untenable, and for the last twenty years or so has been discarded by every scientific man who specialises in the localisation of cerebral function. When, in the first German edition of this book, I criticised this naïve position, friends among brain physiologists pointed out that the notion was completely obsolete, and that it would be an anachronism to deal with it. Accordingly, in the second German edition, I refrained from referring in detail to such " mythological " views, as Rieger calls them. If the mere refutation of such antiquated notions be anachronous, what must be thought of their application to our attempts to place the phenomena of organic reproduction on a common physiological basis ?

Finally, let me say a few words on an objection advanced by O. Hertwig, who claims that " the material bases of the brain-substance and of the hereditary matter are fundamentally distinct," and that, therefore, " the processes going on in each are of different kinds." First, I question whether the material foundations of brain substance and hereditary matter are " fundamentally distinct." For are not these foundations in both cases nuclear elements—*cells ?* Touching this point, Hertwig has written : " The distinction of the material foundations arises from the fact that the single cell itself manifests the phenomena of heredity, while the phenomena of memory are dependent on a nexus between many cells, that is, on the development of a highly complicated nervous system and specifically of the cerebral cortex." But in this Hertwig appears to me to concede that the difference is not fundamental—that is, a difference in essence—but that it is simply a difference in complexity.

I admit that a fundamental difference in the material

foundation of these processes would exist if the descriptions and illustrations of the formation of brain-engrams, given by H. E. Ziegler, were not hypothetical, but the results of actual observation. He represents these engrams as changes in the ramifications of cell-processes—terminals of the dendrites and neurites—and as formations or strengthening of neurofibrils. As we have good reason for the assumption that the engrams of the germ-cells are largely, if not altogether, localised in the cell-nucleus, and as it has been definitely established that the germ-cells have neither the tree-like terminals nor the fibrillary structure which characterise the nerve-cells, a fundamental difference of the material foundations for the engraphic changes of the germ-cell and of the nerve-cell would seem thereby to be given. Unfortunately, no human eye has as yet seen those engraphic changes of the brain-cells which Ziegler by word and diagram so eloquently depicts. They do not possess reality. In my opinion, the strong probability is that the actual engraphic changes are in every respect different from those Ziegler surmises. It is futile, however, to quarrel over histological problems which lies so entirely beyond the boundaries of actual observation, and for which even indirect evidence is lacking. If Ziegler (p. 38) postulates that every " physiological explanation must be based on anatomical and histological states," then I reply that it is quite justifiable, and, in fact, necessary, to treat all faculties and functions of the organism in their correlations with corresponding morphological structures, so long as this is done without straining and without the use of purely arbitrary hypothesis. But I maintain that enquiry into this correlation is impracticable as long as an anatomical basis, ascertained by specific observation, is still wanting ; for, in the absence of such a basis, one is dealing only with statements which, like the representation of the brain-engrams by Ziegler, are merely the outcome of imagination.

At this place I will make a passing reference to one objection, which is directed against a somewhat unimportant point in my evidence, but which has been advanced by many writers, notably by Ziegler, who writes : " Semon bases his theory on some of his experiments on plants. The accuracy of his observations, however, is flatly denied by the famous botanist, Prof. Pfeffer." The readers of this book will be able to judge how far it is true to say that the Mnemic theory is based entirely on my experiments on the sleeping movements of plants. For the evidence derived therefrom is but a fragment of an accumulated mass based on other phenomena observed and recorded by many workers, such as Chauvin, Kammerer, Standfuss, Fischer, Schröder, Przibram, Sumner, Blaringhem, Klebs, Bordage, etc., and which I have always recognized as far more convincing than my investigations on the diurnal period of plants, and such evidence as is not entirely open to experimental verification. But, after all, the essential point is that Pfeffer has in no way denied my conclusions on the only matter which is here relevant, but on the contrary has confirmed them, as the reader may see for himself by reference to the treatise by Pfeffer (see Index).

In conclusion, I may refer to the argument that the Mneme theory stands in contradiction to Mendelian laws. If that were true, it would certainly be so much the worse for my theory. That it is not true has already been sufficiently shown in Chapter XIV of this work, wherein it is made clear that our conception of the phenomena of organic reproduction as resting on a common physiological basis furnishes a necessary complement to the research work on variation and hybridisation—work which is concerned with problems other than those dealt with by the Mnemic theory.

If Mendelian research had actually proved that the gametes bear either one or the other, but not both, of the allelomorphic pair of unit-characters, and that the germ-cell at some point of cell-division in the formation of gametes divides into two definitely dissimilar parts, and that the process must be interpreted—as the Mendelians say—as a " segregration " of characters, then we should have to accept this as a fact and draw the necessary consequence from it, namely, that the separate determining factors, the engrams, were isolable structures. To me, however, the available evidence is unconvincing. The elimination at the formation of the gametes of one of the two allelomorphic characters can be explained otherwise. But I should like to say that the explanation may be regarded as quite independent of the ideas developed in this book.

In any case the Mneme theory is not adversely affected by the Mendelian theory. The incompatibility of the two would follow, not from the mere statement of the possibility of isolation, but from the proving of an actual isolation existing from the beginning, and from the demonstration of the lack of orderly connection between the determinants, that is, the engrams.

By certain modern scientific workers this isolation is assumed. They see in the hereditary factors a mass of blindly-shuffled particles, each of which possesses its special chemical constitution. Because specific factors, under certain circumstances, cause the formation of enzymes, they are by some described as enzymes. But, as I have shown on pages 263–265, that view stands in contradiction to evidence gathered from the physiology of development, and from the phenomena of regulation and of periodicity, and therefore cannot be used as an argument against the position outlined in this book.

In my judgment, none of the criticisms hitherto raised has stood the test of examination. I admit, however, that much work has yet to be done in the experimental investigation of the principles that govern the somatic induction of the germ-cell. I do not forget that we are as yet only at the opening of a new and, as I trust, promising avenue, and that the main journey lies still before us. If I have succeeded in demonstrating that no obstacle exists to prevent us from using these fundamental mnemic laws as a uniform physiological foundation in the investigation of the phenomena of organic reproduction, my purpose will have been achieved.

CHAPTER XVII

THE MNEME AS THE PERSISTING ELEMENT IN THE CHANGE OF ORGANIC PHENOMENA

I HAVE now, I hope, given sufficient proof that the same fundamental physiological laws are valid for all organic reproduction, and that an identical principle underlies all organic phenomena which confront us in such manifold diversity of garb. I now conclude by asking what we have gained thereby, and how far we have arrived at a better understanding of the evolved and ceaselessly evolving organic world in which we live.

The influences in the external world effect changes in the organism in a twofold manner : first, in the sense of a merely synchronous alteration, secondly, through and beyond this, by affecting the organism engraphic-ally and so permanently transforming it. The external energetic condition, for ever changing, never repeating itself exactly, thus acts as a transforming factor ; whilst, in the faculty of the organic substance to retain traces of the synchronous excitations in the form of engrams, we have the factor whereby transformations effected during the " flight of phenomena " are conserved.

But are these two principles sufficient to render the aspect of the organic world scientifically intelligible to us ? We venture to think they are not. We find the organisms in a peculiar, harmonious relation to the outer world, a relation which has been fitly described as one of adaptation or adaptability to the conditions of life. Neither the transforming action of the external world nor the purely conserving mnemic faculty of the organic substance can account for this adaptation. An additional principle is required to explain it.

The necessity for this has so far been recognised that two attempts have been made to explain the nature of this additional principle. First, a mere paraphrase of the necessary principle was offered in terms of indefinite or indefinable factors such as " internal causes," or " impulses " or " desire " on the part of the organism to adapt itself to such external condition and to develop in this or that direction. This interpretation seems to us not only ineffective but also prohibitive of further enquiry. Lamarck and Nägeli may be noted as the most prominent representatives of this forlorn and barren explanation.

The second and more adequate attempt to solve this problem was successfully made by Darwin and Wallace who, in my opinion, achieved thereby one of the greatest triumphs of the human mind. The riddle was solved by adducing evidence of an operative selective principle whereby the unfit were eliminated and the fit survived through succeeding generations.

This foundation laid by Darwin has turned out to be a thoroughly solid one, and though it gets amplified and deepened by the results of more modern experimental research, it is not shaken, even where corrections have to be made.

Darwin was not, however, in a position to distinguish, as we can to-day, the different kinds of variation since revealed by recent experimental research. He set the direction and traced the first steps ; further progress had to be left to his fellow labourers and successors. That this subsequent work was taken in hand comparatively late was not his fault ; that new fundamental data were brought to light by it was only to be expected. The greatest advances which have been made are due, first, to the more precise distinction between the inheritable and non-inheritable characters of the variations, a point which had engaged Darwin's attention, but which was not exhaustively worked out by him ; and secondly, to

19

the discovery that though selection may serve to isolate already existing types in the mixture of individuals of a "population," it is unable actually to create new characters.

New characters are created exclusively by the organic reaction against stimuli, which continually spring from the ever changing external world. Darwin recognised the existence of this organic reaction against stimuli ; he never denied the direct influence of the external world, and he always guarded himself against such an over-estimate of the principle of selection as was made by Weismann under the cry of "The All Sufficiency of Natural Selection." It is not Darwin, but Weismann, who has been refuted by the more recent data acquired in the course of experimental research into the laws of heredity.

The action of natural selection is indeed but a negative one, yet it exercises in the change of organic phenomena an exceedingly effective, and in a limited sense a creative influence. The operations of a sculptor who chisels a figure from a block of marble are, it may be said, entirely of a negative character. Yet just as we see in the group of Laocoon a creative achievement, so we may regard many of the astonishing adaptations that confront us everywhere in organic nature as the shaping work of Natural Selection, although the latter has just as little created its material (the hereditary variations) as the sculptor the marble out of which he models his creation.

Natural Selection simply weeds out the unfit, but as the process is ceaselessly at work, we are not surprised to find everywhere organisms which are adapted to their environment. In the wonderful phenomena whereby the adaptation is achieved, not all the elements which in our generalising terminology we describe as "useful" can be exclusively traced to Natural Selection. In truth, these astonishing processes of regeneration and regulation, to which many antagonists of the doctrine of Selection appeal, require for their explanation the principle of Mnemic Persistence, and are not, as Weismann claimed for regeneration, involved in the action of Natural Selection.

What we are accustomed to describe as " usefulness " in the organic world is therefore a product of at least two factors, Natural Selection and Mnemic Persistence. Both conceptions are the outcome of biological research, and are based exclusively on the principle of causality, which also suffices for the exploration of the inorganic world. There is no need for " final causes," or " entelechies," and the like. The appeal to a vitalistic principle is rendered superfluous.

Neither in the Mneme nor in Natural Selection is to be discovered an all-sufficient principle furnishing a universal key to the understanding of all organic phenomena. But in the Mneme there is to be found a conserving principle which is indispensable for organic development, in so far as it preserves the transformations which the external world unceasingly creates. Its conserving influence is, of course, restricted by that indirect factor of the external world, Natural Selection, for, in the long run, only fit transformations survive.

This insight into the activity of the Mneme in ontogenesis supplies also the key to a fuller understanding of the biogenetic law, in the formulation of which Haeckel has to a surprising extent deepened and enlarged the foundations of comparative morphology. That the ancestral path of development has to be trodden by each descendant in an approximately equal manner (Palinogenesis) is the obvious consequence of the action of the mnemic factor in ontogenesis. That in course of time this path, especially in its oldest and therefore most frequently traversed initial stages, becomes shortened here and there and otherwise changed (Caenogenesis) is equally obvious, if we consider that during each ontogenesis new original stimuli act on the organism, and in favourable cases (that is with stimuli of sufficient strength or of sufficient frequency of repetition in the lines of generations) add their engraphic effects to the old mnemic stock.

Moreover, the study of the Mneme is of the greatest importance, not only for the problems of genetics, but quite as much for the correct interpretation of the functions of the living organism.

Restriction to the study of synchronous stimulation leads to quite a one-sided conception of physiological phenomena, and, what is worse, to an entire misconception of the so-called " formative " stimuli. In the great majority of these it is merely a case of an ecphoric action of certain stimuli on inherited engrams. Further, the disappointment ensuing on the realised impossibility of understanding many physiological phenomena solely on the basis of synchronous stimulation leads many thinkers back to vitalism. This disappointment and this relapse may be avoided, if the engraphic effects of stimulation are duly recognised as such, and if it is realised that the ecphory of inherited and individually acquired engrams affects many physiological phenomena. We have to abstain from trying to investigate the physiology of organisms as if they were isolated from their previous experiences and those of their ancestors.

We are still far from being able to *describe* the phenomena of life on a purely physico-chemical basis. But progress in that direction will be made if we regard regeneration and regulation, which have hitherto baffled all mechanistic analysis, as adjusting processes of co-operating original and mnemic excitations.

By the extension of this conception, certain profound enigmas of the organic world may become intelligible by reference to the mnemic properties of the irritable substance, a process the main features of which we have attempted to trace' in the preceding pages.

At the same time, to reach our goal, research work in physics and chemistry would have to be undertaken in order to discover whether, and how far, evidence could be adduced for something corresponding in the inorganic world to engraphy and ecphory. So far no results in that direction have been obtained.

Confining ourselves for the present to the investigation

of the organic world, we see, on adequate consideration of engraphic stimulations, how the area of the physiology of stimuli widens out in an extroardinary manner. We have found that the phenomena of organic reproduction, whether of an hereditary or non-hereditary character, are subject to the same laws, and that they possess the same physiological basis. Physiology as the science of actual life cannot dispense with the investigation of the past. This claim is met by the study of the Mneme, which in the organic world links the past and present in a living bond.

INDEX OF LITERATURE

CHAPTER I

p. 22. Fr. Darwin and D. F. M. Pertz, On the artificial Production of Rhythm in Plants. Annals of Botany, vol. xvii, 1903, page 104.

CHAPTER II

p. 28. Francis Darwin, Lectures on the physiology of movement in plants. 1. Associated stimuli. The New Phytologist, vol. v, No 9, 1906

p. 29. C. B. Davenport and W. B. Cannon, On the determination of the direction and rate of movement of organisms by light. Journ. of Physiol., vol. xxi, 1897, page 32.

p. 29. F. Oltmanns, Ueber positiven und negativen Heliotropismus. Flora oder Allgemeine Botanische Zeitung, vol. 83, 1897.

p. 33. W. Biedermann, Electrophysiologie, Jena, 1895, page 101.

p. 34. E. Steinach, Die Summation einzeln unwirksamer Reize als allgemeine Lebenserscheinung. Pflugers Archiv für Physiologie, vol. 125, Heft 5–7, 1908.

p. 47. C. Lloyd Morgan, Habit and instinct. London, New York, 1896.

p. 48. L. Edinger, Haben die Fische ein Gedachtniss ? Munchen, 1899. Buchdruckerei der " Allgemeinen Zeitung."

CHAPTER III

p. 57. P. Kammerer, Vererbung erzwungener Fortpflanzungsanpassungen I u. II Mitt. im Archiv für Entwicklungsmechanik, vol. 25, 1907.

p. 61. M. von Chauvin, Ueber die Verwandlungsfähigkeit der mexikanischen Axolotl. Zeitschrift fur wiss. Zoologie, vol. 41, 1885.

p. 61. A. Pictet, Influence d'alimentation et de l'humidité sur la variation des papillons. Mém. Soc. de Phys. et de l'Hist. nat. de Genève, vol. 35, 1905.

p. 61. Chr. Schröder, Ueber experimentell erzeugte Instinktvariationen. Verhandl. d. D zool., Gesellschaft, 1903.

p. 61. P. Kammerer, Vererbung erzwungener Fortpflanzungsanpassungen III Mitt. Archiv fur Entwicklungsmechanik, vol. 28, 1909.

p. 61. E. Fischer, Experimentelle Untersuchungen über die Vererbung erworbener Eigenschaften. Allgemeine Zeitschrift fur Entomologie, vol. 6, 1901.

p. 61. M. Standfuss, Experimentelle zoologische Studien mit Lepidopteren. Neue Denkschrift der allg. Schweiz. Naturforscher Gesell, vol. 36, 1898 ; also : Zur Frage der Gestaltung und Vererbung auf Grund 28 jahriger Experimente. Vortrag, Zurich, 1905.

p. 63.　E. Bordage, A propos de l'hérédité des caractères acquis.,
　　　　Bulletin scientifique, 7 série, T. 44. Paris, 1910.
p. 73.　W. Pfeffer, Der Einfluss von mechanischer Hemmung und von
　　　　Belastung auf die Schlafbewegungen. Abhandl. d. math-
　　　　phys. Klasse der kgl. sächs. Gesellschaft der Wissenschaften,
　　　　vol. 32, Leipzig, 1911. See also :
　　　　R. Stoppel, Zeitschrift für Botanik, 2 ter Jahrgang, Jena, 1910.
　　　　R. Stoppel und H. Kniep, Zeitschrift fur Botanik, Jena, 1911.
p. 74.　W. Pfeffer, Biol. Centralblatt, vol. 28, 1908, page 389–415.
p. 74.　P. W. Gamble and F. W. Keeble, Hyppolyte varians. Quarterly
　　　　Journal Microscop. Science, N.S., vol. 43, 1900.
p. 74.　P. W. Gamble aod F. W. Keeble, Philosoph. Transact. Royal
　　　　Soc. London (B), vol. 196, 1904.
p. 74.　G. Bohn, Bull. Institut gén. psycholog., 3, 1903 ; 7, 1907.
p. 74.　W. Schleip, Der Farbenwechsel bei Dixippus morosus. Zool.,
　　　　Jahrbuch Abt. f. allg. Zoologie und Physiologie, vol 30,
　　　　Heft 1, 1910.
p. 77.　Th. H. Morgan, Studies of the "partial" larvæ of Sphaerechinus.
　　　　Archiv fur Entw. Mechanik, vol. 2, 1896.
　　　　H. Driesch, Neue Antworten und neue Fragen der Entwicke-
　　　　lungsphysiologie. Ergebnisse der Anat. und Entw. Gesch.,
　　　　vol. 11, 1902.
　　　　Th. Boveri, Zellenstudien, Heft 5, Jena, 1905.
p. 78.　C. Herbst, Formative Reize in der tierischen Ontogenese, Leipzig,
　　　　1901, page 59.
p. 78.　H. Spemann, Sitzungsbericht der Phys.-med. Gesellschaft, Wurz-
　　　　burg, 1901. See further : Anat. Anzeigen, vol. 23, 1903. Zool.
　　　　Anzeigen, vol. 28, 1905.
p. 78.　E. Mencl, Archiv fur Entw. Mech., vol. 16, 1903 ; vol. 25, 1908.
p. 78.　H. Spemann, Zool. Anzeigen, vol. 31, 1907 ; Verhandlung der
　　　　deutschen Zool. Gesellschaft in Rostock und Lübeck, 1907 ;
　　　　Verhandlung der Zool. Ges. in Stuttgart, 1908.
p. 78.　H. D. King, Archiv fur Entw. Mech., vol. 19, 1905.
p. 79.　W. H. Lewis, American Journal Anat., vol. 3, 1904, and vol. 7,
　　　　1907.
p. 79.　G. Ekman, Experimentelle Beiträge zum Linsenbildungsproblem
　　　　bei den Anuren. Archiv fur Entwicklungsmechanik, vol. 39,
　　　　Heft 2 and 3, 1914.

CHAPTER IV

p. 93.　The Life and Letters of Charles Darwin, vol. 1, page 84.
p. 104.　E. Wasmann, Die psychologischen Fahigkeiten der Ameisen,
　　　　Stuttgart, 1899.
p. 105.　H. Ebbinghaus, Ueber das Gedächtnis. Untersuchungen zur
　　　　experimentellen Psychologie, Leipzig, 1885.
p. 108.　J. Fabre, Souvenirs entomologiques, Paris, 1879–1882.

CHAPTER V

p. 128.　C. von Monakow, Ueber die Lokalisation der Hirnfunctionen,
　　　　Wiesbaden, E. F. Bergmann, 1910.
p. 130.　Marie von Chauvin, Ueber die Verwandlungsfähigkeit des mexi-
　　　　kanischen Axolotl. Zeitschrift für wissensch. Zoologie, vol. 41,
　　　　1885.

p. 230. P. Kammerer, Vererbung erzwungener Fortpflanzungsanpassungen. 3. Mitteil. Archiv für Entw. Mechanik, vol. 28, 1908, page 526. Also Zeitschrift für induktive Abstammungs- und Vererbungslehre, vol. 1, 1909, page 139.

p. 132. P. Kammerer, Direkt induzierte Farbanpassungen und deren Vererbung Zeitschrift für induktive Abstammungs und Vererbungslehre, vol. 4, Heft 3 and 4, 1911.

p. 132. H. Przibram, Aufzucht Farbwechsel und Regeneration der Gottesanbeterin (Mantidæ) III. Archiv für Entw. Mech., vol. 28, 1909. See also the same author's Experimentelle Zoologie, vol. 3, Phylogenese, Leipzig and Wien, 1910, page 161.

p. 133. C. Detto, Die Theorie der direkten Anpassung, Jena, 1904.

p. 133. A. Weismann, Aufsätze über Vererbung, Jena, 1892, page 323.

p. 134. F. B. Sumner, An experimental study of somatic modifications and their reappearance in the offspring, Arch. f. Entw. Mechanik, vol. 30, II Teil, 1910.

CHAPTER IX

p. 193. J. Loeb, The dynamics of living matter, New York, 1906, page 171.

p. 193. J. Loeb, Ueber das Wesen der formativen Reizung, Berlin, 1909.

p. 193. J. Loeb, Die chemische Entwicklungserregung des tierischen Eies. (Künstliche Parthenogenese), Berlin, 1909.

CHAPTER XI

p. 210. Th. Boveri, Ueber die Polarität des Seeigel-Eies. Verhandl. der Phys.-Med. Ges., Wurzburg N.F., vol. 34, 1901.

p. 211. H. Driesch, Neue Ergänzungen zur Entwickelungsphysiologie des Echinidenkeimes. Archiv f. Entwicklungsmechan, vol. 14, 1902.

p. 213. P. Kammerer, Centralblatt für Physiologie, vol. 19, 1905.

p. 214. P. Kammerer, Archiv f. Entw. Mech., vol. 19, Heft 2, 1905.

p. 219. H. Przibram, Experimental Zoologie, vol. II, Regeneration, pages 117–119, Leipzig und Berlin, 1909. Also : Die Homoeosis bei Arthropoden. Archiv für Entwicklungsmech., vol. 29, 1910.

CHAPTER XII

p. 223. Klein, Futterbrei und weibliche Bienenlarve. "Die Bienenpflege," 26 Jahrg., Ludwigsburg, 1904, page 80.

p. 223. H. v. Buttel-Reepen, Atavistische Erscheinungen im Bienenstaat. C.R.d.I., Congres internat. d'entomologie à Bruxelles, 1910 ; Brüssel, 1911.

p. 225. A Forel, Les fourmis de la Suisse. Neue Denkschrift d. allg. Schweiz. Ges. f.d. allg. Naturw., vol. 26, 1874.

p. 225. E. Wasmann, Ergatogyne Formen bei den Ameisen. Biologisches Centralblatt, vol. 15, 1895.

p. 225. H. Viehmeyer, Experimente zu Wasmanns Pseudogynen-Lomechusa Theorie Allgem. Zeitschr. f. Entom., vol. 9, 1904.

p. 226. H. v. Buttel-Reepen, Die stammesgeschichtliche Entstehung des Bienenstaates. Biol. Centralblatt, vol. 23, 1903. Published also separately with additions by G. Thieme, Leipzig, 1903.

p. 230. Marie v. Chauvin, Zeitschrift f. wissenschaftl. Zoologie, 1875, 1876, 1885.

p. 236. P. Kammerer, Vererbung erzwungener Fortpflanzungsanpassungen III Mitt. Die Nachkommen der nicht brutpflegenden Alytes obstetricans. Archiv. f. Entwicklungsmechanik, vol. 28, 1909.

CHAPTER XIII

p. 241. H. Przibram, Experimentelle Studien uber Regeneration. Archiv fur Entwicklungsmech. vol. 11, 1901.. Also Experimental-Zoologie. 2. Regeneration, Leipzig and Wien, 1909, p. 108.

p. 242. H. Nilsson-Ehle, Ueber Falle spontanen Wegfallens eines Hemmungsfactors beim Hafer. Zeitschr. f. induktive Abstammungs- und Vererbungslehre, vol. 5, Heft 1, April, 1911.

p. 244. E. v. Tschermak, Ueber Zuchtung neuer Getreiderassen mittels kunstlicher Kreuzung, II Mitt. Zeitschr. f.d. landw. Versuchswesen in Oesterreich, 1906.

p. 244. Vernon, Archiv f. Entw. Mech., vol. 9, 1900.

p. 244. Doncaster, Philosoph. transact., vol. 196, 1903.

p. 244. Herbst, Vererbungsstudien, IV, V, VI. Archiv f. Entw. Mech., vol. 22, 1906; vol. 24, 1907; vol. 27, 1910.

p. 244. Tennent, Archiv f Entw. Mech., vol. 29, 1910.

p. 244. Tower, Biological Bulletin, vol. 18, No. 6, 1910.

p. 253. W. L. Tower, The determination of dominance and the modification of behaviour in alternative (Mendelian) inheritance by conditions surrounding or incident upon the germ-cells at fertilisation. Biological bulletin, vol. 18, No. 6, 1910.

CHAPTER XIV

p. 257. W. L. Tower, An investigation of evolution in chrysomelid beetles of the genus Leptinotarsa, Carnegie Institution, Washington, 1906.

p. 257. P. Kammerer, Mendelsche Regeln und Erwerbung erworbener Eigenschaften Verhandl. d. naturf, Vereines in Brunn, vol. 49, 1911. Further: P. Kammerer, Vererbung erworbener Farbenveranderungen. IV Mitt. Das Farbkleid des Feuersalamanders in seiner Abhängigkeit von der Umwelt. Archiv f. Entwicklungsmechanik, vol. 36, 1913.

p. 257. Charles Darwin, The foundations of the origin of species. Two essays written in 1842 and 1844. Edited by his son, Francis Darwin.

p. 258. H. de Vries, Die Mutationstheorie, Leipzig, 1901–1903.

p. 258. W. L. Tower, The determination of dominance, Biological Bulletin, vol. 18, No. 6, 1910.

p. 259. F. B. Sumner, An experimental study of somatic modifications and their reappearance in the offspring. Archiv f. Entw.-Mech., vol. 30, II Teil, 1910.

p. 259. H. Przibram, Versuche an Hitzeratten. Verhdlg d. Ges. deutscher Naturforscher und Aerzte. Versammlung, Salzburg, 1909.

p. 261. H. Nilsson-Ehle, Kreuzungsuntersuchungen an Hafer und Weizen. Lands Universitets Aersskrift N.F. Afd. 2, vol. 5, No. 2, Lund, 1909.

p. 263. W. Bateson, Mendel's Principles of Heredity. Cambridge, 1909, chap. ix.

p. 263. H. Nilsson-Ehle, Ueber Fälle spontanen Wegfallens eines Hemmungsfaktors beim Hafer. Zeitschr. f. induktive Abstammungs-und Vererbungslehre, vol. 5, Heft 1, 1911.

p. 265. W. L. Tower, The determination of dominance. Biological Bulletin, vol. xviii, No. 6, 1910, page 324.

CHAPTER XVI

P. 275. J. R Mayer, Bemerkungen über das Aequivalent der Wärme, 1850. "When a phenomenon has become known in all its aspects, it is already explained thereby and the task of science is complete."

p. 280. O. Hertwig, Die Zelle und die Gewebe, vol. 2, Jena, 1898, pp. 245 and 251, new editions under the title : Allgemeine Biologie, 2nd edition, Jena, 1906, p. 587; 3rd edition, Jena, 1909, p 661.

P. 280. L. Plate, Archiv f. Rassen und Gesellschaftsbiologie, 6 Jahrg. Leipzig and Berlin, 1909, page 92 (Review of Francis Darwin's Presidential Address, Dublin, 1908)

P. 281. L. Plate, Selektionsprincip und Probleme der Artbildung, 3 Auflage, Leipzig, 1908, page 334.

p. 282. H. Driesch, Philosophie des Organischen, Leipzig, 1909, vol. 1, pages 220–223.

P. 282. J. Rosenthal, Biologisches Centralblatt, vol. 25, 1905, page 368, in a critical review of the Mneme

p. 282. L. Plate, Selektionsprincip und Probleme der Artbildung, 3 Auflage, Leipzig, 1908, page 335.

p. 284. O. Hertwig, Die Zelle und die Gewebe, vol. 2, Jena, 1898, page 251.

p. 284. O. Hertwig, Allgemeine Biologie, 3 Auflage, 1909, p. 661.

P. 285. H. E. Ziegler, Theoretisches zur Tierpsychologie und vergleichender Neurophysiologie. Biologisches Centralblatt, vol. 20, 1900. The hypothetical descriptions and illustrations also reappear in the second edition of Ziegler's essay · Der Begriff des Instincts einst und jetzt. Jena, 1910, p. 88, Figs 8 and 9.

Richard Semon, Die Mneme, Leipzig, Wilhelm Engelmann, Erste Auflage, 1904 ; Zweite Auflage, 1908 ; Dritte Auflage, 1911.

INDEX OF AUTHORS

GENERAL INDEX

Printed in Great Britain by
UNWIN BROTHERS, LIMITED, THE GRESHAM PRESS, WOKING AND LONDON

Lightning Source UK Ltd.
Milton Keynes UK
UKHW020616100223
416791UK00005B/117